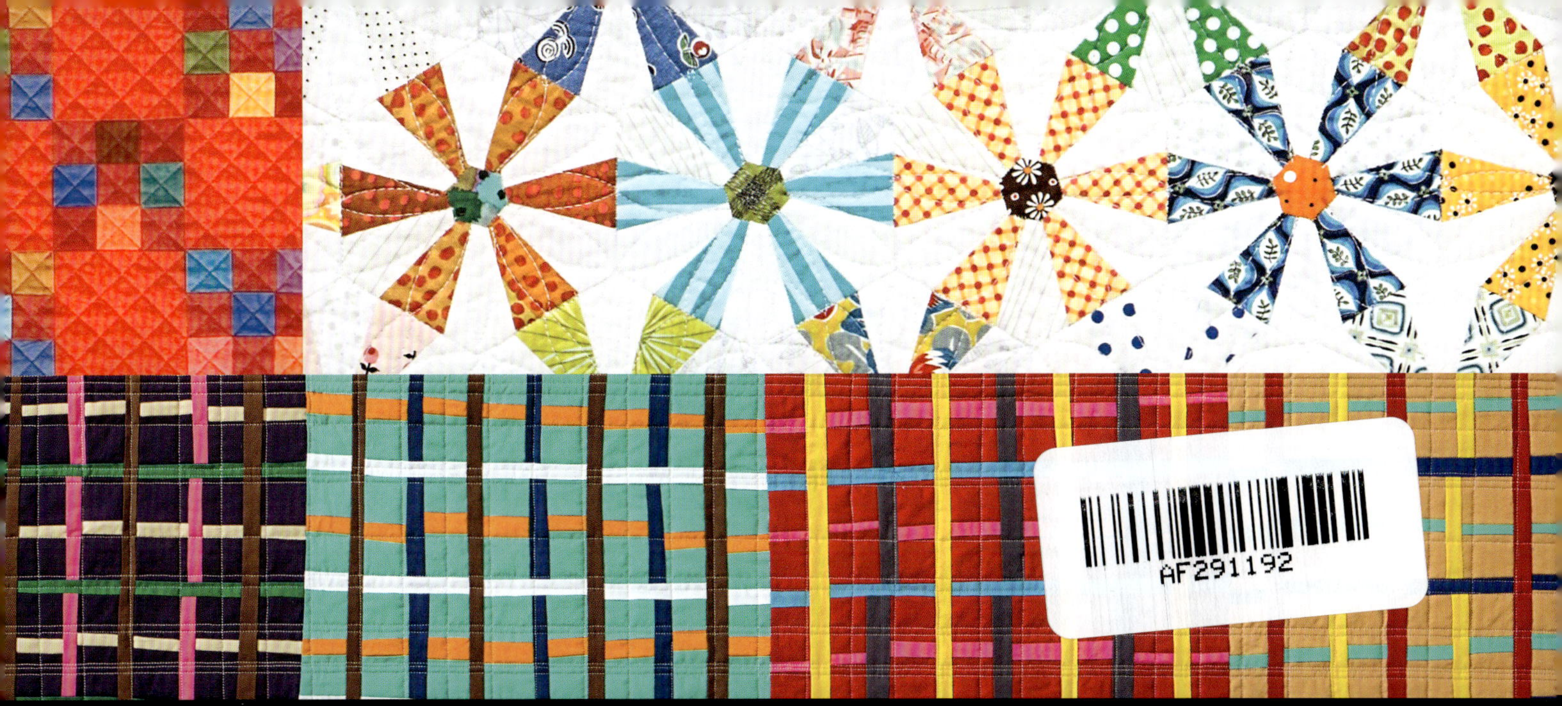

THE QUILTER'S COLOR GUIDE

MASTERING THE ART OF COLOR CONFIDENCE

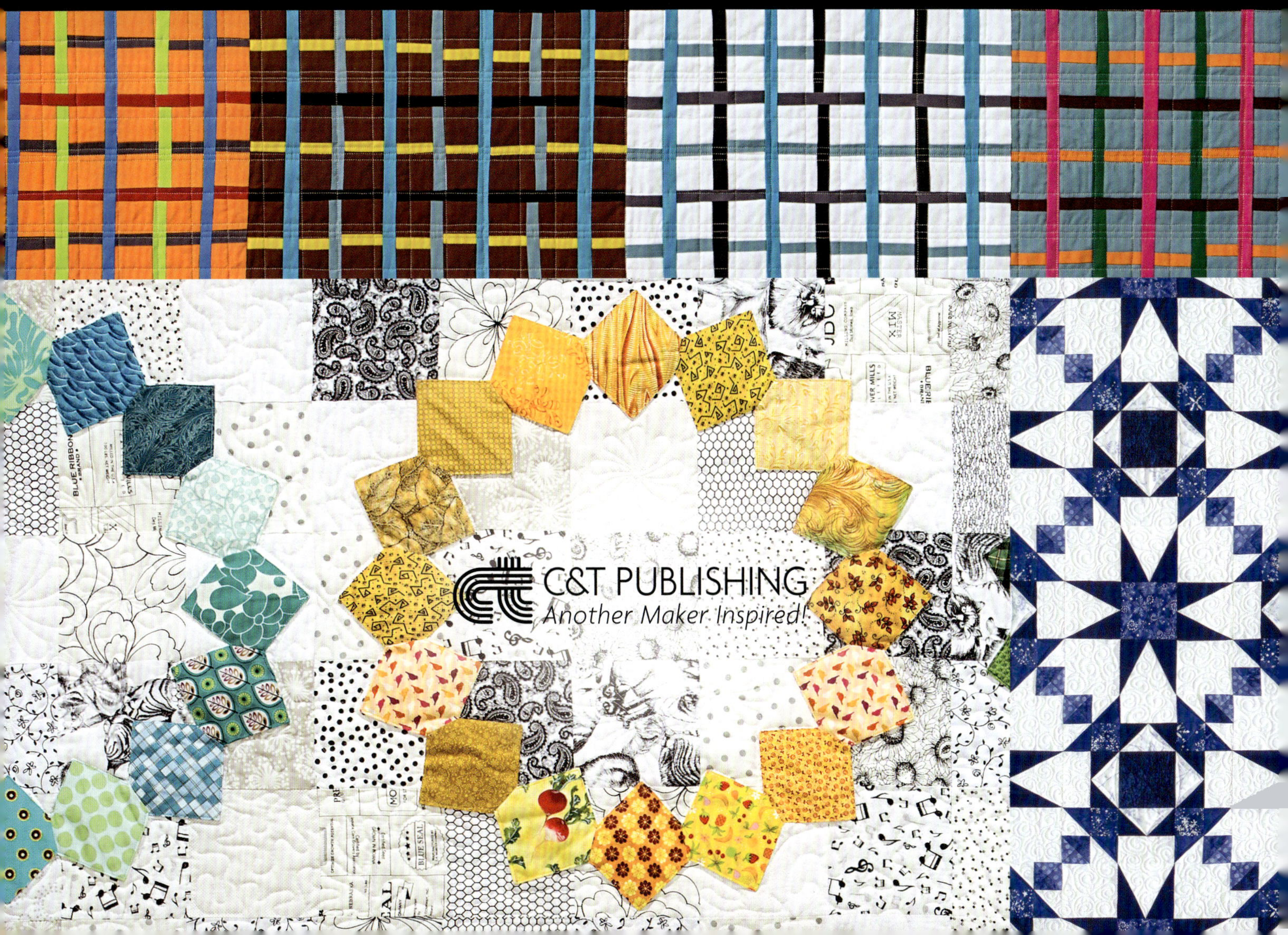

C&T PUBLISHING
Another Maker Inspired!

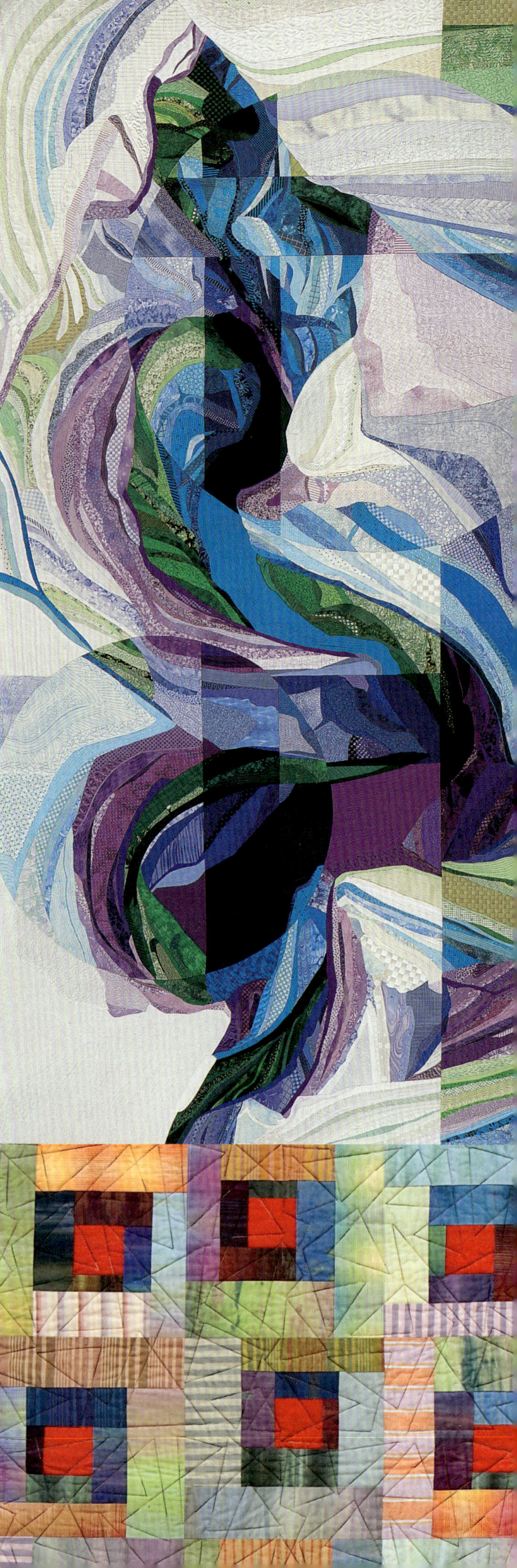

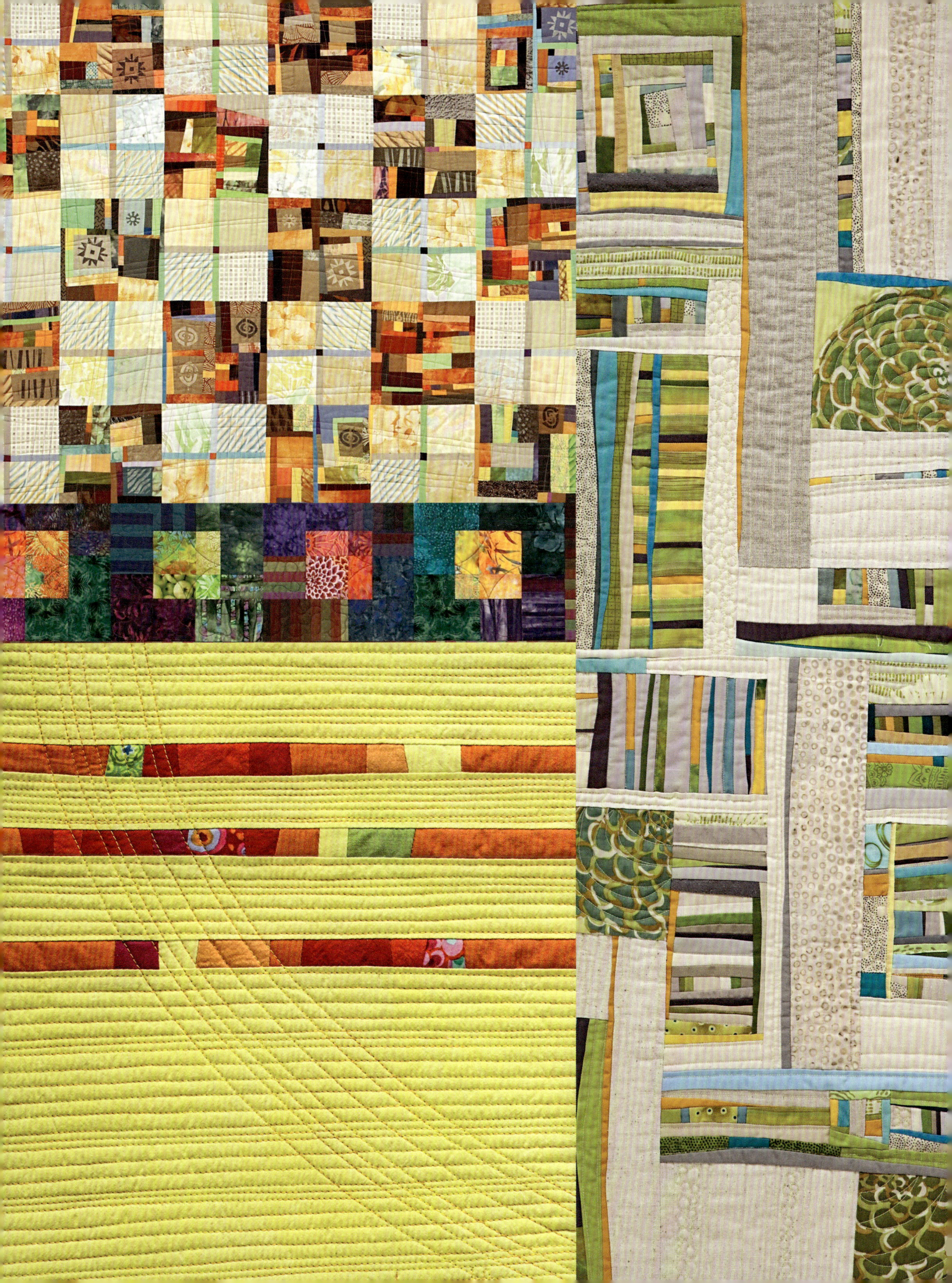

CONTENTS

FOREWORD
By Amy Barrett-Daffin

When I mention color theory the first thing I typically hear is, "I'm not very good at color." What you don't realize is that you are! You match your clothes, decorate your home, and put together pleasing color combinations every day. What you may lack is color confidence. That is something that comes with practice. It is a learned skill, not a mystery or something to shy away from.

I've been teaching Joen Wolfrom's color tools for more than ten years, starting with *The Ultimate 3-in-1 Color Tool*. During that time I have learned so much about color in theory and color in practice. I have learned that there are no color police, that no one is going to tell you your colors don't work. When I started I had no color confidence, so I read the instructions and jumped in (those that know me will not be surprised). I decided to make learning about color part of my quiltmaking practice. After using our tools for every project I make, and demonstrating color to thousands of quilters, it made me curious about how other quilt experts look at color. From hosting color events on Creative Spark Online Learning to talking with other quilters, I learned what they are curious about, their color insecurities, and their fear of making mistakes and only using precuts or kits so they didn't "mess up," the quilt. I can confidently say there is no right or wrong when it comes to color, but there are some helpful guidelines and practical advice that will build your color confidence. To that end, I did a deep dive into our collection and am presenting the information to you here in this book.

Consider this book "everything you didn't know you wanted to know about color"—a master class on color and value featuring Joen Wolfrom, Jean Wells, Katie Pasquini Masopust, Christine Barnes, Becky Goldsmith, Alex Anderson, Cindy Grisdela, Maria Shell, Judy Gauthier, and Teri Lucas. Each section is packed with inspiration, information, and exercises to take your quilts to the next level. The book is divided into three sections: Color Theory, Practical Color, and Special Effects. You will learn about the many facets of the color wheel, the importance of value to create movement, color in fabric, working with neutrals, and more! There are also 18 exercises to help you build your color confidence. I hope you enjoy the essays, exercises, and advice as much as I did collecting it, and remember that practice is what builds our skills so dig into your stash, practice the exercises, and start playing with your fabric!

▶ *The Ugly Fabric Challenge* pieced by Becky Goldsmith, Machine quilted by Angela Walters, 52″ × 60″

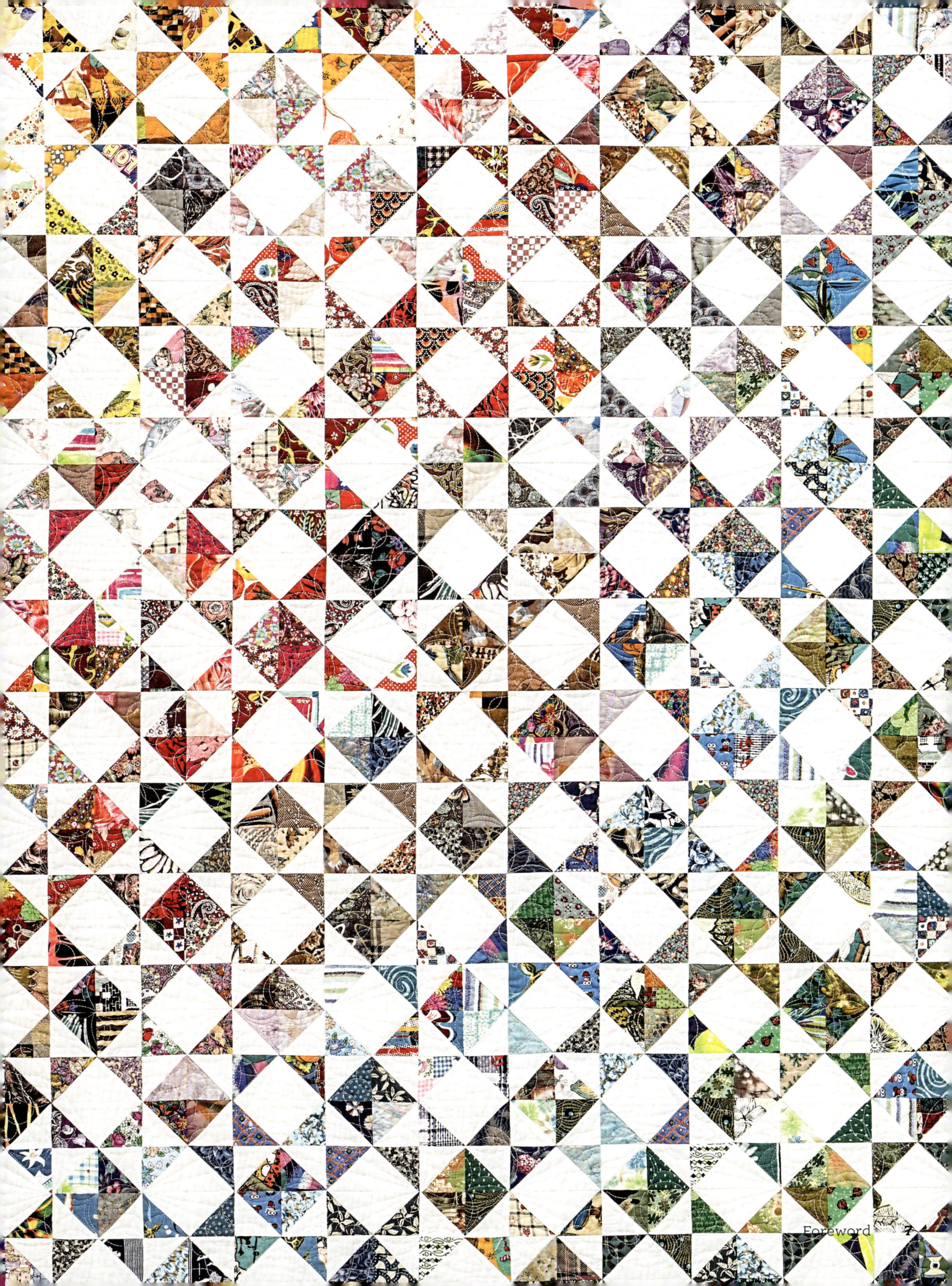
Foreword

CREATING A COLOR RECIPE
By Cindy Grisdela

Color choice is very personal, and it's a decision that many quilters struggle with. I like to cook, and creating a color scheme for a quilt feels a lot like putting together a recipe. The basic structure of your design might be shades of red, from the fiery orange of a tomato, to deep burgundy, all the way to warm cinnamon. If you leave it at that, it might look fine but lack the zing that really makes the recipe special. For spice, you might throw in some contrast such as purple or a dash of lime green.

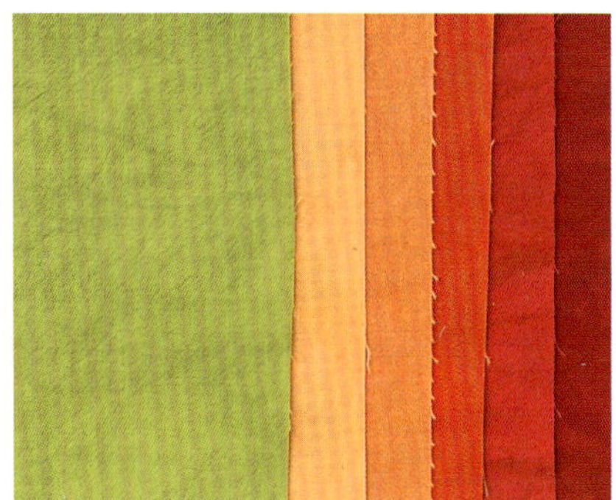

A variety of reds with a green for contrast

You've been putting colors together most of your life, even if you don't think of yourself as having an eye for color. All you need to do is look at the colors you wear and the colors you choose to live with in your home

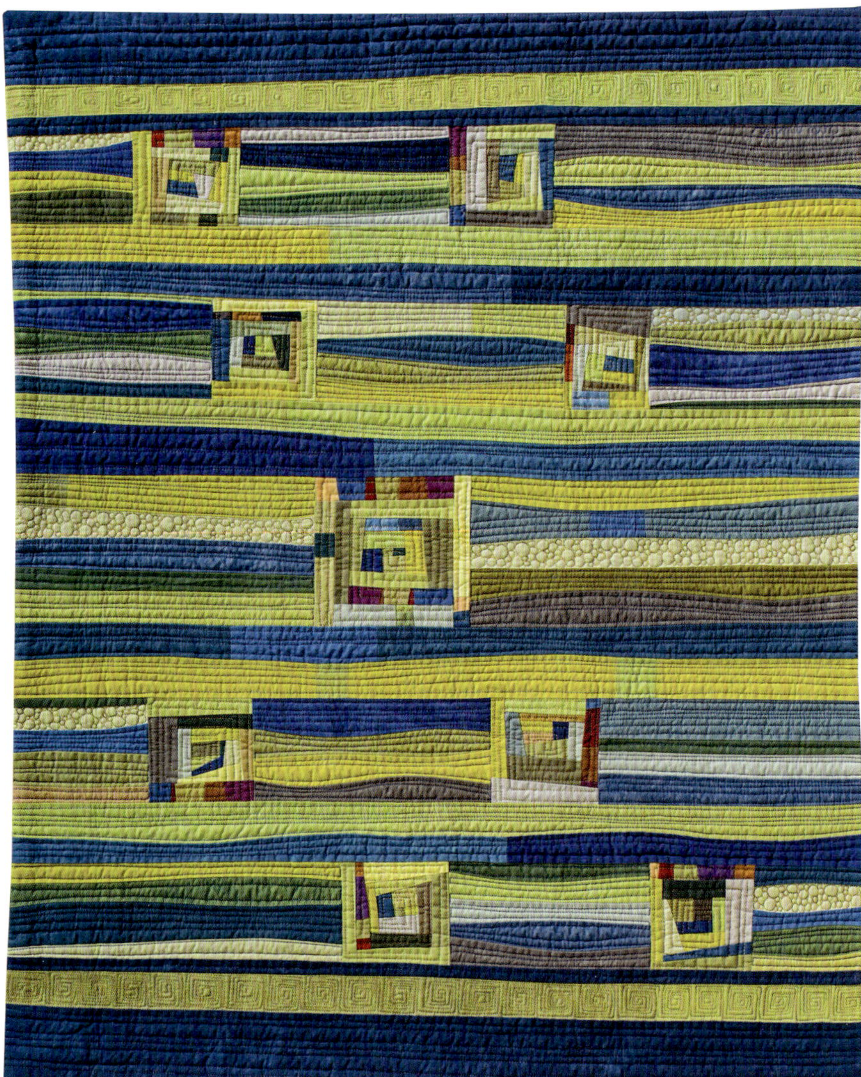

▶ *Island Hopping* by Cindy Grisdela, 28″ × 36″, 2014
This quilt incorporates a variety of blues and greens in an analogous (page 10) color scheme, plus a few accents of red and orange for contrast.

and you have a place to start. Begin where you feel most comfortable and let things evolve from there. For years my comfort zone was blue—sometimes edging over into the violet and red-violet range but rarely to the other side into greens. I made quite a few blue quilts before I was ready to move on to more adventurous combinations.

"How do you know if the colors go together?" is a question I hear fairly often.

My answer is that colors *don't* have to go together, at least in the sense that they don't have to match, and sometimes the composition is better if they don't. If you use a variety of greens in your design, ranging from bright lime to dusky olive, for instance, the eye will move around the quilt looking for connections, and that can make for a more interesting piece of art. *Island Hopping* (above) is a good example of this.

The Color Wheel

Color is one of the major elements of artistic design, and a color wheel is often useful in gaining a basic understanding of color.

There are three primary colors—red, blue, and yellow. Combining these colors gives you secondary colors. Red and blue make violet, blue and yellow make green, and yellow and red make orange. The other colors on the color wheel, called tertiary colors, are combinations of primary and secondary colors—red-violet, blue-green, and yellow-orange, for example.

Looking at the wheel, generally the colors on one side—yellow to orange to red—are considered warm. The colors on the other side—violet to blue to green—are thought of as cool. Warm colors tend to advance and lend energy to a design, while cool colors tend to recede and result in a calmer mood for the piece.

A good starting point can be the tried-and-true color schemes—or color recipes, as I like to call them. There are many more color schemes than the three presented on here, but these will be enough to get you started if you are new to the color wheel.

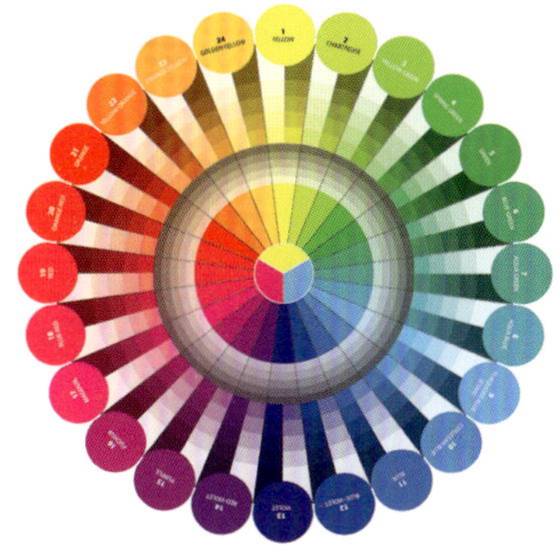

The Essential Color Wheel Companion by Joen Wolfrom (from C&T Publishing) can be a good starting point for using color. See page 106 for additional color tools.

MONOCHROMATIC COLOR RECIPE

In a monochromatic color scheme, all the fabrics come from one color family—green, for example. This is one of the easiest, most comfortable recipes to use because you just need light, medium, and dark fabrics in your chosen color family. A more formal way to think about it is tints, tones, and shades of the basic color, or hue (see Tints, Tones, and Shades, below). Monochromatic color recipes tend to be calm, soothing, and visually cohesive.

Tints, Tones, and Shades

Each color on the color wheel is known as a hue. If you add white to the hue, you get a lighter value, often a pastel, called a **tint**. If you add black to the hue, you get a **shade**, which is obviously darker than the original. And if you add both black and white to the hue, you get a **tone**, which is usually a softer, subtler variation of the color. A tone may be lighter or darker than the original hue.

Value

In the monochromatic color scheme the idea of **value** is particularly important. The value of a given fabric, whether it reads as light, dark, or medium, often depends on the value of the pieces surrounding it. Value is often more important than actual color in making a composition work, and using a variety of values is important in creating an interesting design, particularly with a

monochromatic color recipe. In *Seahorses* (below), I used a range of greens with different values, from deep hunter green to light pastel seafoam. In addition, there are some bluish-green shapes that push the green out toward blue on the color wheel, and some lime green ones that push out toward yellow on the other side. The contrasts keep the composition from becoming static and boring, which is often a risk with monochromatic color recipes.

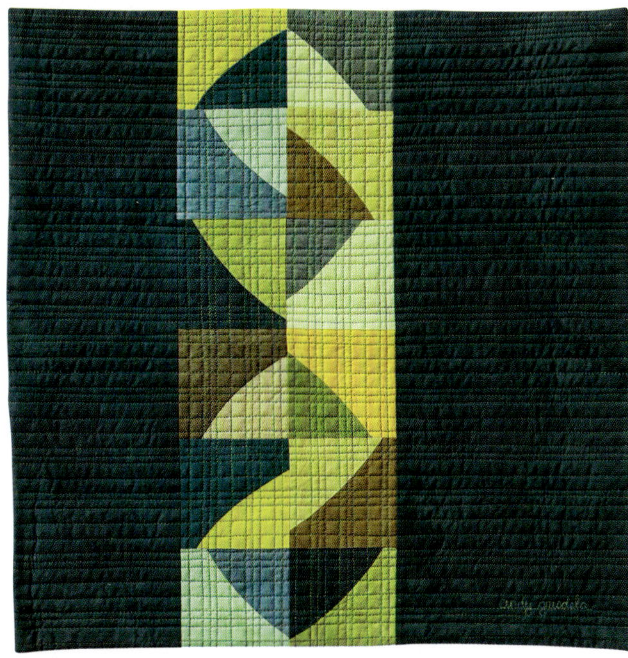

▶ *Seahorses* by Cindy Grisdela, 20″ × 20″, 2015
This quilt uses a monochromatic color recipe with a variety of greens.

ANALOGOUS COLOR RECIPE

Another color recipe that is comfortable to use, but usually more visually interesting, is known as analogous. This scheme uses colors that are close to each other on the color wheel, such as purple, blue, and green, or red, orange, and yellow. Often this recipe uses primarily two of the colors, say, blue and purple, with just an accent of the third one, green in the color run below.

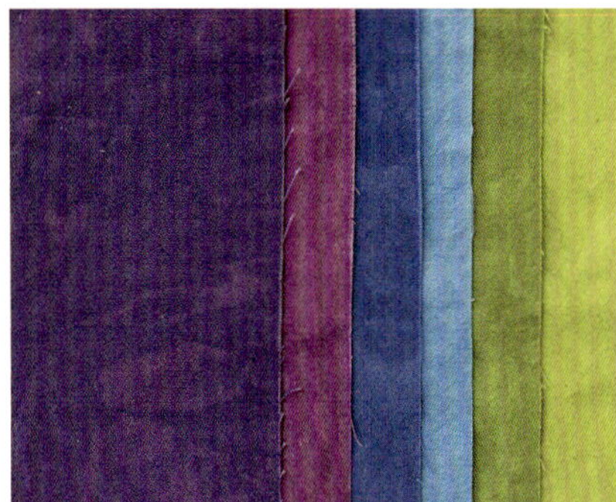

Analogous color recipe with blue, purple, and green

Analogous color recipes are usually richer and more nuanced than monochromatic ones, with controlled harmony. See *Island Hopping* (page 8) and *Summer* (page 11) for examples of analogous color schemes.

COMPLEMENTARY COLOR RECIPE

Complementary colors are opposite each other on the color wheel—think yellow and violet, red and green, blue and orange. Quilts with this color recipe often have a very active, energetic feel because the colors really bounce off one another. If you feel there's too much energy, you can calm things down by using primarily one of the complements with just an accent of the other. *Cosmos* is mostly blue with accents of orange.

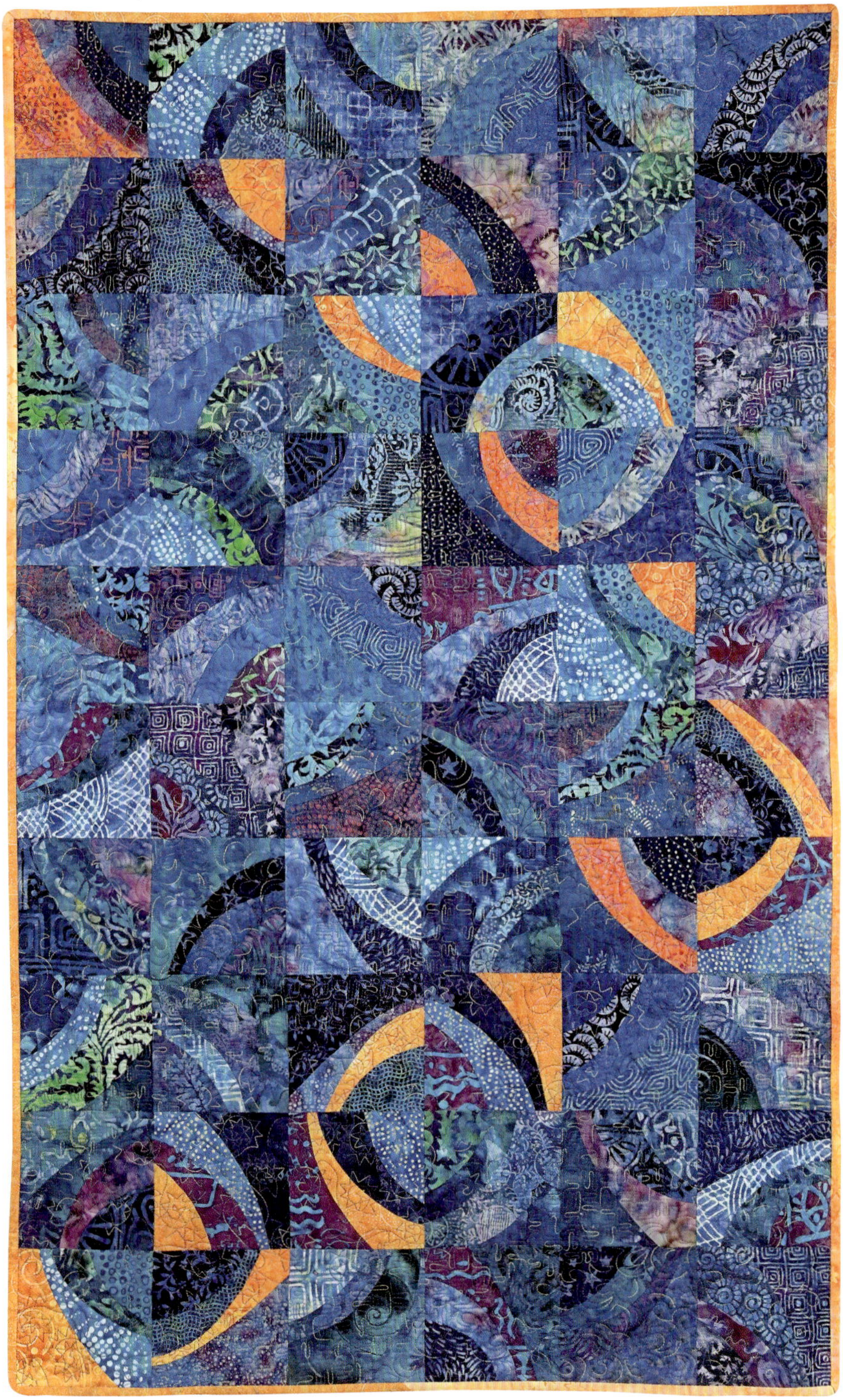

▸ *Cosmos* by Cindy Grisdela, 28″ × 47″, 2009
Complementary color scheme with blue and an accent of orange
Photo by Greg R. Staley

Using a Color Recipe

Use one of these basic schemes as a starting place as you begin to design your art quilt. Ask yourself questions about what you hope to achieve with your piece. Is it a calm, meditative design? Perhaps a monochromatic or analogous recipe using cooler colors would be a good choice. Or is it more assertive? Then you might want to use an analogous scheme on the warm side with reds, oranges, and yellows, or a recipe using complementary colors.

Or maybe you just like purple and lime green together and want to start there and not think about it so much! That's an option too.

ADDING THE SPARK

When you're using a controlled color scheme, such as a monochromatic or analogous recipe, there is a risk of creating a bland design. If your main color is red, try pushing it over to orange and also the other way, to red-purple. Also think about adding a spark to your composition in the form of a contrast to draw the eye in. In an overall warm scheme of red, orange, and yellow, for example, consider throwing in a splash of the complementary green to liven things up and keep the composition from feeling too static. *Summer* uses this type of composition.

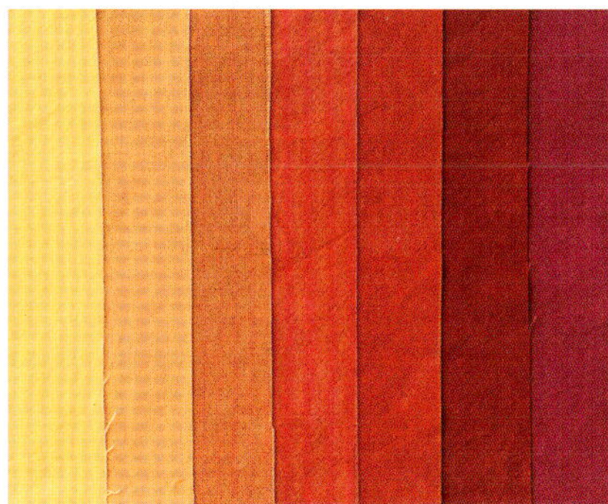

Warm color recipe

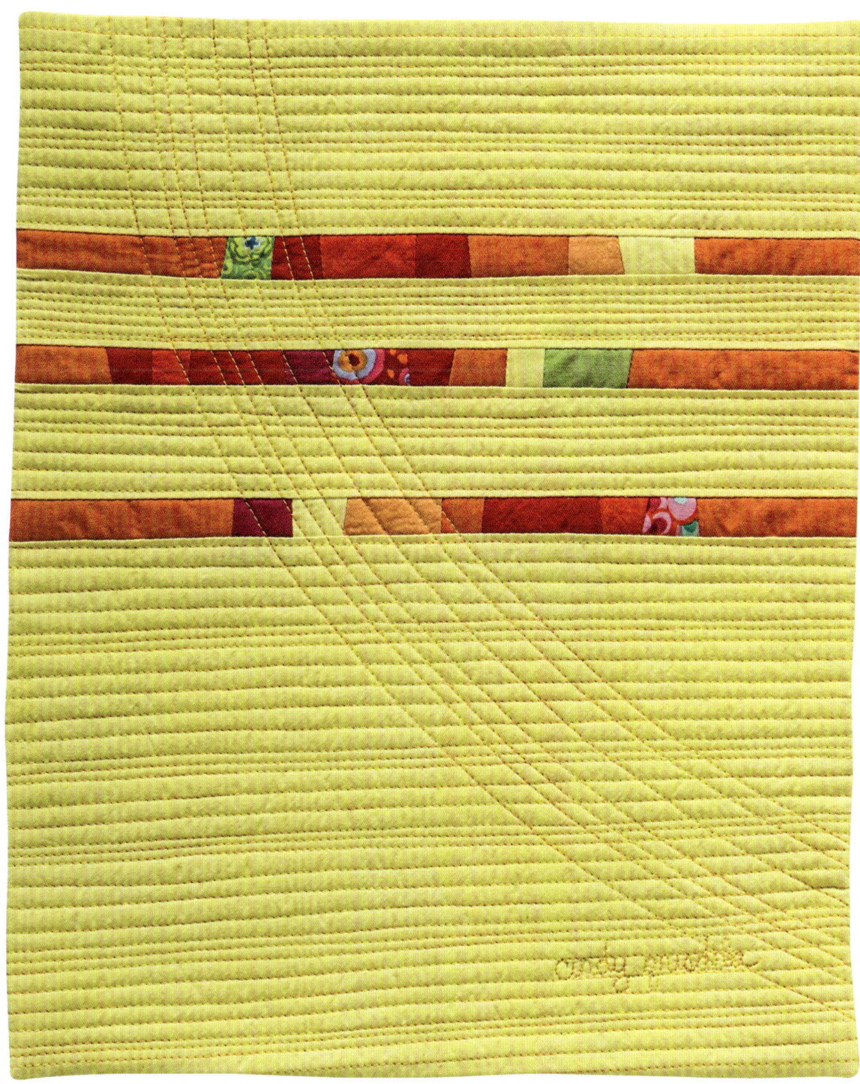

▶ *Summer* by Cindy Grisdela, 12″ × 15″, 2015
Using an analogous color recipe on the warm side with yellow, orange, and red, with an accent of complementary green for the spark

COLOR SCHEMES AND VALUE

By Katie Pasquini Masopust

As textile artists, we use fabric as our palette. I treat my fabrics as I would paints in a paint box. In my studio, they are arranged in the same order as the colors around the color wheel (shown on page 16). Not only do I have composition plans when I design my work, but I have color plans as well—they are the classic color schemes. They make for beautiful color choices. These are the ones I use most often.

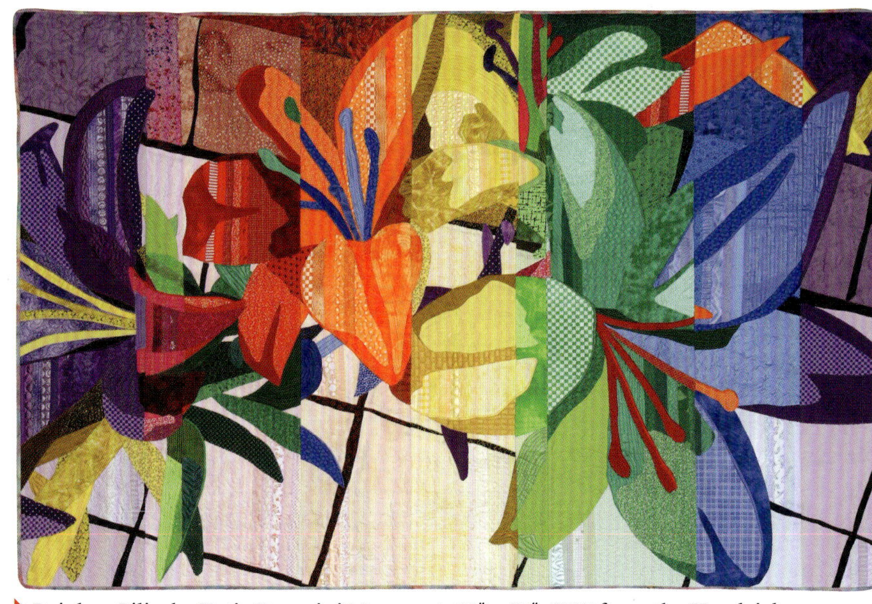

▶ *Rainbow Lilies* by Katie Pasquini Masopust, 54″ × 37″, 2007 from the Hendricks collection

CLASSIC COLOR SCHEMES

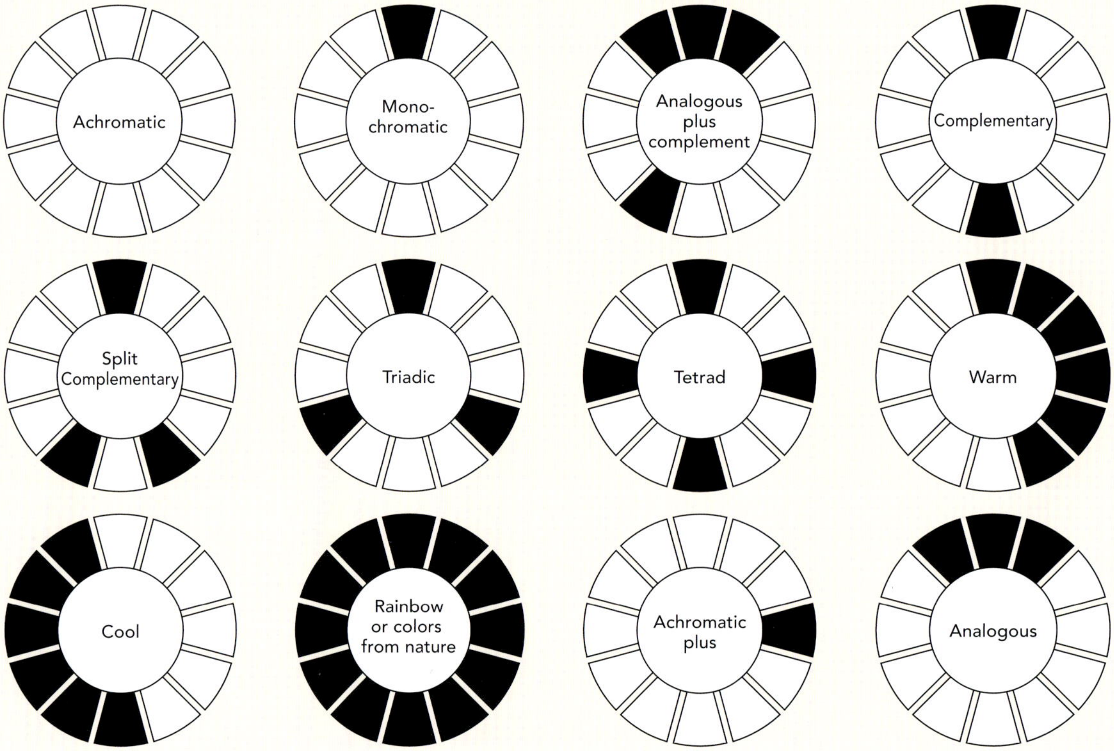

Achromatic

Mono-chromatic

Analogous plus complement

Complementary

Split Complementary

Triadic

Tetrad

Warm

Cool

Rainbow or colors from nature

Achromatic plus

Analogous

Color Schemes

ACHROMATIC

Achromatic is the absence of color. White, black, and all variations of gray make up the gray scale. A graphic gray scale can be created with black-and-white prints sorted to visually make a gray scale when seen from a distance.

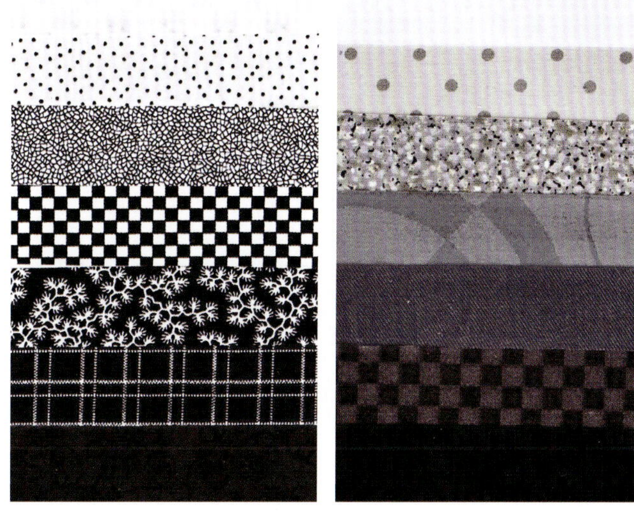

Value 1: white-on-white prints

Value 2: white background with a little bit of black print

Value 3: white background with more black print

Value 4: the middle value, with equal amounts of black and white print

Value 5: black background with a lot of white print

Value 6: black background with a little bit of white print

Value 7: black-on-black prints

ACHROMATIC PLUS

When assigning achromatic exercises to my students, I am often asked if it's okay to add a color—for example, black and white with a bit of red, or black and white with a bit of blue-green. For a true achromatic color scheme, no color should be used. But I have acquiesced on this point; it is more of a quilter's color scheme to use black and white with a bit of color for an accent. I call this scheme achromatic plus. (Two sets shown at right.)

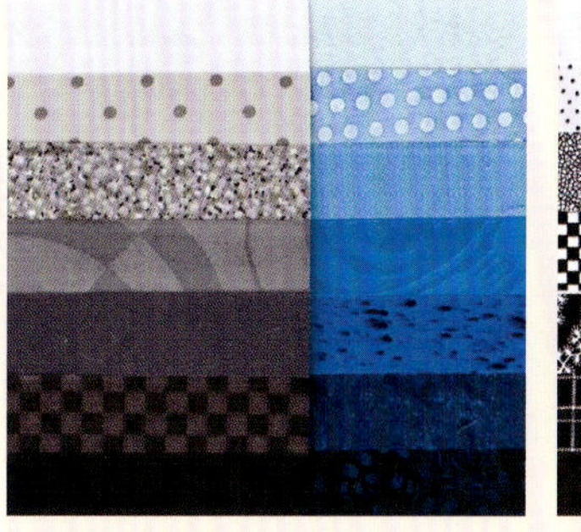
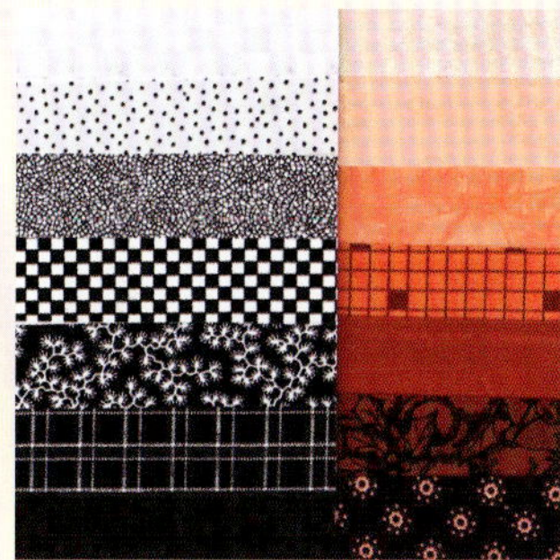

MONOCHROMATIC

Monochromatic is one color and all its values. This is an elegant color scheme and very calming. Contrast is created with value. (Twelve sets shown below.)

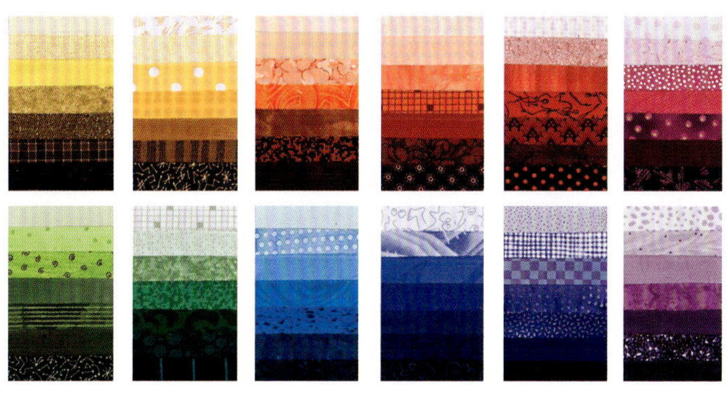

ANALOGOUS

Analogous colors are three to four colors next to each other on the color wheel. This is a harmonious color scheme; the colors are related because they are next to each other, and each color includes a bit of the neighboring color. (Three sets shown below.)

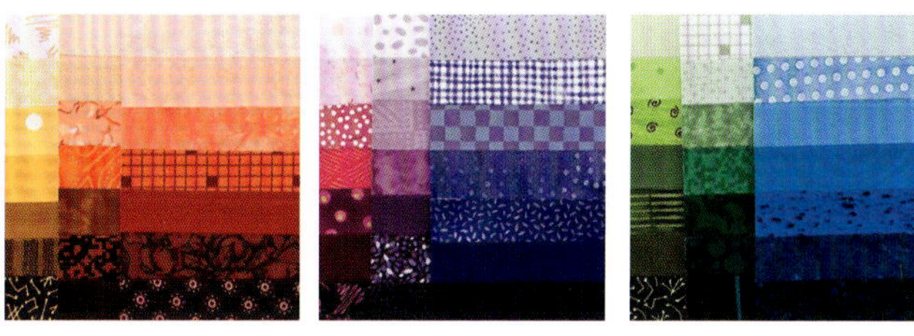

ANALOGOUS PLUS A COMPLEMENT

The analogous plus a complement color scheme uses analogous colors plus the complement of one of the colors added as an accent. (Two sets shown below.)

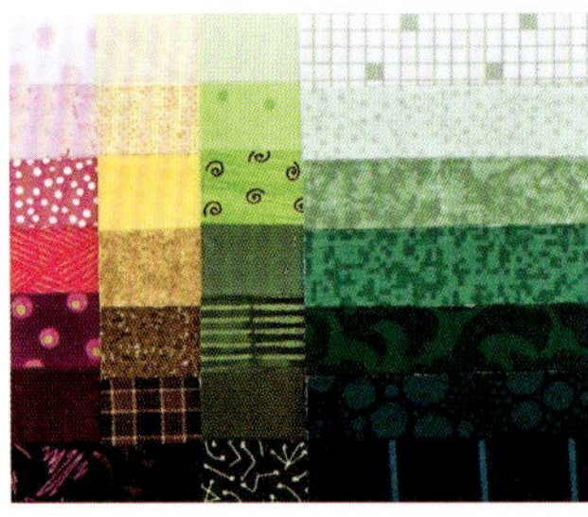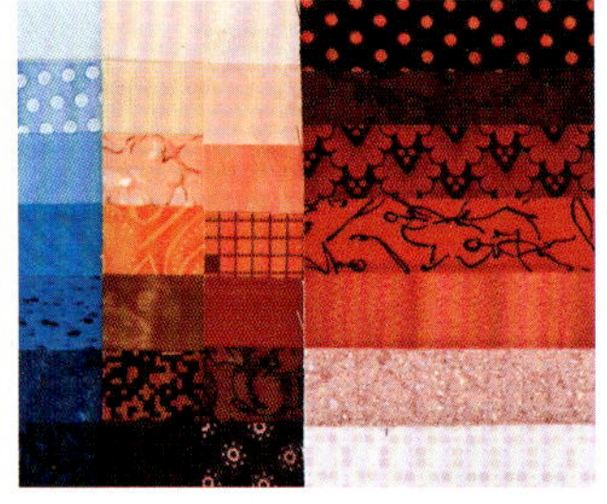

SPLIT COMPLEMENTARY

A split complementary color scheme uses one color and the two colors on either side of that color's complement. This color scheme creates an effect that is similar to but softer than the complementary color scheme. (Three sets shown below.)

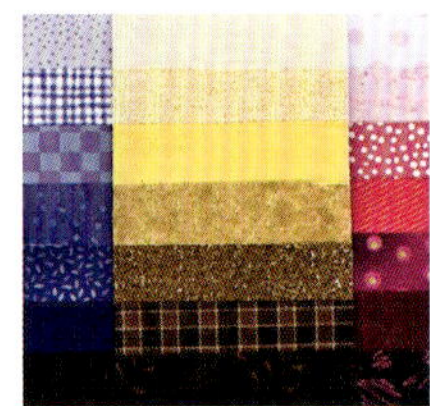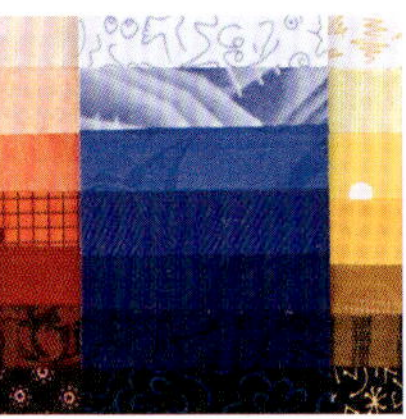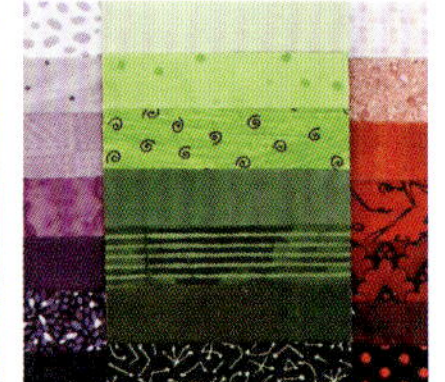

COMPLEMENTARY

The colors opposite each other on the color wheel are complements. These two colors create vibration and tension because they are opposites. When used in a medium value, these colors are very strong and demand attention, but when used with a full range of values, this color scheme can be quite pleasant. The addition of lights and darks creates a calmer composition. (Six sets shown below.)

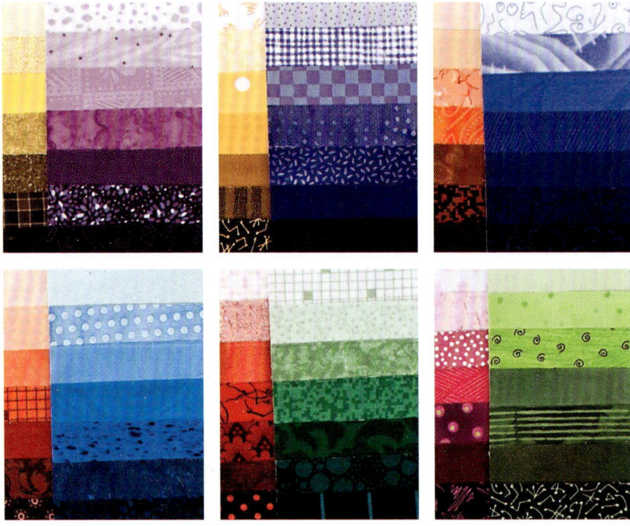

TRIAD

A triad color scheme uses three colors that are an equal distance from each other on the color wheel (i.e., separated by three colors). Red, yellow, and blue make up the primary triad color scheme. Orange, green, and violet make up the secondary triad color scheme. Two different triad color schemes are created from the tertiary colors (the colors between the primary and secondary colors). (Four sets shown below.)

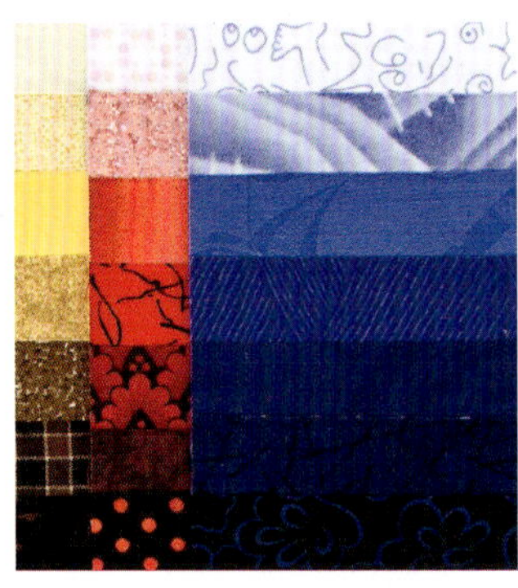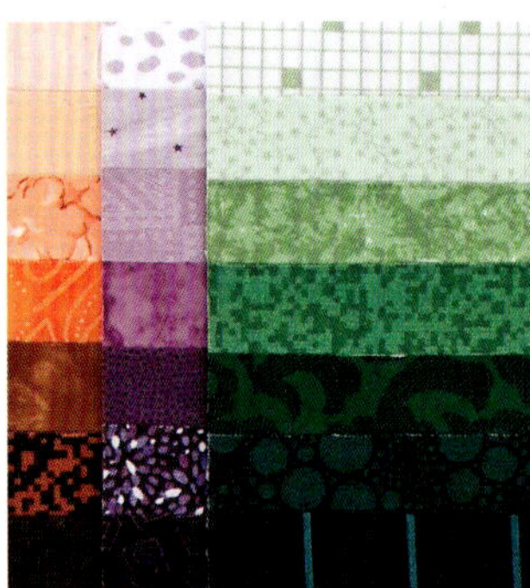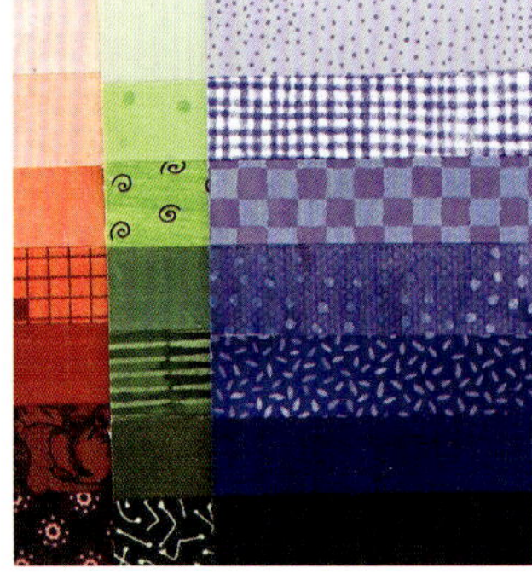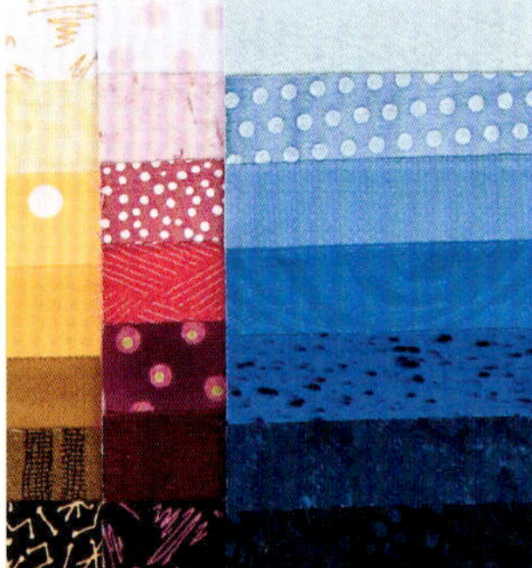

TETRAD

A tetrad arrangement uses colors at four points on the color wheel, in either a rectangle or a square—in other words, two pairs of complementary colors. A dual complementary color scheme is a variation of a tetrad but uses two colors next to each other on the color wheel and their complements. This color scheme is very lively because of the use of two complements, but it can be toned down by using a full value run (covered later in this chapter). (Three sets shown below.)

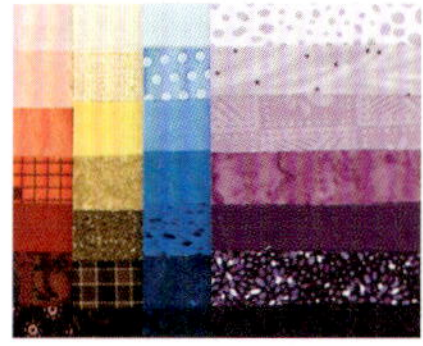 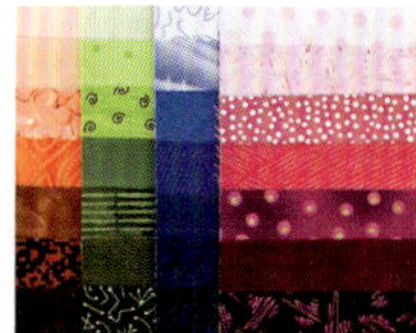 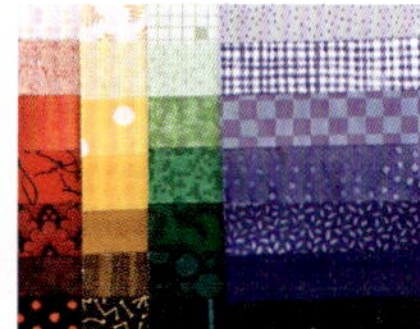

COOL

Cool colors are yellow-green through violet—the other half of the color wheel. Cool colors are colors that are seen in water.

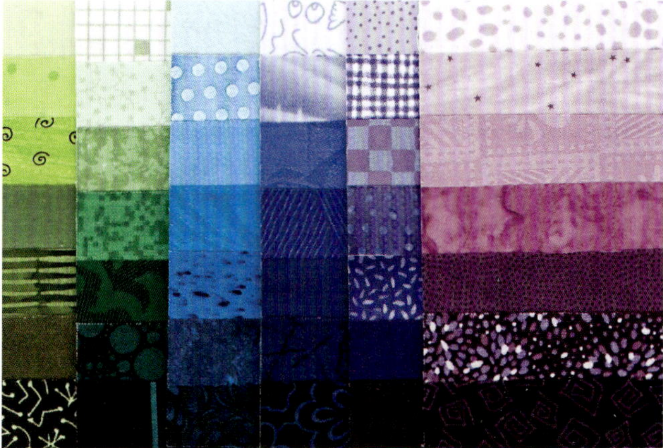

WARM

Warm colors are yellow through red-violet, comprising one half of the color wheel. Warm colors are colors that are seen in fire.

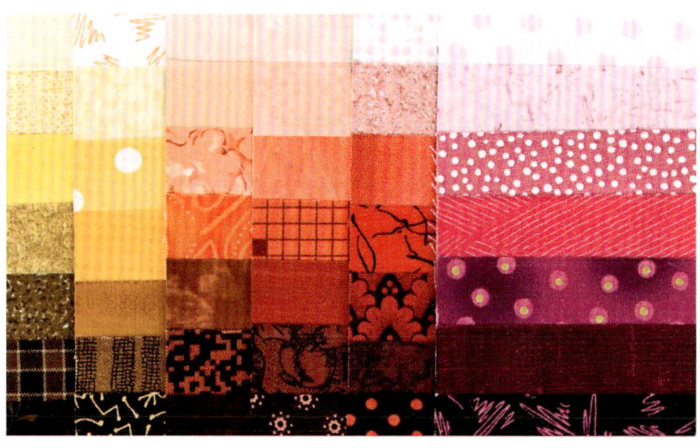

RAINBOW

Rainbow colors are the twelve colors on the color wheel. This color scheme creates a rainbow effect. Warm colors come forward and cool colors recede when all the colors are used.

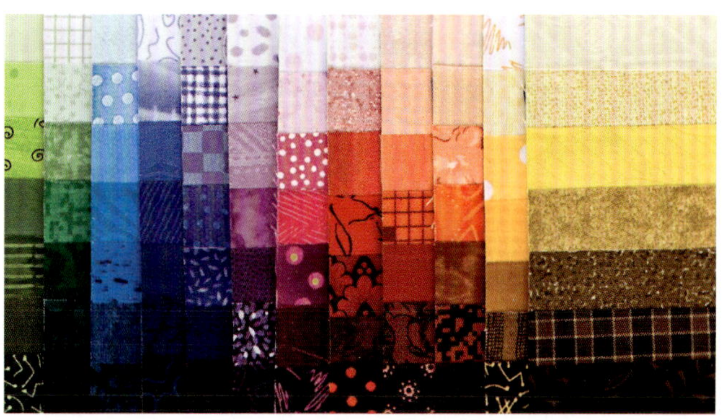

COLORS FROM NATURE

This color scheme is used for realistic landscapes, creating the image in the true colors of the original subject.

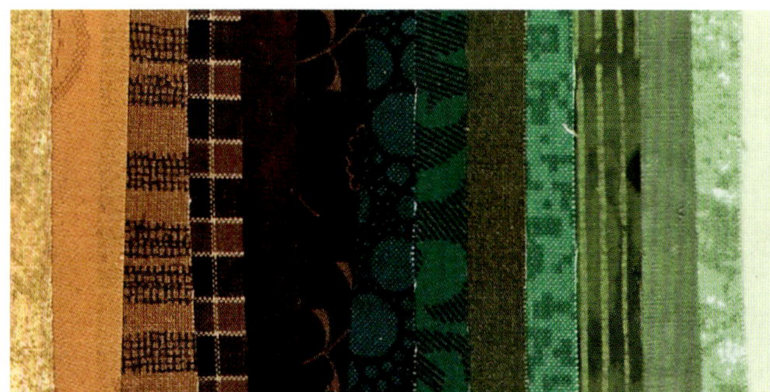 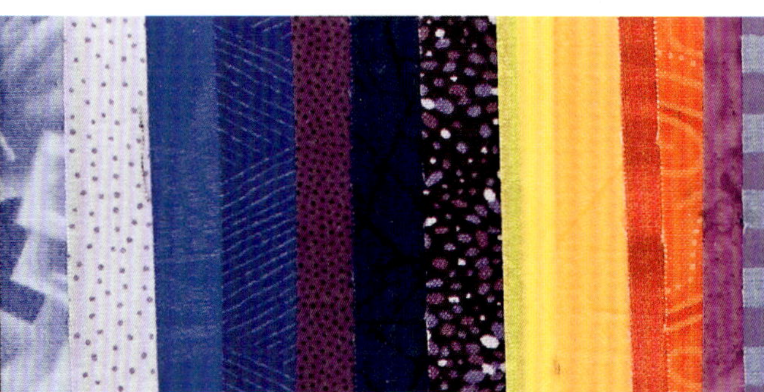

Value

Value is as important as the colors you choose. It is often said that color gets all the credit while value does all the work.

I store my fabrics in racks of open bins in my design studio, separated into primary and secondary colors—yellow, orange, red, violet, blue, and green. I then sort each color further into seven value steps, from light (value 1) through the pure color to dark (value 7). Pure colors have an inherent value: yellow, yellow-green, and yellow orange are value 3; violet and blue-violet are value 5; and the rest are value 4.

I use fabrics that read as one color. The fabric may include more than one color, but the overall impression is that of a single color. Busy fabric with too much pattern or color will compete with the lines of the design.

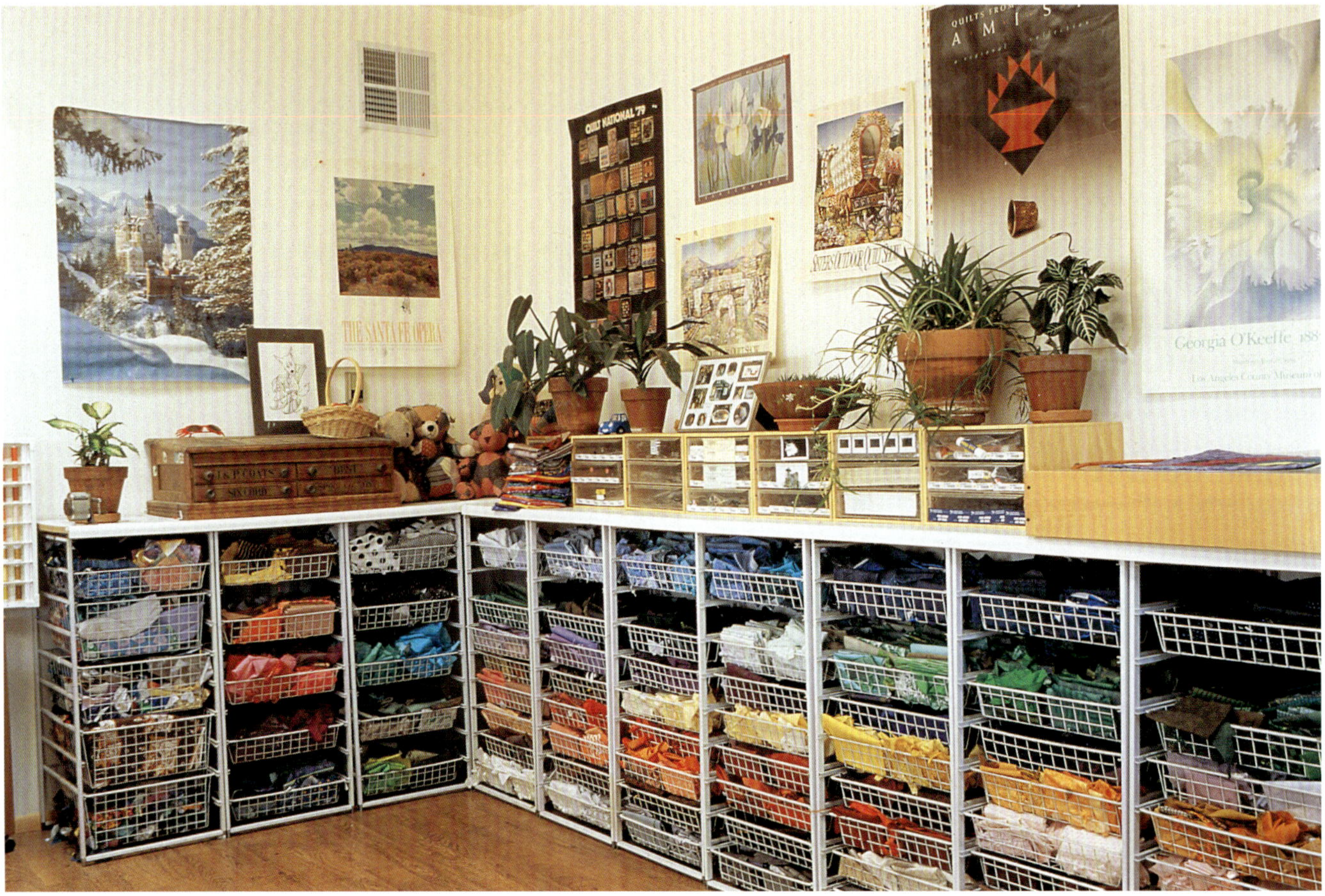

Seven-step system for sorting fabric in wire drawers

Photo by Hawthorne Studio

USING VALUE

I typically use three value ranges in my designs:

Full value range: A complete value range, or run, starts with the lightest value of a color, which is the color plus white (value 1), runs through the pure color, and ends with the darkest value, the color plus black (value 7). (Three sets shown at right.)

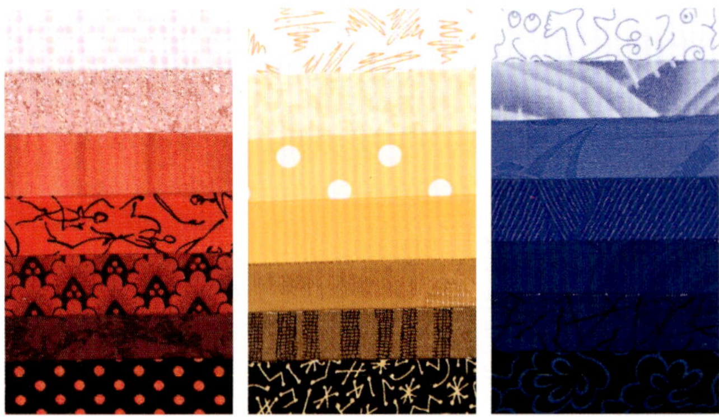

Light value range: A light value range runs from the lightest value of a color (value 1) through to the midrange (value 3 to 5, depending on the color). It does not include the very darkest values of the color. This value scheme will create a light, cheerful quilt.

Dark value range: A dark value range runs from the midrange value of the color (value 3 to 5, depending on the color) to the very darkest (value 7). It does not include the light end of the value run. This value scheme will create a somber or mysterious quilt.

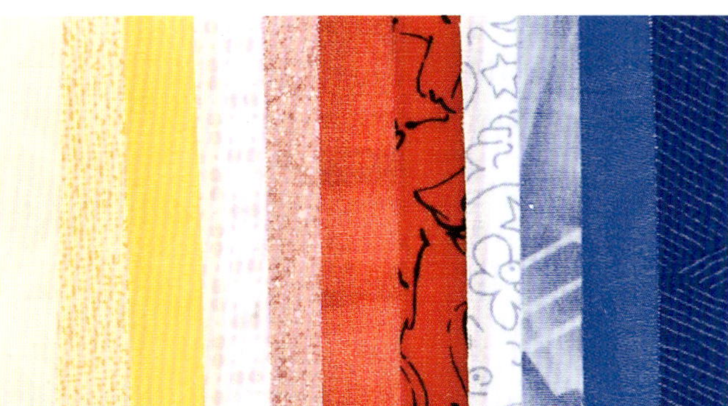

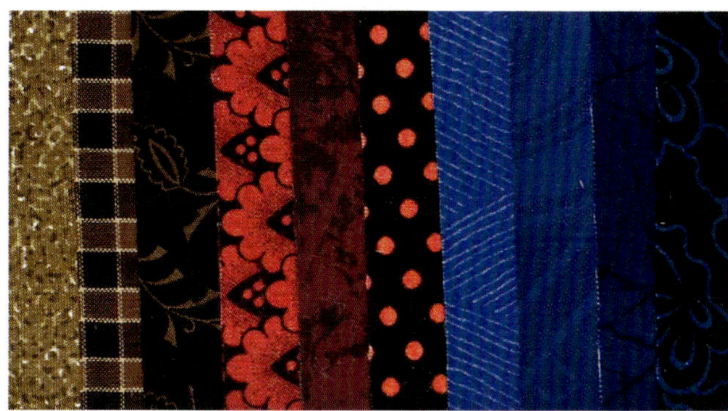

USING THE SEVEN-STEP VALUE RANGE

I recommend that you try to arrange your fabrics into seven-step value ranges. Don't be too concerned with each piece being in the perfect order. If you can't decide if a piece goes in value 3 or 4, then it is close to where it should be and you can pick one or the other. Color and value will change depending on the lighting and the adjacent color choices. I use the seven steps as a guide, not as an absolute.

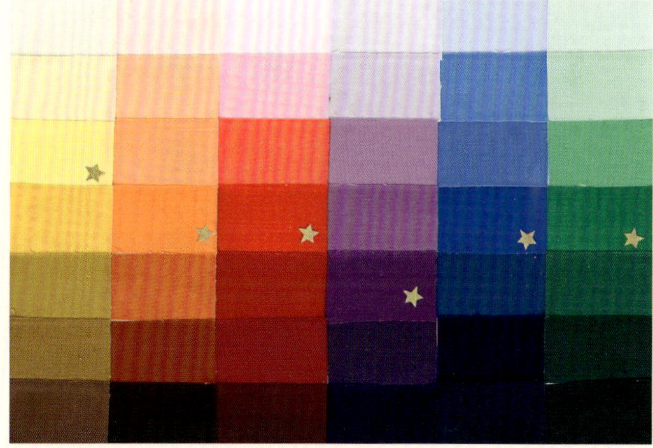

Pure color positioning

Choosing a Color Scheme

When choosing a color scheme, begin by deciding on one color that you want to use. Find that color on the color wheel. Refer to the chart of color schemes and find all the other colors that would be needed for each scheme. You will know the right color scheme when you find the one that excites you. For the explorations based on painting, you will need to choose the color scheme before doing the painting. For the explorations based on drawing, this decision will be made after the design is complete. If you are working with a design based on a photograph, you will have additional information to help you in your decision making. For example, if the design is based on a flower or a landscape, decide whether you want to use colors from nature; if you do, create the design in the colors in the photograph. However, using an unexpected color scheme is one way of making a realistic design more abstract. For example, if the image is a red flower with green foliage, consider recreating it in a monochromatic color scheme using only purples, or possibly a triadic color scheme of red, blue, and yellow. An unusual color scheme will create a unique quilt that will catch people's attention and amaze them because the quilt is so different.

VALUE AND COLOR EXERCISES

By Katie Pasquini Masopust and Brett Barker

Value is the most important aspect of color. A full range of values, from light to dark, makes the difference between a mediocre quilt and a true piece of art. Usually the very lights and the deepest darks are forgotten. Because lighter colors can illuminate a quilt and darks can add depth and richness, we encourage the use of a seven-step value run in art pieces.

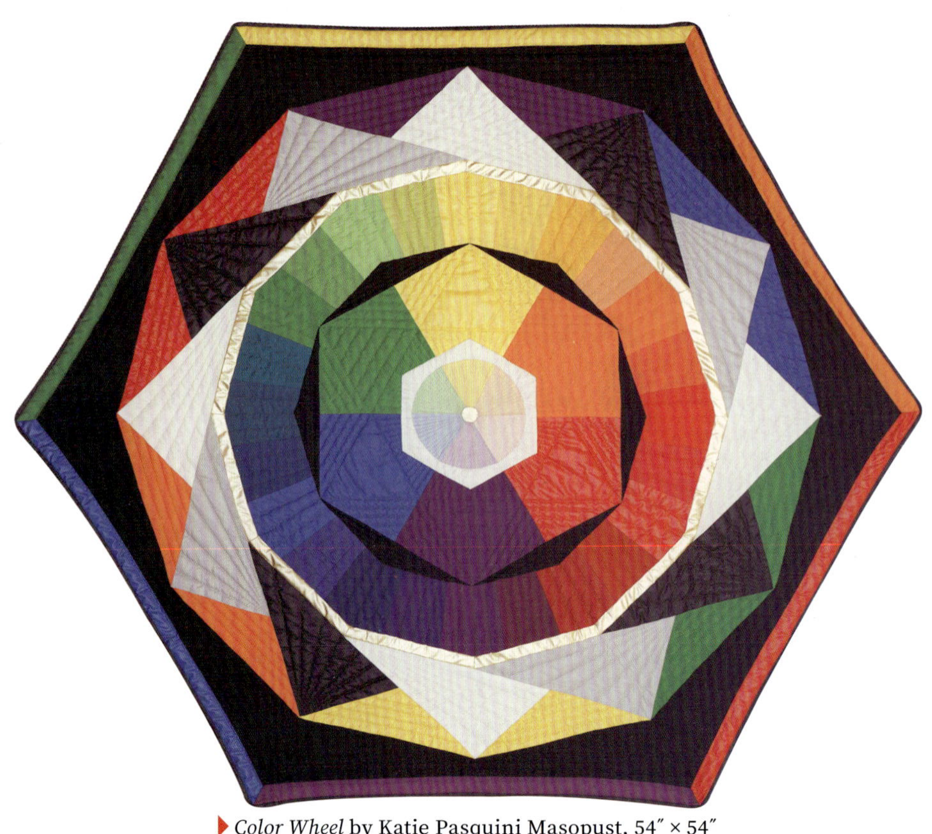

▶ *Color Wheel* by Katie Pasquini Masopust, 54″ × 54″
Photo By Lindsay Olsen

Exercise: Gray-Scale Value Run

This arrangement of gray values is one of the most important tools you can possess as an art quilter. It will help you evaluate each color's value.

Materials

Fused fabrics in a seven-step value run from white through grays to black

Medium gray fabric: 1 square 18″ × 18″ for background foundation

Rotary cutting ruler

Rotary cutter

Cutting mat

Iron

DIRECTIONS

1. Evaluate your fabrics to produce 7 gradations that transition smoothly in even steps from white as Value 1 to black as Value 7.

2. Cut 1 square 2″ × 2″ from each of the selected fabrics.

3. Remove the paper backing from the fused fabric, and place your 2″ squares in order, from light to dark, on the left edge of the gray fabric. Put the light square at the top and the dark at the bottom.

4. Fuse the squares in place.

Gray-scale value run

Exercise: Graphic Gray-Scale

You'll add energy and vibration to the gray scale by using blackand-white graphic prints.

Materials

Fused fabrics in black-andwhite prints in a seven-step value run (Your fabrics need to be true black-and-white prints—no creams, grays, or solids.)

Rotary cutting ruler

Rotary cutter

Cutting mat

Iron

Seven-Step Value Run

It is important to have the seven-step value run as a full palette to work with. The solid gray scale allows you to more easily see value difference as you train your eye. The graphic gray scale shows you how to use black-and-white prints. Keep these two scales as a reference tool in your studio.

DIRECTIONS

1. Evaluate your print fabrics to produce 7 gradations that transition smoothly:

Value 1: the lightest value—white print on white background

Value 2: white background with a little bit of black print

Value 3: white background with more black print

Value 4: equal amounts of black and white

Value 5: black background with a lot of white print

Value 6: black background with a bit of white print

Value 7: the darkest value—black print on black background

2. Cut 1 square 2″ × 2″ from each of the selected fabrics, remove the paper backing from the fused fabrics, and place them on the far right side of the gray foundation used in Exercise 1. The lightest value should be on the top and the darkest value at the bottom.

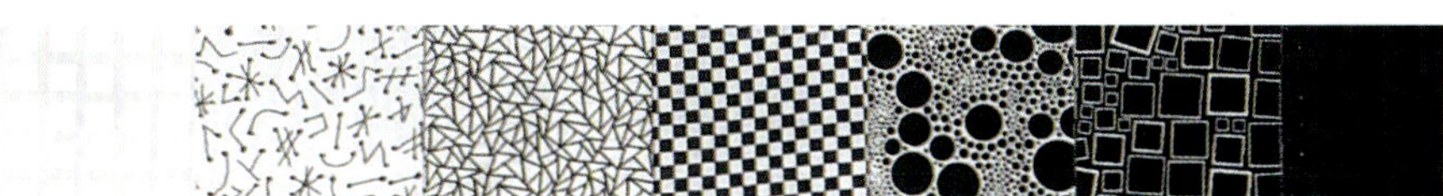

Graphic gray-scale value run

3. Fuse the squares in place.

Exercise: Color Wheel

A personal color wheel that you create from fabric gives you a much better sense of color theory than a printed color wheel that you simply purchase from an art store. Your color wheel will have 12 **medium value** colors (sometimes called the **true hues**). The primary colors will have lighter versions, called **pastels** or **tints**, and darker versions, called **shades**.

Materials

Fused fabric in all the following colors:

Yellow, light yellow, dark yellow	Violet, light violet, dark violet	Rotary cutting ruler
Yellow-orange	Blue-violet	Rotary cutter
Orange, light orange, dark orange	Blue, light blue, dark blue	Cutting mat
Red-orange	Blue-green	Iron
Red, light red (pink), dark red	Green, light green, dark green	
Red-violet	Yellow-green	

1. Evaluate your colors carefully—you are making a reference tool that you will use in the future. Compare your selected colors with the completed color wheel (on page 21) to make sure you have the right selection of colors. Cut 1 square 2″ × 2″ from each fabric you choose.

2. Create a color wheel in the center of the gray fabric that has the two gray scales. Start by placing the yellow, red, and blue squares in position as if on a clock: yellow at 12 o'clock, red at 4 o'clock, and blue at 8 o'clock. These three colors are the **primary** colors.

3. Place the orange square at 2 o'clock, violet at 6 o'clock, and green at 10 o'clock. These are the secondary colors, the midway points between primaries.

4. Add **tints** and **shades** to these primaries and secondaries. Place the lighter value, the tint, to the inside of each color on your wheel to make an interior ring. Place the darker values, the shades, to the outside of the medium-valued, true primaries and secondaries to make an outer ring of 6 shades.

5. Complete the wheel by adding the tertiary colors. Place the pure values of:

    yellow-orange at 1 o'clock

    red-orange at 3 o'clock

    red-violet at 5 o'clock

    blue-violet at 7 o'clock

    blue-green at 9 o'clock

    yellow-green at 11 o'clock

See how the tertiary colors contain equal amount of the colors they are between.

6. Fuse the squares in place.

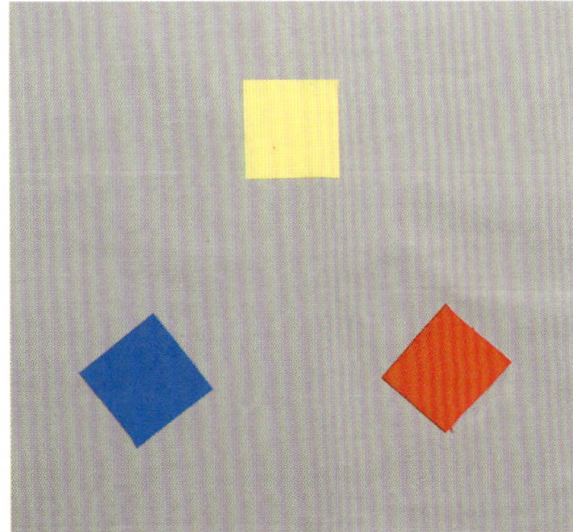

Primaries

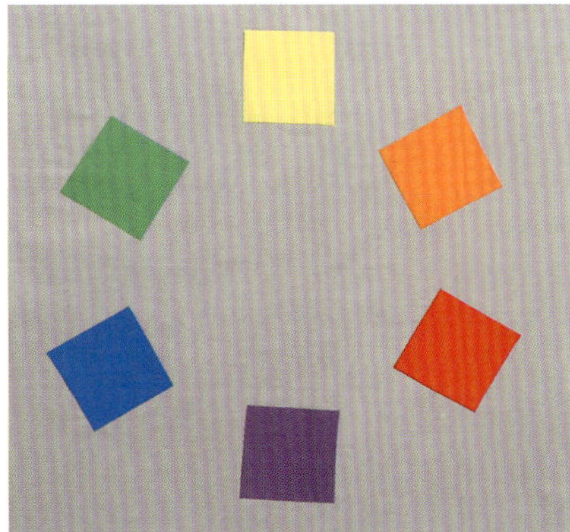

Secondaries

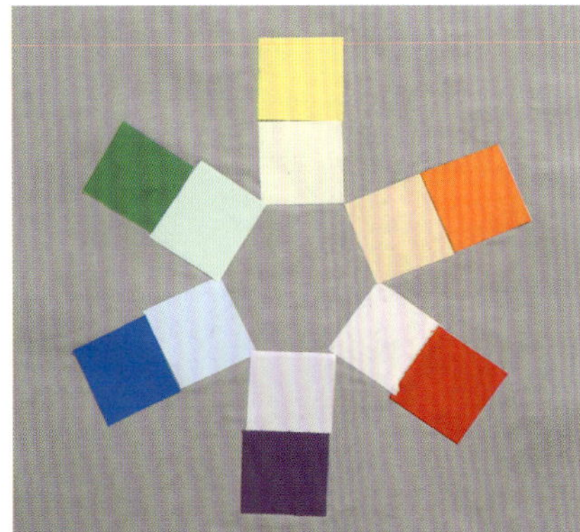

Tints

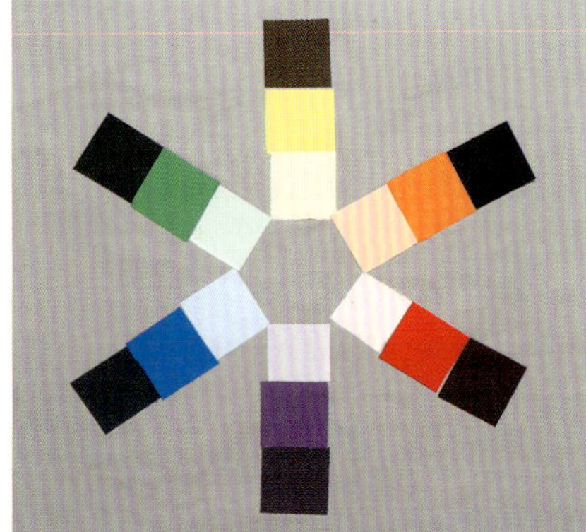

Shades

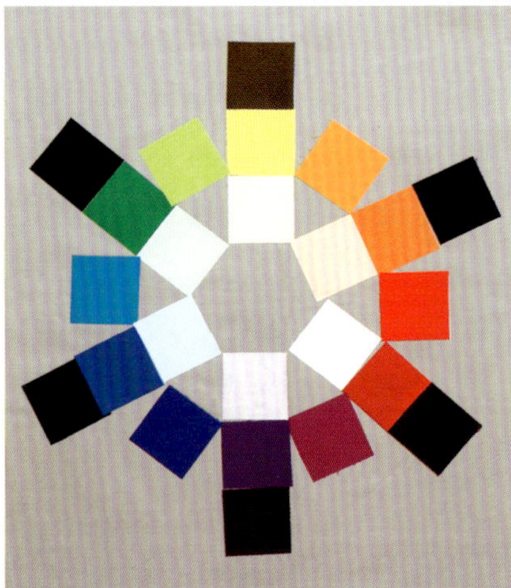

Complete color wheel

OPTIONAL EXERCISE

If you'd like to add tints and shades of the tertiary colors, cut out lighter-value triangles, and place them in the inner ring for the tertiary tints. Cut out darker value 2″ squares, and place them in the outer ring for the shades. Fuse the squares and triangles in place.

The Importance of the Wheels

Creating a color wheel and gray-scale value run tool from fabric is essential for understanding colors and value changes. The way in which color and value relate to each other is at the heart of artistic creation. Hang this tool on your wall. Use it to identify the color and value schemes used in future chapters. A fabric color wheel will help you develop your eye for color faster than any other tool in the marketplace today.

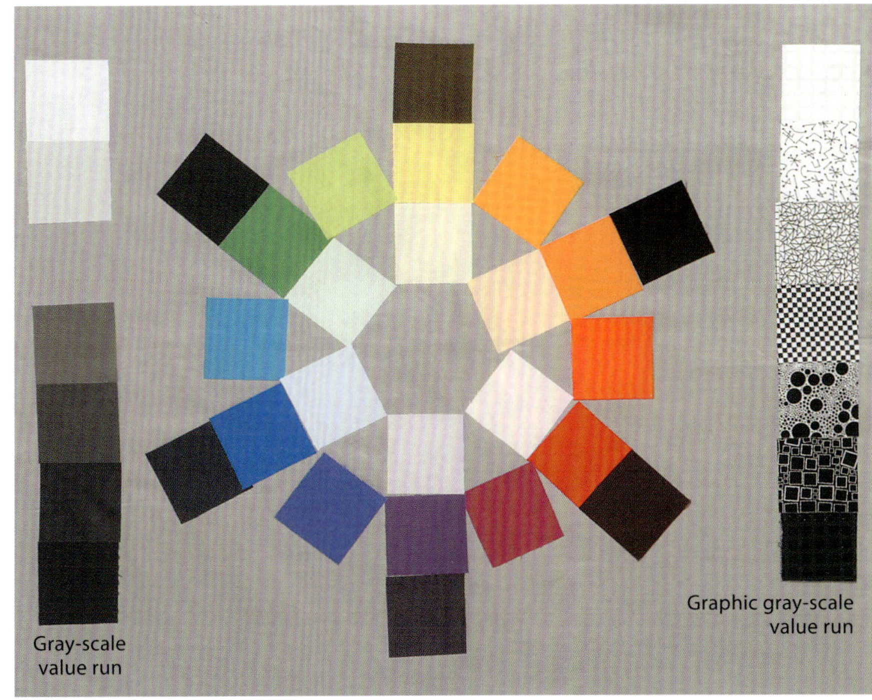

Color wheel and gray-scales value tool

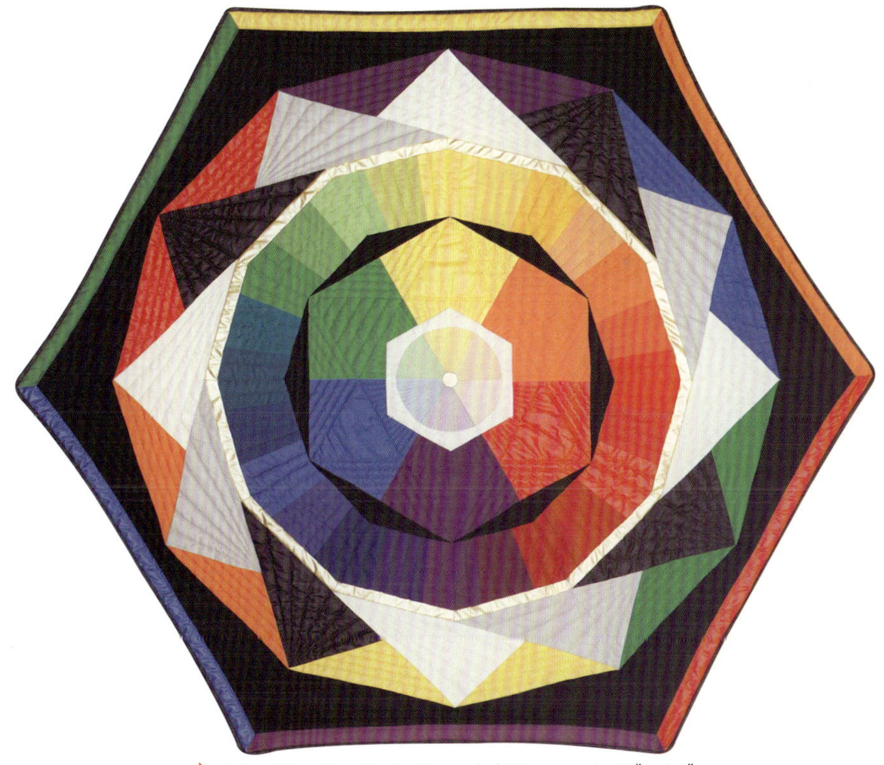

Color Wheel by Katie Pasquini Masopust, 54″ × 54″
Photo By Lindsay Olsen

COLOR—THE QUILTMAKER'S FOUNDATION

By Maria Shell

Your job as a quiltmaker is to harness the power of color and use it to create vivid compositions.

In order to do that, you need to understand some basic color concepts. There will be enough information in this chapter to get you started, but I heartily encourage you to make this the starting point in a lifelong quest to understand what color is and what it does.

First of all, color, also known as *hue,* is *relative.* This is the most important thing for you to know about color. The perception of a color can change depending upon the other colors around it. Color is also affected by the light in which it is viewed. The truth is even our own eyesight can affect the way color is perceived. We do not all see color the same way.

Using A Color Wheel

A color wheel helps you understand the colors and their relationships. Even if you choose your color palette intuitively or from a specific inspiration, using a color wheel can help you with your color choices.

Colors opposite from each other on the wheel are called *complementary colors*—this color scheme is bold and high contrast. Colors that form a triangle on the color wheel work well together and are called *triadic.* Colors next to each other create a soothing color scheme and are called *analogous.*

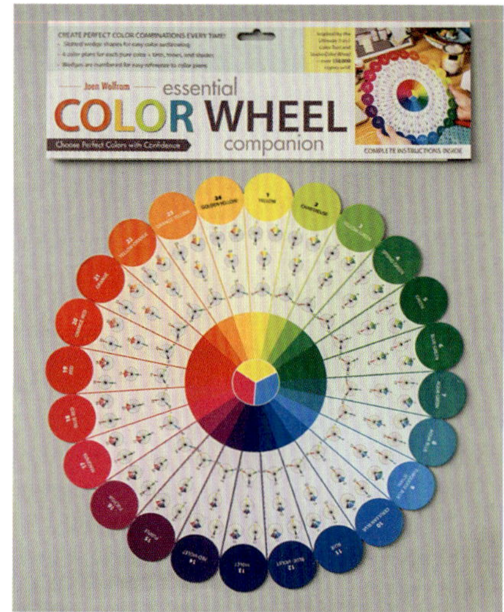

A well-stocked quiltmaking toolbox includes a color wheel and value finders.

DEVELOP YOUR PERSONAL COLOR IDENTITY

Try not only to observe color but also articulate to yourself what you are seeing.

Identify how you want to use color. I call this "creating your own personal color identity." Do you like muted palettes? Or are you a graphic quiltmaker using bold colors? Do you gravitate toward cheerful color palettes or are you more somber? Knowing this will help guide you in building palettes.

While selecting your palette, try very hard to shut off any analytical or critical voices in your head. Try to work only with your eyes and emotions. How does that color palette feel? Does it create the feeling you want to evoke?

Practice, practice, practice. Developing a strong personal color identity takes time. It is as much a part of your voice as a quiltmaker as the compositional and technical choices you make in your work.

Color From A Quilter's Perspective

It is useful to know that when you mix blue and yellow, you will get green, but as a quiltmaker you don't necessarily need to have that information. Unlike a painter or fabric dyer, who actually mixes colors, a quiltmaker uses already-colored fabric.

But it's imperative for successful quiltmaking to understand and pay attention to how colors work in relationship to each other.

It's also useful to know that when you mix black with a color you get a shade, and when you mix gray with a color you get a tone. While these shades and tones may be just what you are looking for in a color palette, they can also look muted and dead, sucking the life out of other colors or making a color palette murky or dull. On the other hand, pure colors (with no black or gray in them) will be more lively. Keep these characteristics in mind when you are pulling together a color palette.

Most quilters come to quilting with a natural inclination toward a particular palette. You may be very fond of earth tones or you may love the primary colors. It is helpful to identify where your comfort zone is and then grow. We all have colors we don't like. Challenge yourself to use them. I find maroon disturbingly ugly and for years wouldn't touch a shade of brown. After I welcomed brown into my palette, my work immediately gained a level of sophistication that it had been missing.

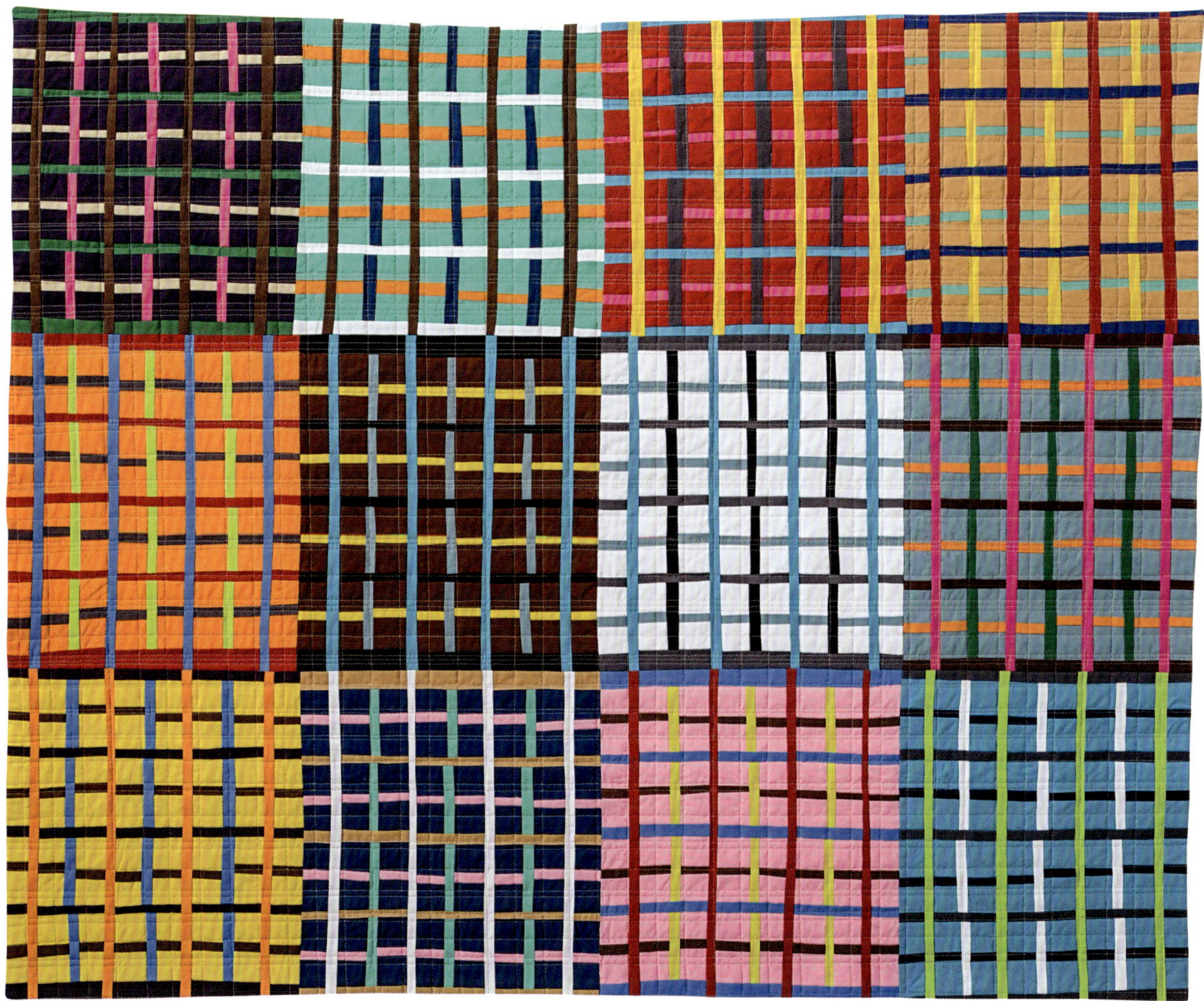

▶ *Big Rad Plaid* by Maria Shell, 2017, 48″ × 54″
This quilt was made with Designer Essentials solids by FreeSpirit Fabric.

Building A Color Palette

Selecting fabrics to begin a new quilt can be daunting. In my early years as a quilter, I would take hours (sometimes days) to select a palette, and even then I frequently felt that I failed. Over the years, I have slowly gotten better and better at this crucial step, and you will, too, if you are willing to be thoughtful in your decisions.

When you select a palette think about three things:

Creating a *beautiful* palette

Creating an *unusual* palette

Creating a palette where each color *holds its own* (By that I mean that no matter where a color lands in the composition it still has the ability to be seen.)

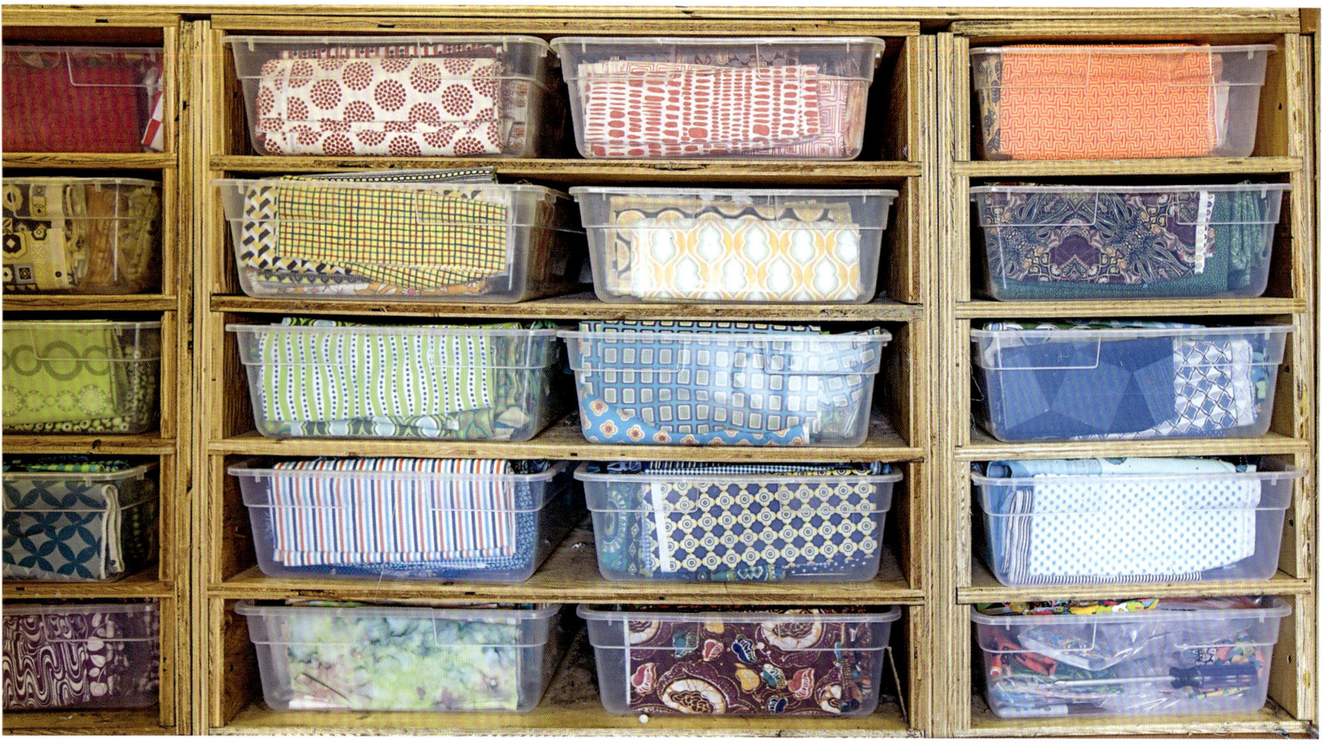

My filing system

Photo by Paul Scannell

I store my fabric in what I call my fabric filing system. I have about 80 files/bins in my studio. As I work on a palette, I pull my files/bins out and look through them, searching for interesting combinations.

After you select a palette that you think might work, fold the fabrics and rest them on top of each other. You want an *equal* amount of each color to be visible—about 2″—to do a color test. With my process, these fabrics will all exist together in equal amounts in the final composition. If you don't like how they look now, you won't like them later. Selecting a palette is the most important step when beginning a composition. After you've started, you can take away fabrics and splice in new ones, but it is always better to start out strong with a lovely palette that you love.

If you don't like what you see, add and subtract until you do. This can be a challenging process. Listen to your intuition.

After you find a palette that is both *beautiful* and *unusual*, you must challenge it to see if each color *holds its own*. Move the fabrics around and see how they interact with each other. Quiltmaking involves joining many fabrics together—all of the colors that you use in a quilt have to get along and work well with all of the other colors.

To test your palette, look at it in a variety of ways using both a value finder and a black-and-white or grayscale setting or filter on your camera. The bottom line is to make sure that each fabric can hold its own with all the other selected fabrics. Each method of viewing values provides you with different information.

1. Arrange the palette by value, moving from dark to light.

This palette is arranged by value, with the darkest fabrics on the left.

2. Examine what these fabrics look like using a black-and-white or grayscale setting or filter on your camera.

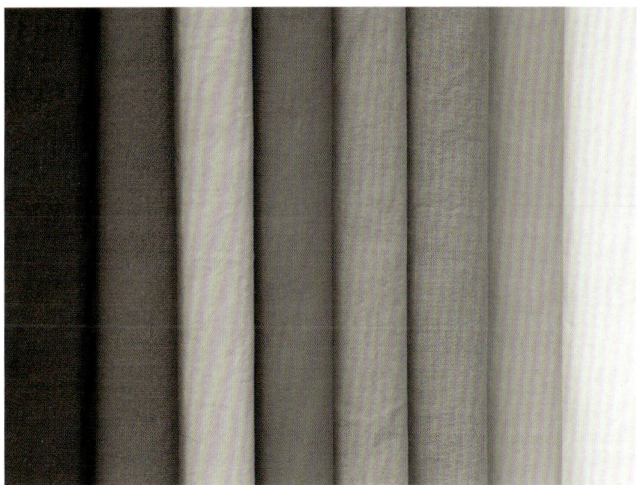

This tells me I have a range of values in my palette and that it is half dark and half light in value.

3. Use a value finder to see what it can tell you. *Note: Because the value finder is red, it doesn't work well on red and some yellow fabrics. You can also use a green value finder to get better readings on reds.*

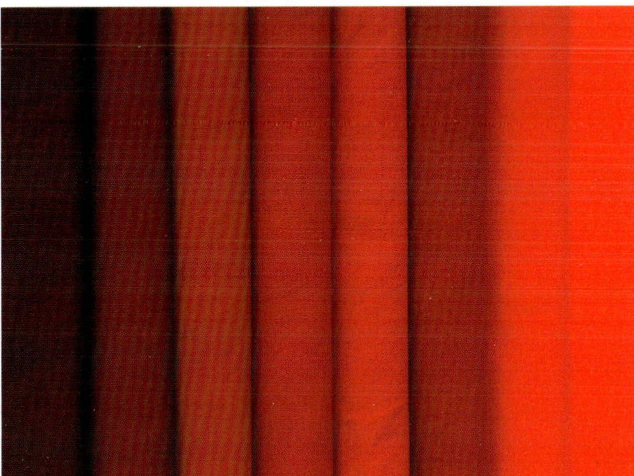

Using a red value finder tells me that the four colors on the right are very close in value. If they are not wildly different in their colors (as opposed to values), this might not work.

4. To further test your palette, arrange the fabrics so that they alternate between dark and light values.

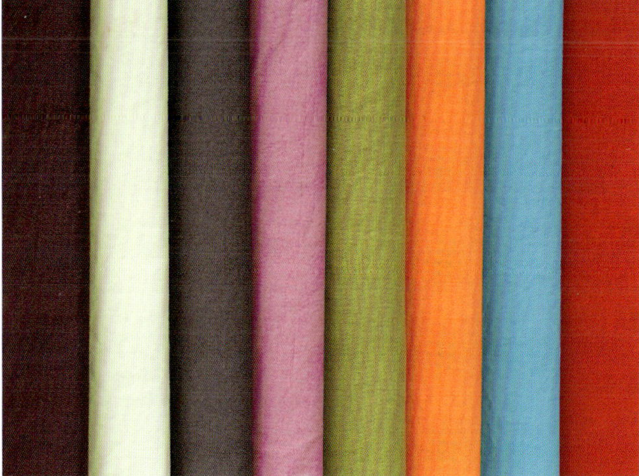

Each time I move the fabrics, I check to make sure that there is always good contrast between the colors and values.

5. View this arrangement using a black-and-white or grayscale setting or filter on your camera to see how these fabric values are getting along.

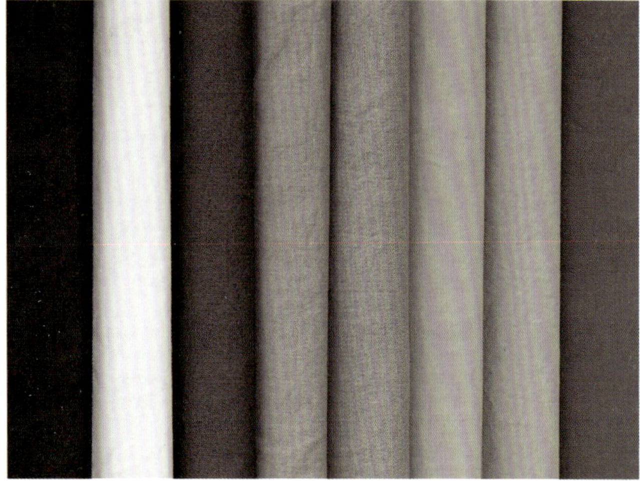

This image tells me that I have good contrast and each color is holding its own.

6. Look at the color combination with the value finder.

As long as what I am looking at feels interesting, I know I am moving in the right direction.

Do this over and over again. Add and subtract colors until you get a palette that excites you. It can be helpful to work toward a palette that evokes a particular season, culture, or time period. The book *Colorscape: An Around-the-World Guide to Color* by Naomi Kuno is a great resource for creating color palettes based on themes, cultures, or ideas.

Sometimes I will generate several palettes to be used in one quilt. Do a Little Dance (right) has five separate color palettes.

NOTE

When selecting fabric, I do not like to use nor do I recommend batiks or fabrics that read as solids but in reality have a light print or texture to them. These fabrics are not predictable when cut up. To create the most successful prints and patterns, use pure, solid fabrics.

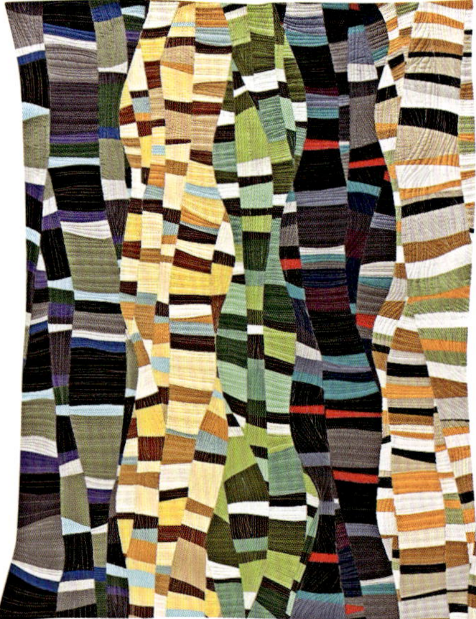

▶ *Do a Little Dance* by Maria Shell, 2010, 28″ × 38″
When building several palettes to be used together, they must all hold their own.

Photo by Chris Arend

TIPS ON BEING FEARLESS WITH COLOR

- Predictable is boring; challenge yourself to be unpredictable.

- Look in nature and in urban environments for color combinations that excite you. Take photos so you can recreate that palette with fabric.

- Think about why you like a particular color combination—try to put it in words.

- Color is its own form of memory. Did you have a favorite dress growing up? Or did your grandmother have a wild 1970s tablecloth? What about the curtains in your dorm room? If you were to see those colors and prints now, it would produce a memory. Use your color memories in your work.

- Cultivate your own signature way to use color. I call this "creating your own personal color identity." Many years ago, I decided that in addition to using the primary and secondary colors, I would also always use turquoise and pink. Doing this dramatically changed the look of my quilts for the better.

- Practice, through making quilts and observing color in all things, is the best way to learn how to create dynamic palettes.

- Just because you haven't seen it before doesn't mean you shouldn't do it.

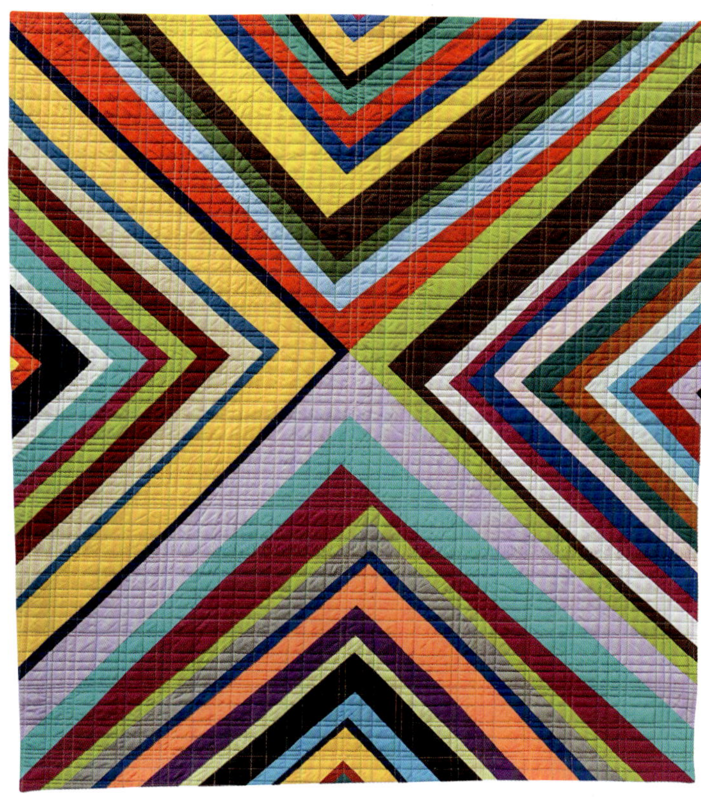

▶ *BIG TRI* by Maria Shell, 2016, 48″ × 55″

Say the word color, and many quilters think first of the color wheel. But it might surprise you that *characteristics* of color—value, visual temperature, and intensity—as much as color itself, determine the impact of a quilt. Let's start with value, the most influential aspect of color.

Value

"Value does all of the work, and color gets all of the credit." The first time I heard that statement, I was startled and excited by its truth. In a nutshell, value is about the *lightness* or *darkness* of a color, not the color itself. An infinite number of values exist—from the lightest lights through mediums to the darkest darks—but for simplicity I think of values as light, medium, or dark. Value performs two important functions in quilt design: It creates a sense of depth, and it makes the design read.

VALUE CREATES DEPTH

We perceive some values as closer, and others farther away. In most pieced quilts—

- light values appear to recede, and

- dark values seem to advance.

Look at the star blocks shown below. The block with dark value star points and a light-value background appears to float against a light backdrop, giving the block a strong sense of foreground and background. But if you reverse the light and dark values—with the light fabric as the star points and the dark fabric as the background—it's as if you're looking through a cut-out star, into the distance. A sense of depth exists, but it is very different.

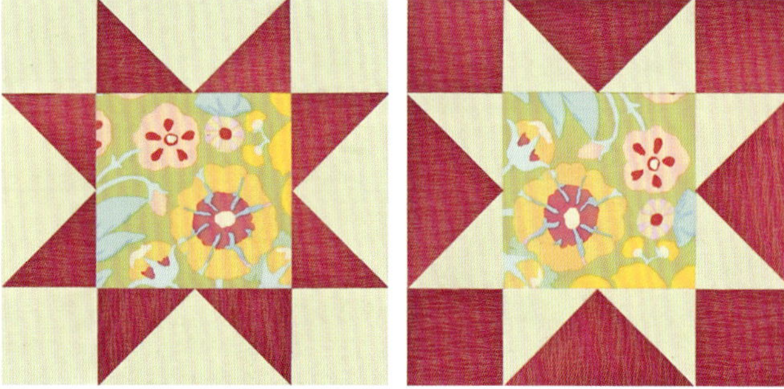

Placement of values—light, medium, and dark—affects depth in a traditional quilt block.

Light values don't always recede and dark values don't always come forward, of course. In appliqué, light shapes on a darker background will appear closer because they literally lie on top. An abstract or contemporary design can reverse the traditional advancing/receding aspect of value; see *Doors of Rome* (below).

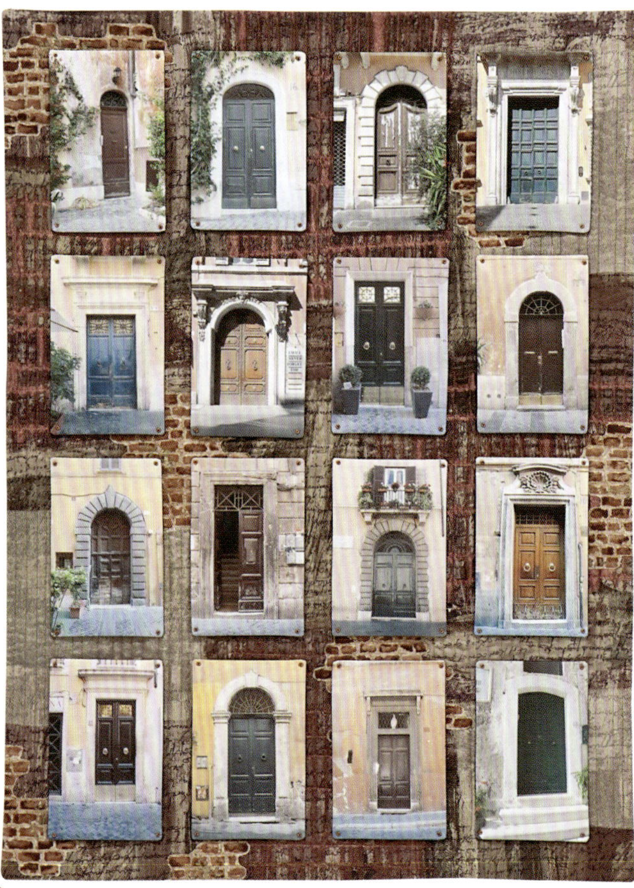

▶ *Doors of Rome* by Kim Butterworth, 24½″ × 33½″, 2007

VALUE MAKES A PATTERN READ

Now take a look at the role that value plays in establishing the design. In *Tropical Crossroads* (below), the dark triangles anchor the blocks, while the paler triangles shimmer in the distance. If all the triangles were medium in value, you would never see the pattern and the quilt would look flat.

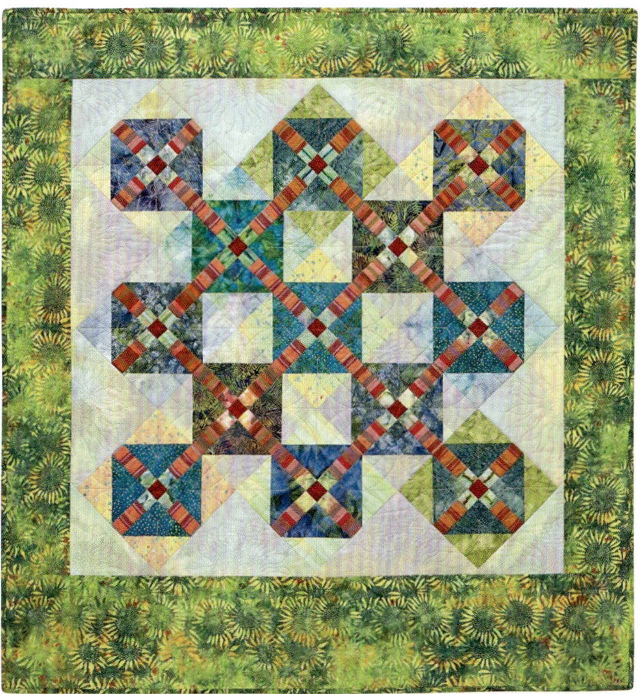

▶ *Tropical Crossroads* pieced by Christine E. Barnes, machine quilted by Teresa Leavitt, 51½″ × 55½″, 2003

As you gather fabrics for a quilt, ask yourself, Will these colors separate enough to read as distinct pieces, or will they merge into one? Fabric on bolts is deceiving because you're seeing large areas of color and pattern. The best way to find out is to make sample blocks.

Finally, if you think only novices need to consider value, think again. Experienced quilters often determine value placement before ever thinking about which colors to use. As one quilter put it, "You can use any colors as long as the values are right."

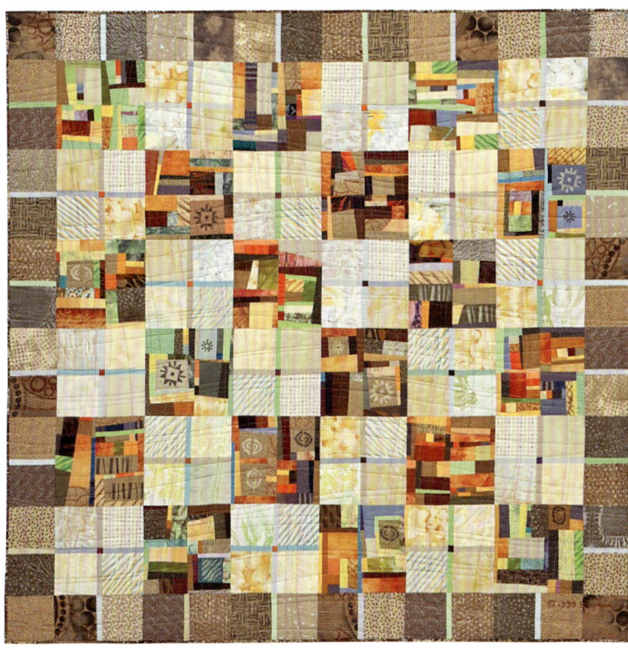

▶ *Inside Looking Out* pieced and machine quilted by Elaine Plogman, 56″ × 56″, 1999

Light values recede and dark values come forward in this original-block quilt. Hand-dyed, painted, discharged, and stamped fabrics add texture and pattern to the layers.

Exercise: Give Value a Try!

Ask everyone in your Color Club (page 80) to bring at least one photo of a quilt that achieves depth through the placement of light, medium, and dark values. If you're working on your own, look for several photos. Do the lighter values read as background and the darker values as foreground? In quilts with mostly medium values, what other aspects—such as pattern—help to create depth and establish the design?

Disregarding color, create two simple 8″ × 8″ star sample blocks, placing the values as shown in the background and star points. Use the same medium-value fabric for the center square. Notice how much the sense of depth changes when you reverse the background and the star-point values.

Visual Temperature

Of the three color concepts, visual temperature is the easiest for quilters to comprehend. Why? We naturally associate the warm colors—yellow, red, and orange—with the sun, heat, and fire. The cool colors—green, blue, and violet—suggest meadows, water, and sky. It's just as easy to apply this aspect of color to your quilts.

To understand the concept of visual temperature, turn to the color wheel (page 19). If you draw an imaginary line from red-violet to yellow-green, the colors on the left—yellows, oranges, and reds—are considered warm. The colors to the right of the imaginary line—greens, blues, and violets—are regarded as cool. Yellowgreen and red-violet can be either warm or cool, depending on other colors in the block or quilt. Red-violet next to blue, for example, appears warm in comparison, but red-violet next to orange feels cooler.

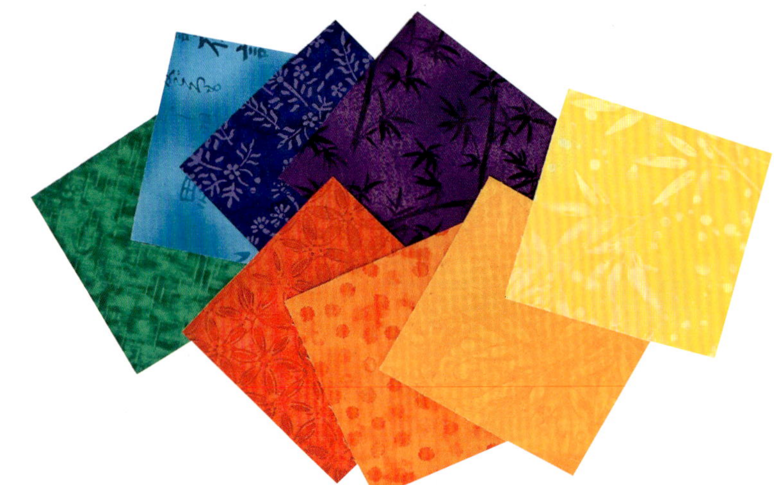

Warm and cool colors are easy to distinguish when you look at them side by side.

Like value, temperature has an advancing/receding quality; it also sets the mood. Warm colors advance and seem lively. Cool colors recede and feel calm.

Temperature varies within a color family, too. Green is cool, but yellow-green is warmer (thanks to the greater presence of yellow), and blue-green is even cooler (thanks to the greater presence of blue). In the red family, red-orange feels warmer than red-violet.

What's the take-away lesson of visual temperature? From watching people's reactions to quilts over the years, I've concluded that the eye craves both warm and cool colors, with one or the other temperature predominating. All-warm quilts can be aggressive, while all-cool quilts may, well, leave you cold. The key to applying the concept of visual temperature is balance and proportion. To an all-orange quilt, add touches of cool blue-violet to bring down the temperature. To a blue-and-green quilt, introduce accents of red-orange or red. Quilts that sparkle, traditional or contemporary, almost always have a mix of warm and cool colors.

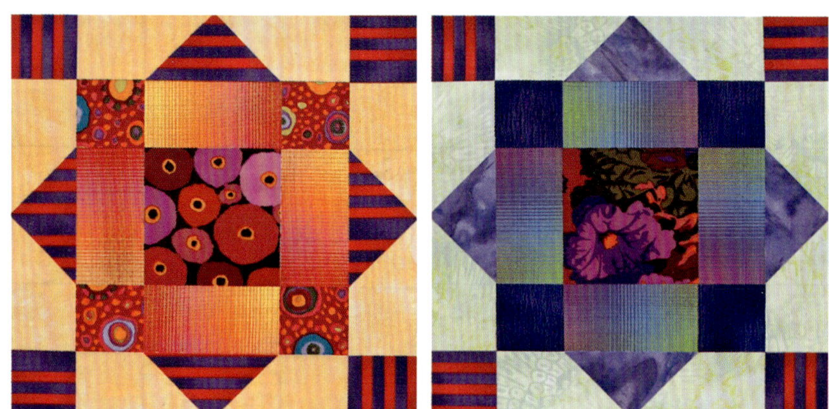

What a difference visual temperature makes! The Oregon Trail block on the left almost sizzles; in the righthand block, cooler hues calm things down. Only the corner squares are the same fabric in these two blocks.

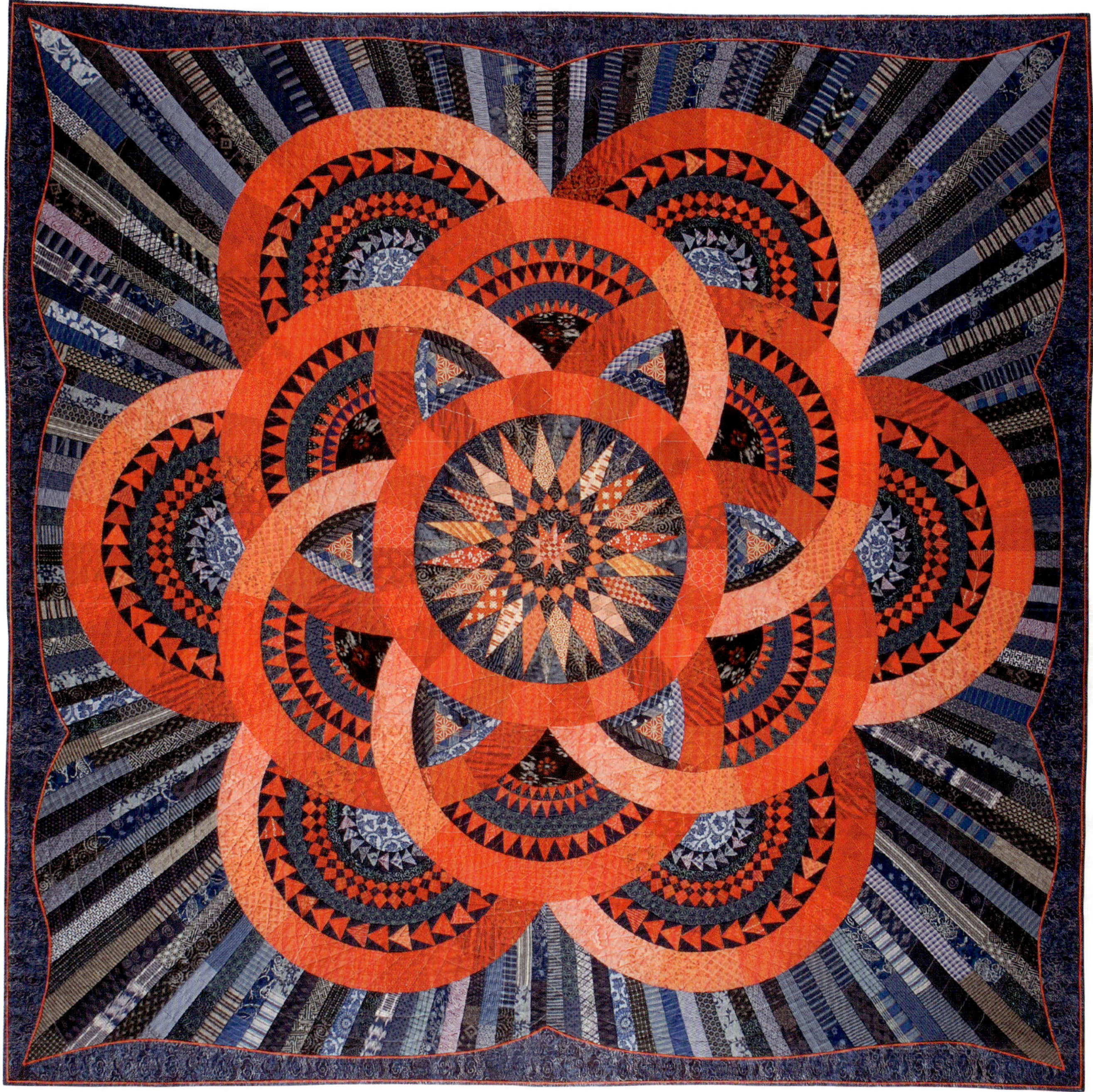

▶ *Cinnabar and Indigo* pieced and machine quilted by Judy Mathieson, 77″ × 77″, 2009
Warm red-orange advances dramatically, while cool indigos read as background in Judy's dynamic design. Angled strips in alternating values create a visual vortex and enhance the sense of depth. Judy was inspired by an image of an ancient Roman tile floor.

Exercise: Give Visual Temperature a Try!

- On your own or as a group, find a photo of a mostly warm quilt, a mostly cool quilt, and one with both warm and cool colors. Which quilts appeal to you the most? In the quilt that contains both warm and cool colors, which temperature Predominates?

- From your stash, pull five or six warm fabrics and another batch of cool ones. To the warm group add one or two of the cool fabrics, and to the cool group add one or two warm ones. Notice how each group changes with the addition of a few opposite-temperature colors.

Intensity

Value and temperature are relatively easy to grasp; intensity can be a bit more challenging. In your group sessions or on your own, spend the time it takes to master this aspect of color—your understanding will pay off in more satisfying, sophisticated quilts.

Simply put, intensity is about how brilliant or dull a color is. Synonyms for intensity are saturation, purity, and clarity. Tempera-paint colors from childhood are intense and lively. In contrast, low-intensity colors are often described as muted or dull. Some colors are decidedly intense and others are very dull, but most fall somewhere in between. Many of the fabrics shown in this book are medium in intensity.

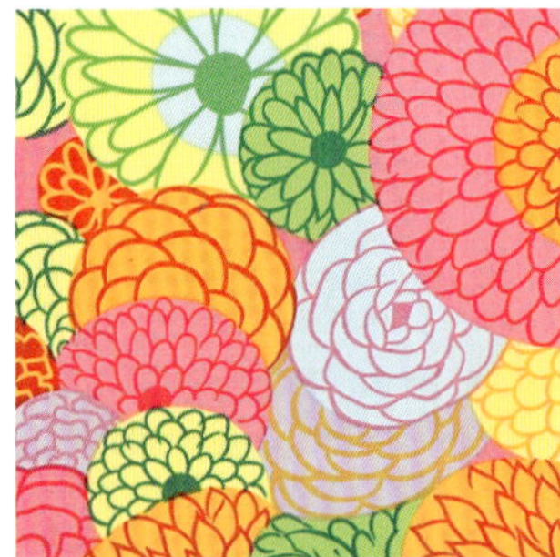

Bright and muted versions of similar colors illustrate the power of intensity to set the mood of a fabric.

It should come as no surprise that intensity, like value and temperature, has an advancing/receding quality. Intense colors appear to be closer, while low-intensity colors seem farther away. Imagine intense circles appliquéd to a less intense background—the circles will seem to float above the quilt.

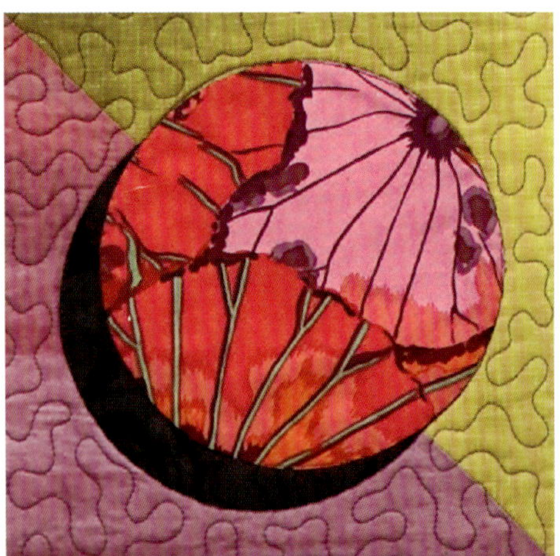

In this block from Elegant Circles (full quilt on page 83), the intense circle appears to float.

Following are a few tips for working with intensity:

- Although bright colors advance and dull colors recede, value can override intensity. A dull, dark blue, although cool and muted, will probably still advance because it's dark in value.

- Colors set against black appear more intense than the same colors on a white background. That's why some Amish quilts with bright colors surrounded by black look so vibrant.

- Intensity is relative: A color will look intense when placed among duller colors; the same color appears less intense among purer hues.

- Having just learned about value, you may wonder: What's the difference between value and intensity? Value has to do with the lightness or darkness of a color, while intensity has to do with its purity or dullness. As you evaluate a fabric, ask yourself: Is it light or dark? Then, is it bright or dull? You'll soon be able to tell the difference.

- Choose three intense fabrics and three low-intensity fabrics, and then find another three or four fabrics that fall somewhere in between. Arrange the fabrics from the most intense (brightest) to the least intense (dullest). If working in a group, let members weigh in on (and perhaps argue about) the relative intensity of the colors.

- Make two 9″ Ohio Star sample blocks, one using intense fabrics, and the other using duller ones. Stick to traditional values to make your task easier—medium center square, medium-light surrounding triangles, dark star points, and light background. If you're working as a group, arrange the intense blocks to make one paper quilt, and the low intensity blocks to make another. Analyze the role intensity plays in the impact of each grouping of blocks.

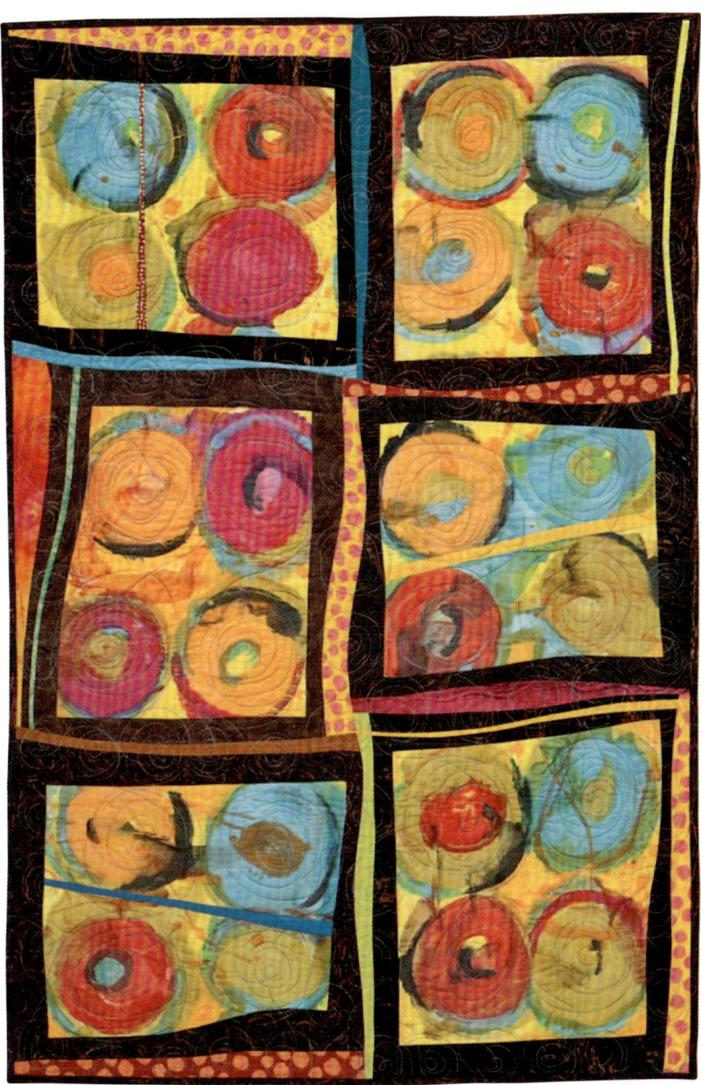

▶ *Eurythmia*, 39″ × 60″,
pieced and machine quilted
by Rene Steinpress, 2008

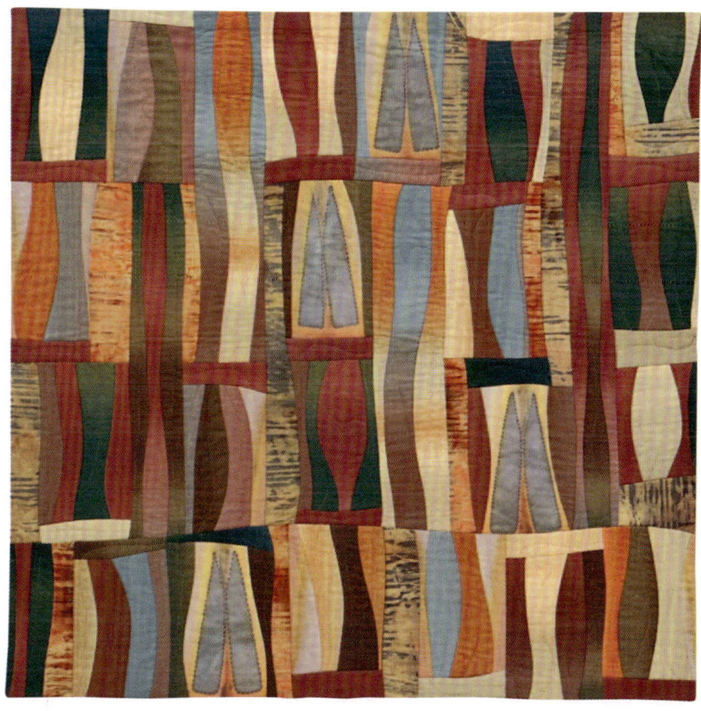

▶ *Elin in Athens*, 38″ × 38″,
pieced and hand and machine
quilted by Joan Dyer, 2009

An Introduction to Color Concepts   **33**

YOU ARE THE BOSS OF COLOR

By Becky Goldsmith

When I design a quilt, I am not working from a pattern or photograph. I don't have a "map" to go by. Sometimes a quilt will "feel" like a particular color to me before I have it all on paper. At other times, fabrics that have been sitting on my work table for a while wave at me, saying that it is their turn to be used. But one way or another, on the day I need to start cutting, I've decided on the colors I am going to use for that quilt.

When *you* start a quilt, *you* have to decide on the colors that *you* want to use. I wish I could tell you what you like, but really—do you want anyone to have that kind of power over you? Not likely. You do not have to use the colors shown in a pattern. Feel free to change the colors of any quilt you are making—including the quilts in this book.

If you have trouble deciding on colors, my very best advice is to choose at least one color that you really want to work with, and then add to it. Keep in mind what you've read so far, and continue reading.

PRACTICAL ADVICE

Choosing colors for a quilt does not have to be difficult. I rarely overthink it. Either I am in the mood to work with a particular color or fabric, or the quilt suggests the color to me.

When I made *Simply Delicious*, my thinking went like this: fruit goes in the kitchen; kitchens are blue and white. I chose light blue-and-white fabrics for the background. As it turns out, they bring to mind Delft tiles, but that was obvious to me only after the quilt was made.

When I use many different fabrics in a background, I am careful to choose ones that are similar enough in color and value to be read together as background. I keep a close eye on how the different fabrics are working together as I build the quilt on my design wall.

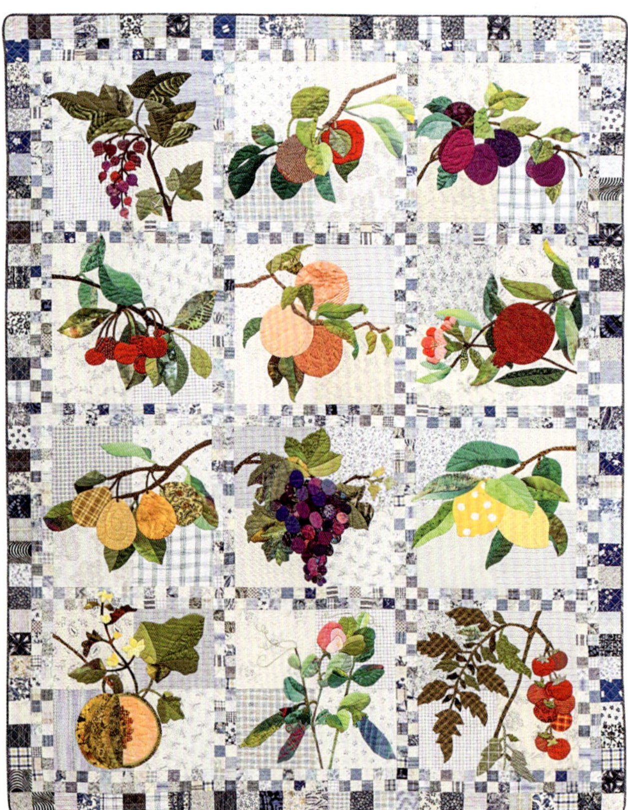

▶ *Simply Delicious* by Becky Goldsmith, 54″ × 70″, 2007
I chose blue-and-white fabrics for the background because they reminded me of kitchen colors—and fruit goes in the kitchen.

Choosing the colors for fruit in the foreground was equally easy: brown branches, green leaves, red apples, and so on. Again, you might want to play with the colors of the fruit.

Help—I've Fallen In Love With A Photo

Quilters often begin a project with a picture of a quilt. You can learn a lot about how to combine colors and values by studying these pictures. However, it is very difficult to reproduce a quilt from a photo exactly as it appears in the image.

An often overlooked fact is that the color you see on the printed page—or online—may not be the color of the fabric as it is in the actual quilt. What may look like true blue in the picture could in fact be periwinkle or turquoise.

If you want to reproduce a quilt from a photo, begin with the knowledge that you will be making fabric substitutions. Embrace the fabric hunt. Use the photo as a guide, but pay attention to the fabrics you are accumulating. The colors may be a little (or a lot) different from those in the photo. At some point it's a good idea to put the picture away and focus on how your actual fabric looks together.

Using Colors You Do Not Like

Have you ever been told that in order to grow as a quilter, you should work with a color that you don't like? I heard that when I was a new quilter, and I accepted that it was true. I became more skeptical as time wore on.

As I set about writing this, I thought a lot about how I work with color. I always work with fabric that I like. I had never considered making a quilt from fabrics that I didn't choose and did not particularly like.

Overall, my palette is made up of colors that are clear and clean. I am comfortable with a wide range of colors and prints inside this spectrum. I rarely use muddy or grayed colors. For example, you won't find Civil War reproduction fabrics in my stash. It's not that these grayed colors are bad—I just don't like them for my own quilts.

Change and challenge can be invigorating, so I decided to challenge myself. I asked readers of my blog to send me small pieces of their ugliest fabric. Some of the pieces I received were not bad, but others … oh my. It's not just that the motifs printed

on the fabrics were odd, but also the horrible mix of colors—from insanely bright to the muddiest grays.

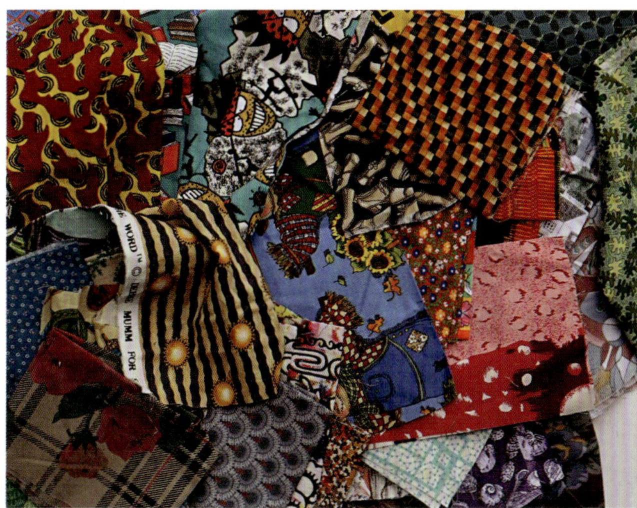

Have you ever seen so much awfulness in one pile of fabric?
Photo by Becky Goldsmith

My promise was to use every fabric given to me. The question was—how? I tried separating the uglies into dark and light stacks, and it quickly became obvious that that was not going to work—there wasn't enough light fabric to work with.

I changed the rules and allowed myself to add one fabric to use in the background. All the ugly fabric became the foreground, and solid white, the background.

Why white? First, using a neutral background unified the ugly fabrics. White was lighter than all of the ugly fabrics, and it brightened them up. The light against-dark value contrast allowed the piecing pattern to shine.

Could I have chosen something other than white? Yes. I considered black, dark brown, and charcoal gray, but I knew that the darker uglies would disappear against them. A bright color, such as red, might have been fun—or it could have been a hot mess. I didn't have enough ugly fabric to risk having to start over.

Could I have changed the rules and used more than one fabric for the background? Yes, but it would have made for a much busier quilt. The ugly fabric is busy enough on its own.

Once committed to the white background, I made half-square triangles and began playing with them on the design wall.

Everyone needs to use a design wall—including me. I arranged and rearranged the half-square triangles until I settled on the Broken Dishes block.

I had planned to treat this as a scrap quilt, not paying particular attention to color placement. Eventually I realized that I needed to group similar colors together in ribbons across the quilt, which brought order from chaos. After that, it became fun to look at.

The whole experience surprised me. This quilt, which was hard for me to make, has become one of my favorites. The most awful fabrics became my friends and are the most fun to spot.

I realized that there is value in expanding your color range—to putting more crayons in your box, so to speak. I still prefer to work with fabric and colors of my own choosing, but the stretch was worth the effort.

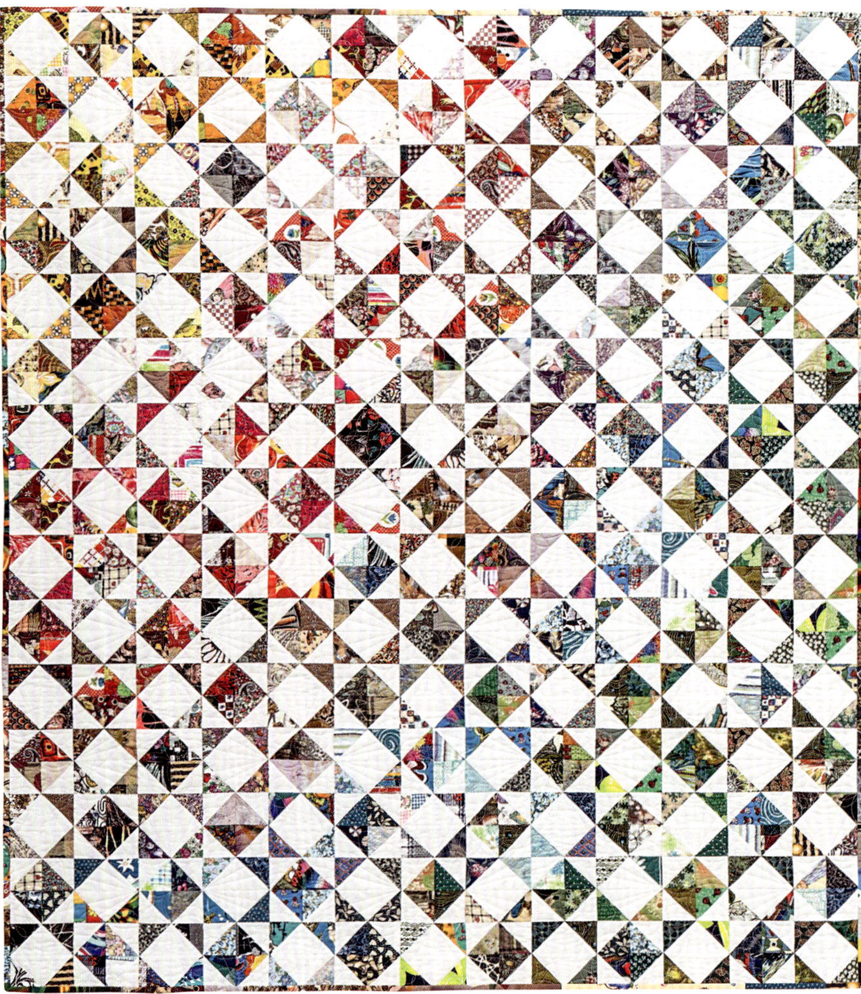

▶ *The Ugly Fabric Challenge* pieced by Becky Goldsmith, Machine quilted by Angela Walters, 52″ × 60″

Exercise: Try An Ugly Fabric Challenge

You can hold your own Ugly Fabric Challenge! Here are some tips for making it work:

· Keep the piecing simple and repetitive.

· Cut the ugly fabric into small pieces to hide truly awful designs in the prints.

· A quiet, neutral background can unify wild foreground fabrics.

· Use your design wall. Take the time to play with the pieces on the wall before sewing units together.

· Look at old scrap quilts for inspiration.

· You may find yourself liking the odd or ugly color combinations you Smile and embrace the unusual.

Building Stacks

I build at least two stacks of fabric for every quilt. The first stack is made up of background fabrics. If I plan to use only one background fabric, this is a very short stack. When I use more than one background fabric, as I did in *Tick Tock*, I sort the stack by value.

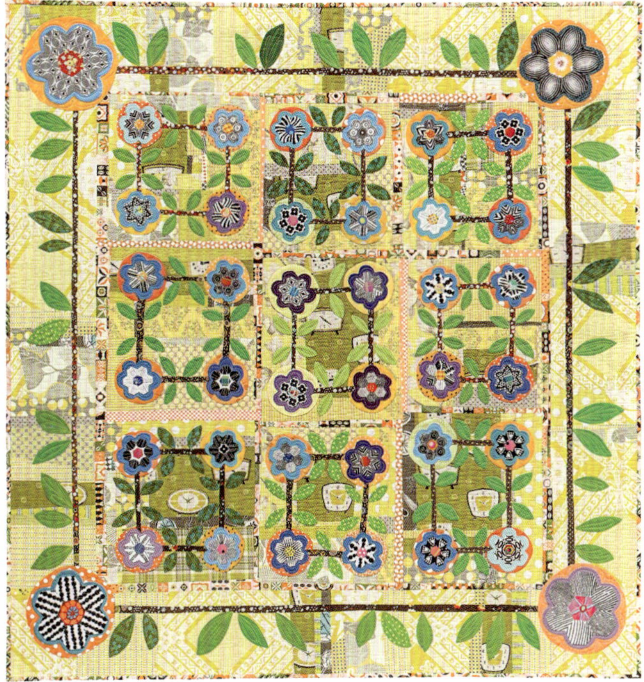

▶ *Tick Tock* made by Becky Goldsmith, 61″ × 61″

To sort by value, look at the fabrics in front of you and choose the darkest piece. Start the stack with this piece. Continue choosing the next-darkest fabric from the pile and place it on the stack, until the pile is gone. (It is also fine to work from light to dark.)

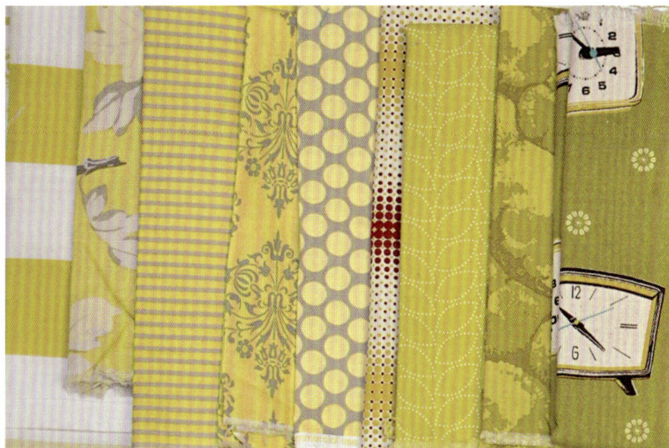

These are the first background fabrics that I chose for *Tick Tock*.

Photo by Becky Goldsmith

If the background has more than one color, I let the colors blend together where possible. In these stacks, the medium gray prints calm down the greenish gold prints that I started with.

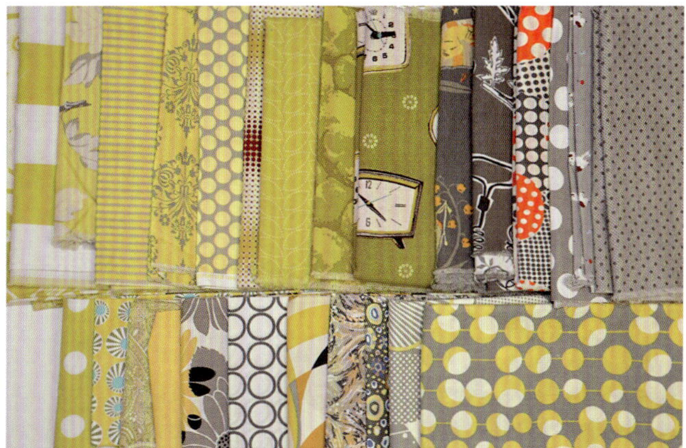

The medium gray colors calm down the greenish gold ones.

Photo by Becky Goldsmith

Next are the foreground fabrics. Focus on the colors, values, and textures that you think might belong in the quilt. You may or may not use all of the fabrics you put into these stacks, but that doesn't matter at this stage. Don't worry about where a particular fabric might go in the quilt; that comes later.

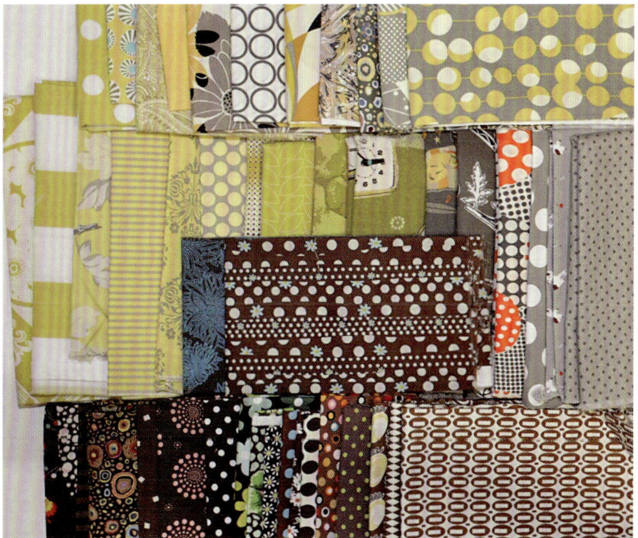

Brown was the first foreground color that I chose for *Tick Tock*.

Photo by Becky Goldsmith

Sort the foreground fabrics by color. You might have a green stack, a red stack, a blue stack, and so on. Sort each of these colors from dark to light.

Place your stacks next to each other on a table or pin them to your design wall. Are the colors working together? Do the background fabrics work with the foreground fabrics? Do you have the necessary light, medium, and dark values to make your quilt? Add and subtract fabric until you think you have enough to begin.

After you have the colors stacked, you can begin to figure out where they will go in your quilt.

Organized Fabrics

What I have found is that it's easier to work from an organized group of fabrics than it is to work from a disorganized pile. The more you arrange and rearrange the background and foreground fabrics, the more color combinations you will discover, and the easier it will be to get your hands on the just the right color and value when you need it.

These are the stacks of fabric for Spinning Wheels, an English paper-pieced quilt. I used a variety of white fabrics in the background and lots of color in the foreground. At this point you don't have to know exactly where each color will go—just that they look good together.

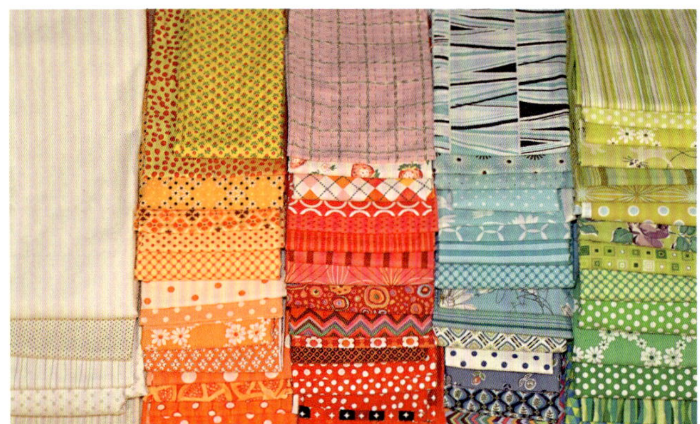

Fabric stacks for my quilt Spinning Wheels

Photo by Becky Goldsmith

Each block in this quilt is made from a different fabric. I didn't know when I pulled the fabrics which ones would be used in the final quilt or where they would be placed. I *did* know that they looked good together.

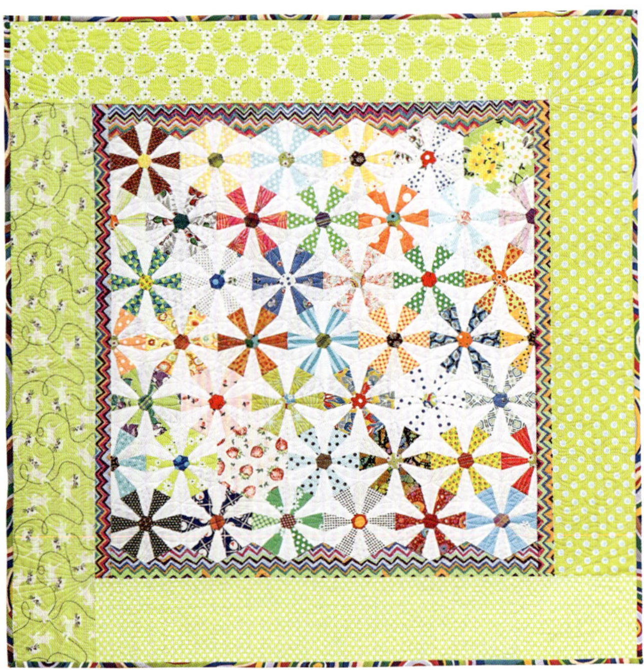

▶ *Spinning Wheels* by Becky Goldsmith, 36″ × 38″, 2013
The fabrics that worked together in the stack work well together in the quilt.

Easy Decisions

When you choose one fabric but not another, don't overthink it. If a fabric looks bad in the stack, discard it. If it looks good (even if you're not sure why), keep it in the stack. Don't be afraid to make these decisions.

Each color choice you make helps to define the direction of your quilt. The quilt you build from the colors you chose will be unique.

Remember that you can always add fabric as you are making your quilt and that you don't have to use every fabric in your stack.

Focus Fabrics

In quilting, a focus fabric is a print that has a combination of colors that you like. Some quilters don't use the focus fabric in the quilt at all; they just pull colors from it. The general wisdom holds that if you use colors taken from the print, they will look as good together as they do in the print.

Be aware that the colors in any print do not exist in a vacuum—they influence each other.

Colors are very rarely used in equal amounts in a print. The proportion of each color has an effect on how the colors look. If you change the proportion of the colors and the proximity of one color to another, the relationships between the colors change. If you choose some colors from a print but not others, they will work together differently than they do in the print.

This print, designed by Kaffe Fassett for Rowan Fabrics, would be a great focus fabric.

Many color combinations from this print would work well together, whether they are used with the focus fabric or not. I am particularly drawn to the blues, greens, and orange.

Some color combinations I would find harder to work with. Although some people would love them, I would have a harder time using these shades of pink, gray, and purple together.

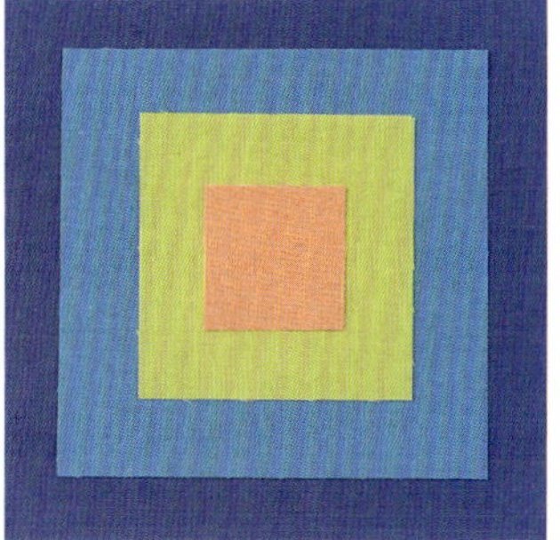

Many wonderful color combinations are possible from the focus fabric.

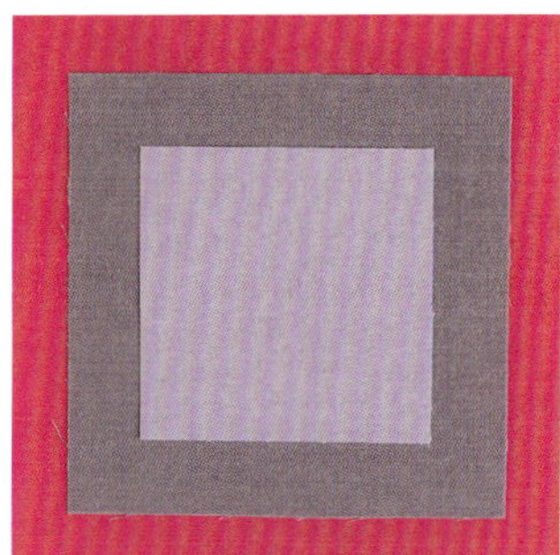

Other color combinations could be a little harder to work with.

The moral of this story is that if you use a focus fabric, please don't assume that doing so will always work. Stop to evaluate how your fabrics are looking together—with or without the focus fabric—as you make your quilt.

COLOR DOTS

Have you ever noticed the little color dots in the selvage of fabric? Those dots show the individual colors in the print. Some quilters use these isolated dots of color when they are trying to match individual colors from the print.

Targets, a lovely fabric designed by Kaffe Fassett, would be a fun focus fabric.

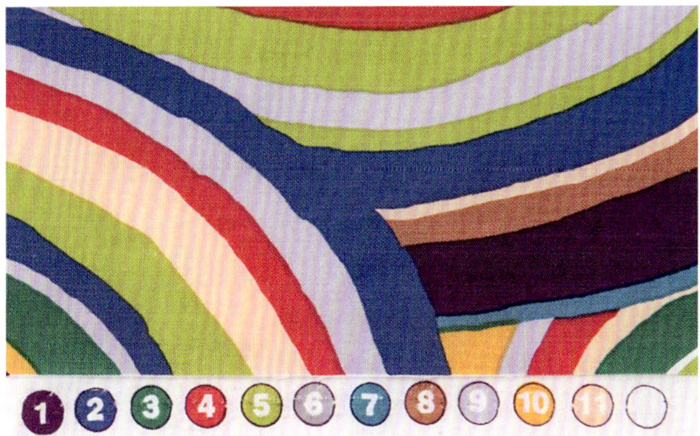

Color dots on the selvage show the individual colors that can be found in the prints.

THE NATURE OF FABRIC

By Becky Goldsmith

Quilters paint with fabric. Just as you would expect a painter to understand how paint works, a quilter needs to understand how fabric works.

Fabric falls into two broad categories: predictable and unpredictable. Predictable fabrics are not better or worse than unpredictable fabrics—they just behave differently.

Most of the fabric that quilters use falls into the predictable category. A **predictable fabric** is one that is not a surprise when you cut it up. If you are making a quilt cut from strips, a predictable fabric is your friend. When you cut a predictable fabric into smaller squares, the print looks basically the same everywhere you place it.

An **unpredictable fabric** is likely to offer surprises when it is cut into small pieces. Unpredictable fabrics are most often large-scale prints or multicolored fabrics with large repeats. These fabrics don't work as well in quilts made from strips of fabric because it is hard to know what color will dominate any particular small piece that is cut from the larger print.

Predictable Fabrics

SOLIDS

Solid-color fabric is the most predictable kind. No matter how you cut it, the color remains the same in every piece.

Solids are very versatile. They can be used with other solids or combined with prints. Depending on how you use them, solids can be quiet and unobtrusive (imagine a white background), or they can take center stage.

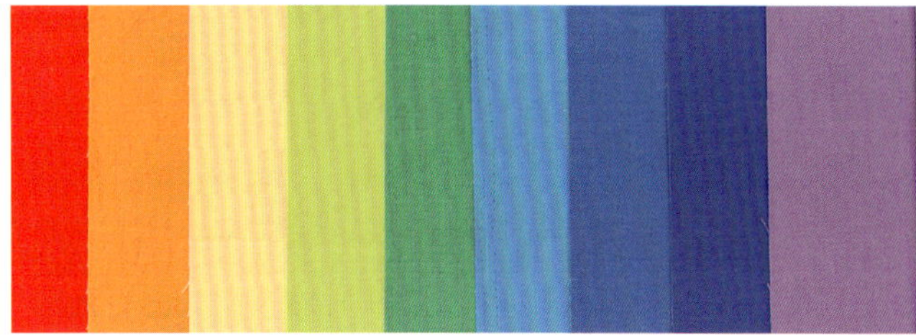

Solid fabric is very versatile and can be used with other solids or with prints.

It's easy to think of solids as boring, but quilts made with only solid fabrics are wonderfully graphic, whether the quilt is traditional or modern in design.

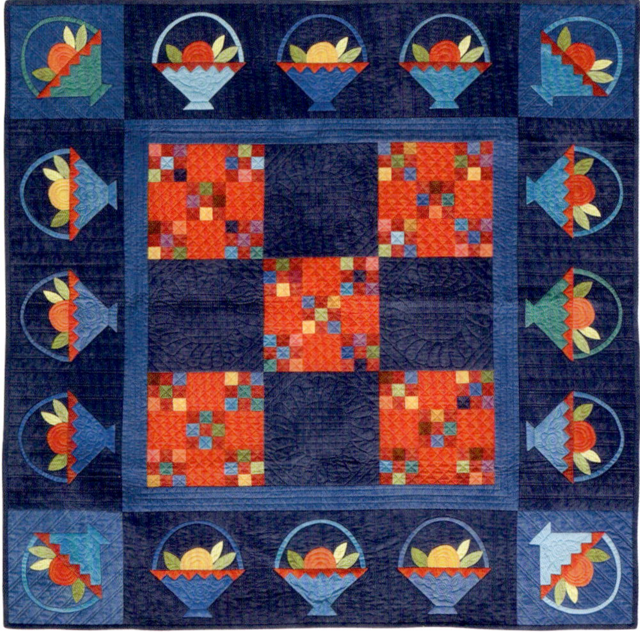

▶ *Amish Baskets* by Linda Jenkins, 2006, 49″ × 49″
Quilts made with only solid fabrics are wonderfully graphic and fresh.

TEXTURED SOLIDS

The Postimpressionist painter Van Gogh used textured brush strokes to give his paintings energy. You can use textured solids in a similar way to add movement to the quieter areas of your quilt.

Textured solids look solid from a distance, and they too are very predictable. Only as you get closer do you see the details in the print. Tone-on-tone prints are the most common kind of textured solid, combining more than one value of the same color.

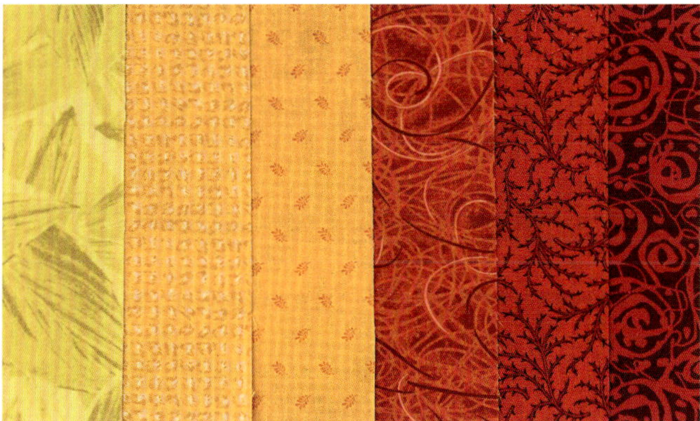

Tone-on-tone prints are active solids.

Single-color, mottled hand-dyes and batiks are another kind of textured solid. They have a fluid visual texture without a distinctive pattern. When you want more than a flat, solid color in your quilt, add some textured solids into the mix.

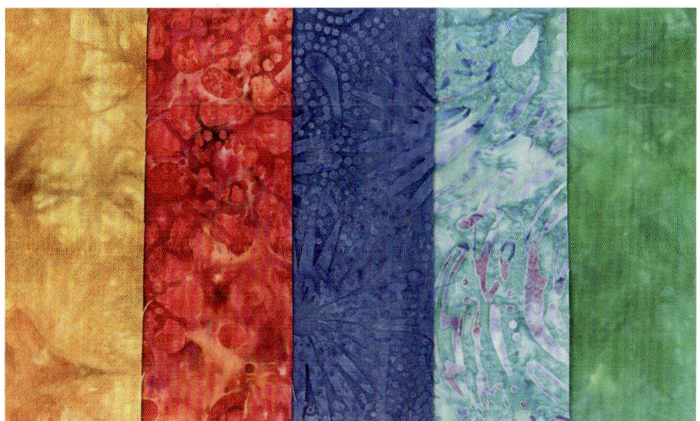

Single-color mottled hand-dyes and batiks have a more fluid visual texture.

Art quilters often create amazing quilts by using solids and textured solids much as they would paint. Laura Wasilowski is an expert at this. In her quilt *Five Sisters*, Laura goes beyond a simple use of solids to create a variety of interesting details. The five orange leaves are not cut from a printed fabric. Laura cut and fused strips and dots to an orange base fabric to create those lovely, complex leafy sisters.

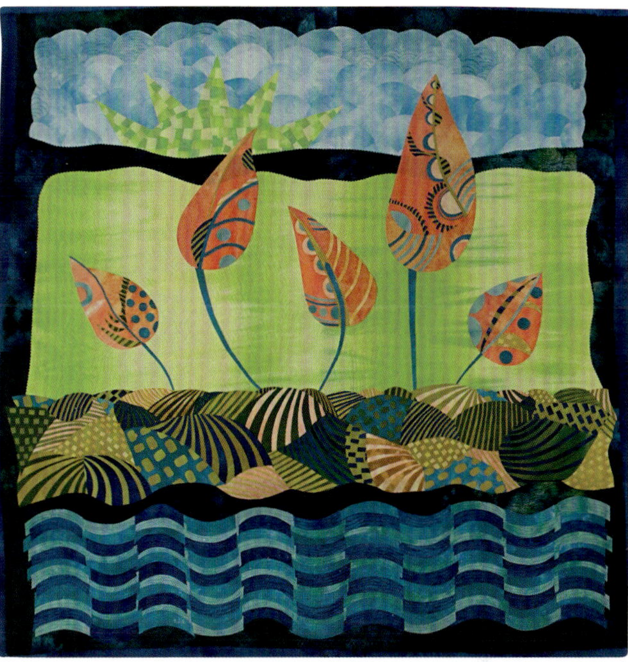

▶ *Five Sisters* by Laura Wasilowski (artfabrik.com), 2006, 51″ × 51″ *Five Sisters* is a marvelous example of the expressiveness of solid fabrics.

Photo by Laura Wasilowski

Practical advice:
Textured solids never go out of style, so it's a good idea to maintain a nice supply of them in your stash. You don't need yards of any one fabric. Instead, collect a wide variety of fat quarters so that you have lots of colors and values to choose from when you want them.

All printed fabric has contrast between the colors and values *inside the print itself*. The contrast found in the print relates directly to how quiet or active the fabric appears to be. Printed fabrics have repeating patterns across the width and length of the fabric. The *repeat* refers to the length of the pattern before it repeats itself again. The repetition of shapes and colors gives the print a cohesive appearance. The smaller the pattern and repeat, the easier it is to predict what the fabric will look like when it is cut up.

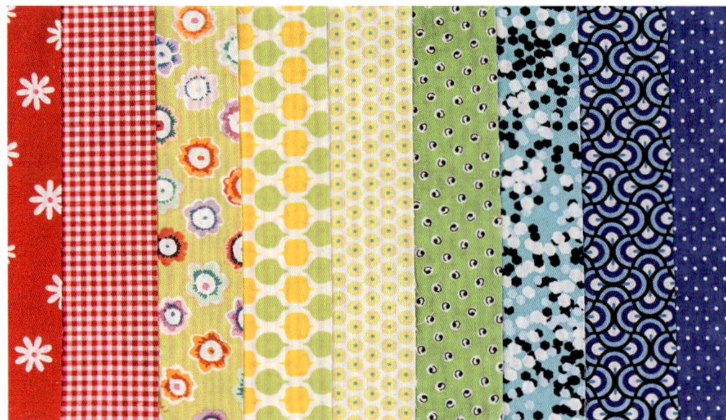

Small, regular prints are predictable.

When you make a pieced quilt, you rarely cut all your individual pieces of fabric to audition together on your design wall. You are more likely to construct units or blocks that you then look at. A predictable print can be cut into big or small pieces and will look the same everywhere it shows up in the quilt. In pieced quilts, that is a very good thing.

LOOKING THROUGH WINDOWS

Looking at fabric through a window template helps you see what that fabric will look like when it is cut into pieces. To make a window template, cut a square of heavy white paper or poster board with a "window" opening in the center. The opening can be any size you like. Leave at least 2″ of paper on each side of the window opening.

Place the window template on the right side of the fabric and see how the print looks. Move the template around on the fabric. If the fabric is predictable, it will look just about the same no matter where you place the window.

When you go to the quilt shop, carry window templates in a variety of sizes with you. Use them on fabric that you might not normally buy. You may be surprised at what you see.

Use a window template to help you visualize what a print will look like when it is cut.

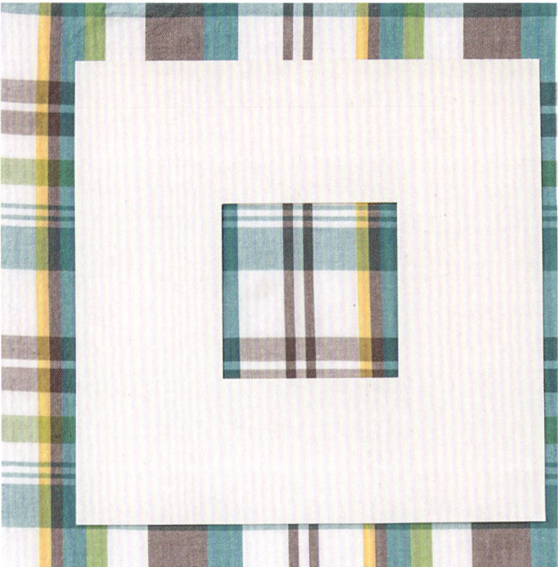

Use a window template to help you visualize what a print will look like when it is cut.

Dots

You don't have to see much of a dotted fabric to know what it is and what it would look like if you could see more of it. That is the essence of predictability.

The smooth edges and the regular shape of dots lend them a calm, yet perky, attitude. In my humble opinion, dots can be used with just about any other fabric.

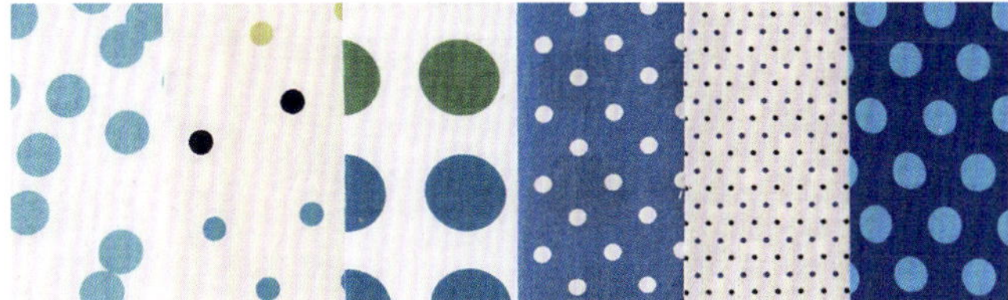

Dots mix well with every other fabric.

Circular Designs

Many predictable prints have circular designs that may not technically be dots but behave in much the same way. A circular design has more visual texture than a traditional, smooth dot, which is what makes circular designs interesting in a composition.

As with other predictable prints, these prints will retain their look whether you cut 2″ × 2″ or 6″ × 6″ squares.

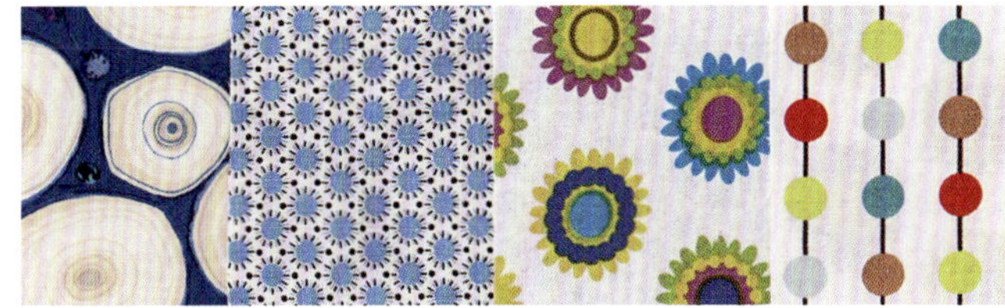

Dotlike prints behave much like smooth dots when cut into small pieces.

Flowers And Zigzags And Penguins—Oh My!

An unlimited number of motifs can be printed on fabric, and any of them can be predictable. However, you may be avoiding some fabrics because, for whatever reason, they feel less safe to you.

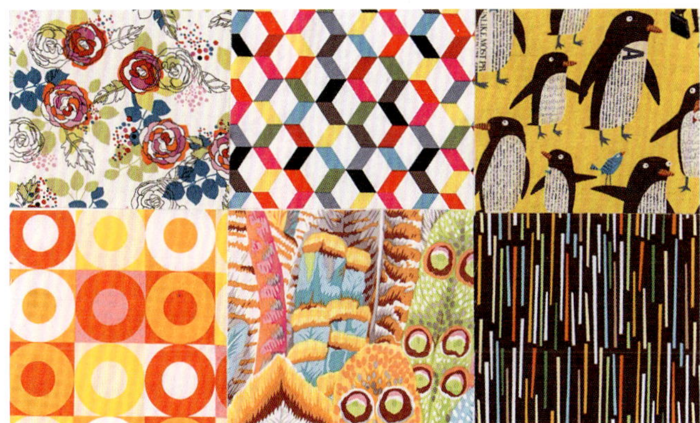

Quilters often avoid prints such as these that feel less safe.

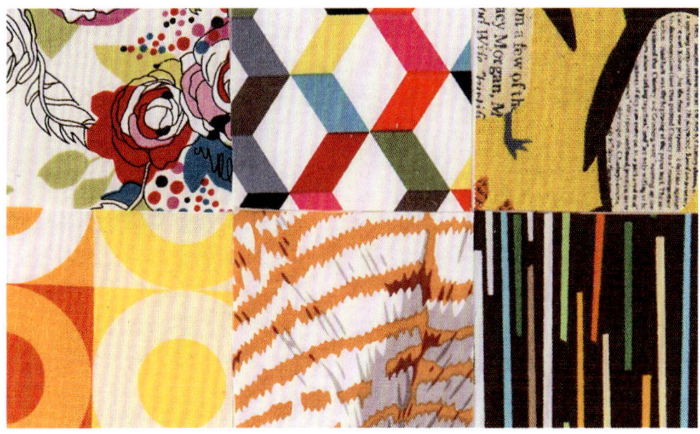

Look again. When cut smaller, these prints still look like the fabric they came from.

I love, love, love interesting and unusual prints! They add a special spark to my quilts. Yes, you have to pick and choose where to use them, but unless you don't use printed fabric at all, you absolutely want to have these kinds of prints in your palette of fabrics.

If a print catches your eye, don't pass it by—even if it is something outside of your comfort zone. Use a window template to see what that fabric will look like when cut into pieces. You may be surprised.

IDENTIFYING PREDICTABLE

How can you tell at a glance if a print is predictable? I look at the density of the printed motifs on the fabric. Are they close together, or are they widely scattered? The closer the motifs are, the more likely it is that small pieces will look like the fabric they were cut from.

I also look at the distribution of colors across the face of the fabric. I ask myself: If I cut this up, will I see the same mix of colors in the smaller pieces?

It may not be easy at first, but identifying predictable prints does get easier with practice and is a good skill to have.

CONVERSATION PRINTS

Conversation prints (sometimes called novelty prints) have identifiable "things" on them: bugs, teddy bears, Mount Rushmore… Whatever the thing is, it is intended to be seen. Viewers notice these things—they might even have a conversation about them.

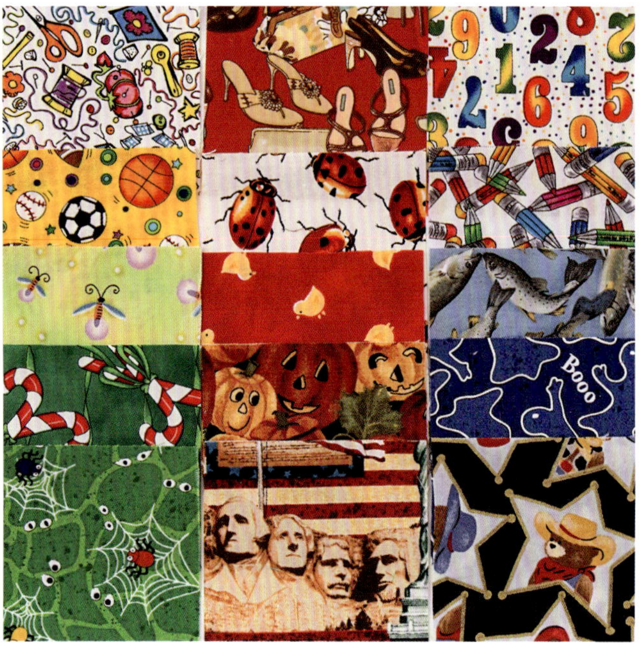

Conversation prints have identifiable, very visible "things" on them.

Conversation prints are perfect for children's quilts, where the intention is for the child to pick out different things in the fabric. These prints can be fun to use in seasonal quilts or in quilts with a theme.

I use conversation prints sparingly because I don't necessarily want the viewer to pick out a bug in the fabric before they see the design of the quilt itself. But these prints are fun to have in your stash.

A Category of Their Own

Conversation prints can be predictable in the same way that other prints can be predictable. When you cut them up, the smaller pieces of the fabric reflect the look of the fabric as a whole.

I have placed conversation prints in their own category because the motifs in the fabric call attention to themselves in a different way from the motifs in most other prints. They don't blend into the larger pattern of the quilt; instead they demand to be noticed. If that is what you want, conversation prints can be fun to use.

DIRECTIONAL FABRIC

Directional fabrics have lines in the design and are, in general, very predictable. Stripes and plaids are the most obvious kinds of directional fabric. Lines—whether they are long or short, smooth or rough—add movement to a composition. Lines point us in one direction or another, and our eyes glide along them, stopping where the lines stop. You can cut the fabric lengthwise to get one look or crosswise for a different look.

Printed Stripes

Stripes can be printed on fabric or woven into the cloth. There are all kinds of printed stripes: simple and smooth, multicolored, stripes with the same or varying widths—the possibilities are endless.

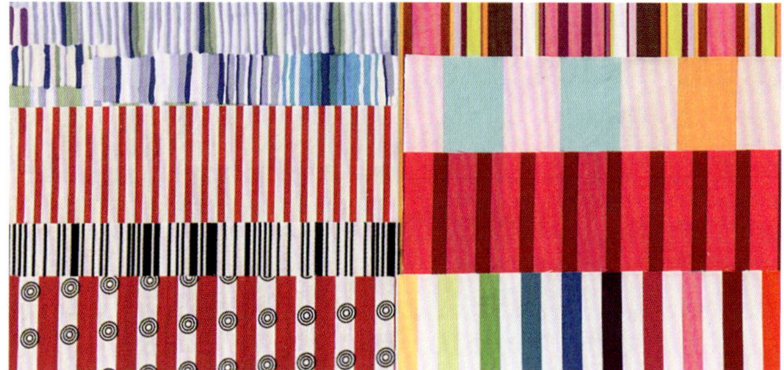

Printed stripes are available in a huge variety of sizes and colors.

Stripes can be made from a variety of motifs that are stacked into lines to create a more complex striped pattern. Our eyes can detect the lines in the overall pattern, and those lines still imply movement.

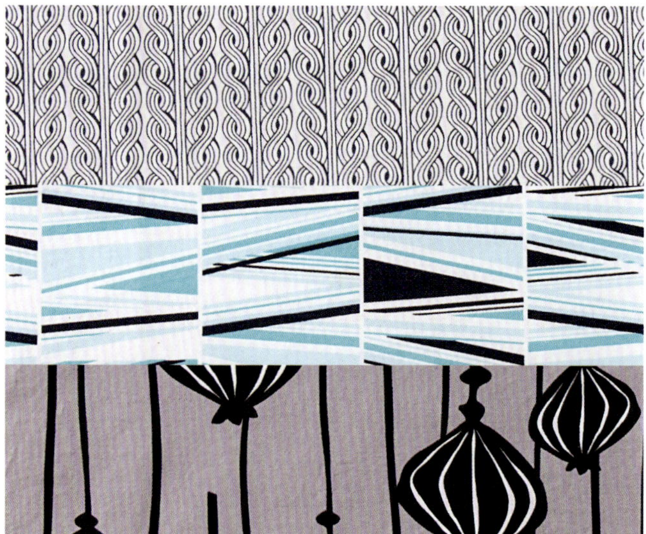

Motifs can be stacked in rows to create a more complex striped pattern.

◼ *Cutting On and Off Grain*

When working with directional fabrics, I do not usually spend time making sure that I am cutting exactly with the grain, on the lines in the fabric. Roberta Horton taught me—and thousands of other quilters—that cutting "casually off-grain" is both lovely and less stressful.

That said, there are times when it is important to cut directional fabric exactly. When the pattern calls for it, I do take the time to do just that.

Woven Stripes

Woven stripes are formed when the lengthwise threads in the fabric are dyed different colors and are woven together. Woven stripes are predictable in the same way that printed stripes are. However, colorwise, woven stripes are a little different.

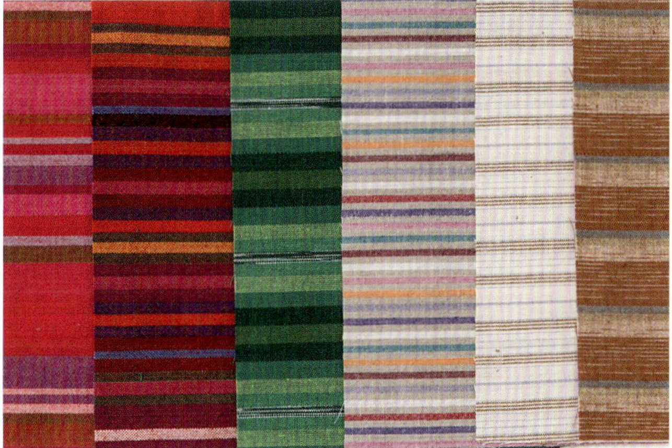

Woven stripes are formed when different colors of thread are woven together.

When the different colors of thread are woven together, they blend to make new colors. The new colors are closely related to the colors that they have been woven from. These more nuanced colors make woven stripes a good choice when you need a fabric to transition from one color to another.

For example, if you are making a quilt from blues and reds and you need a fabric to bridge the color gap between them, a stripe woven from similar blue and red threads will form purple bridge colors.

Plaids

Plaids are made from crossed lines.

Your eyes glide down a long stripe, but your eyes stay put when you look at a plaid because the lines are interrupted. In that sense, a plaid is static, much like any other nondirectional printed fabric. However, the lines in plaids offer a nice counterpoint to curvier prints.

Unfortunately, plaid fabrics are not easy to find. When you find one you like, you should definitely add it to your stash.

Woven Plaids

Woven plaids are formed when different colors of thread are woven across each other to make a pattern. The resulting plaid pattern can be small or large, single colored or multicolored.

Woven plaids are always on the straight of grain. Like woven stripes, the colors blend to make new colors. The lines and colors formed are softer and more nuanced than they are in printed plaids. Plaids, too, make excellent blender fabrics.

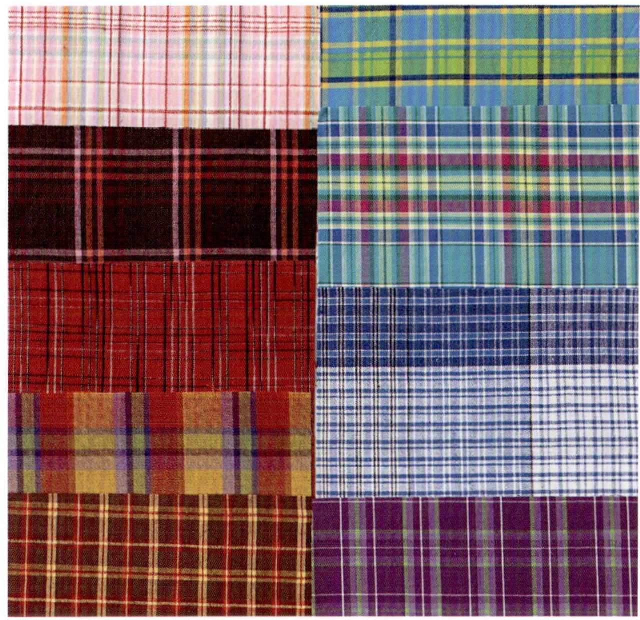

Woven plaids are always on the straight of grain.

Printed Plaids

Printed plaids mimic woven plaids but are not limited by the direction of the threads in the cloth. In fact, the lines in a printed plaid do not have to be "lines" at all. They can be dots or slashes or flowers—the options are limitless.

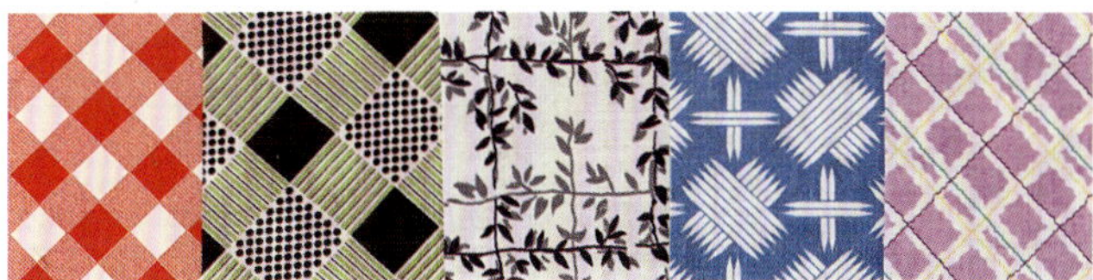

The lines in a printed plaid do not have to be "lines"—and they can be printed on the bias grain of the fabric.

Unpredictable Fabrics

Unpredictable fabrics are often large-scale prints or multicolored fabrics with large repeats. Because the designs in the fabric are big or the colors widely dispersed, it's hard to know what you are going to get when you cut the fabric into smaller pieces.

If you are making a quilt cut from strips, you can't predict which color will end up where, and this can play havoc in repeating blocks. That said, once you understand them, unpredictable prints do have a role to play in Quilting.

Use a Window Template

Remember that you can use a window template to help you evaluate whether or not a particular big print has a predictable pattern. Refer to Looking through Windows (page 42).

BIG PRINTS

Big prints have an expansive feeling that is directly related to their large size. The motifs appear oversized next to other quilt fabric. The colors in these prints are often bold and bright and spaced widely apart. This print, Vivienne from Alexander Henry Fabrics, is a good example.

Big prints can be wild, with big designs and colors widely dispersed.

In appliqué, you can fussy cut shapes from different parts of the print. In piecing, you can fussy cut a fabric, but generally you begin by cutting strips. Strips and other small shapes cut from a large-print fabric are different enough that they could have come from four different fabrics. In a quilt pattern that requires regular color placement, that can be either a problem—or a virtue.

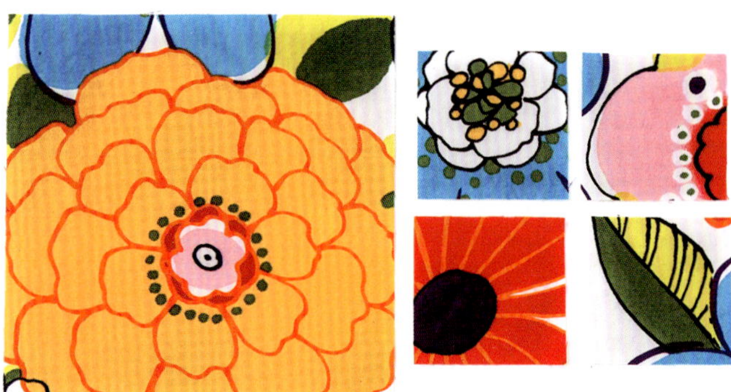

It's hard to tell that these squares came from the same piece of fabric.

The colors in a big print look good together; they don't clash. Different colors may dominate the various shapes cut from a big print, but these shapes will be color coordinated. If you set them against a common background, the results can be exciting.

Needle in a Haystack (below) is a fun, two-fabric quilt. I would have had to work a lot harder to get the same effect from individual red, blue, and yellow fabrics.

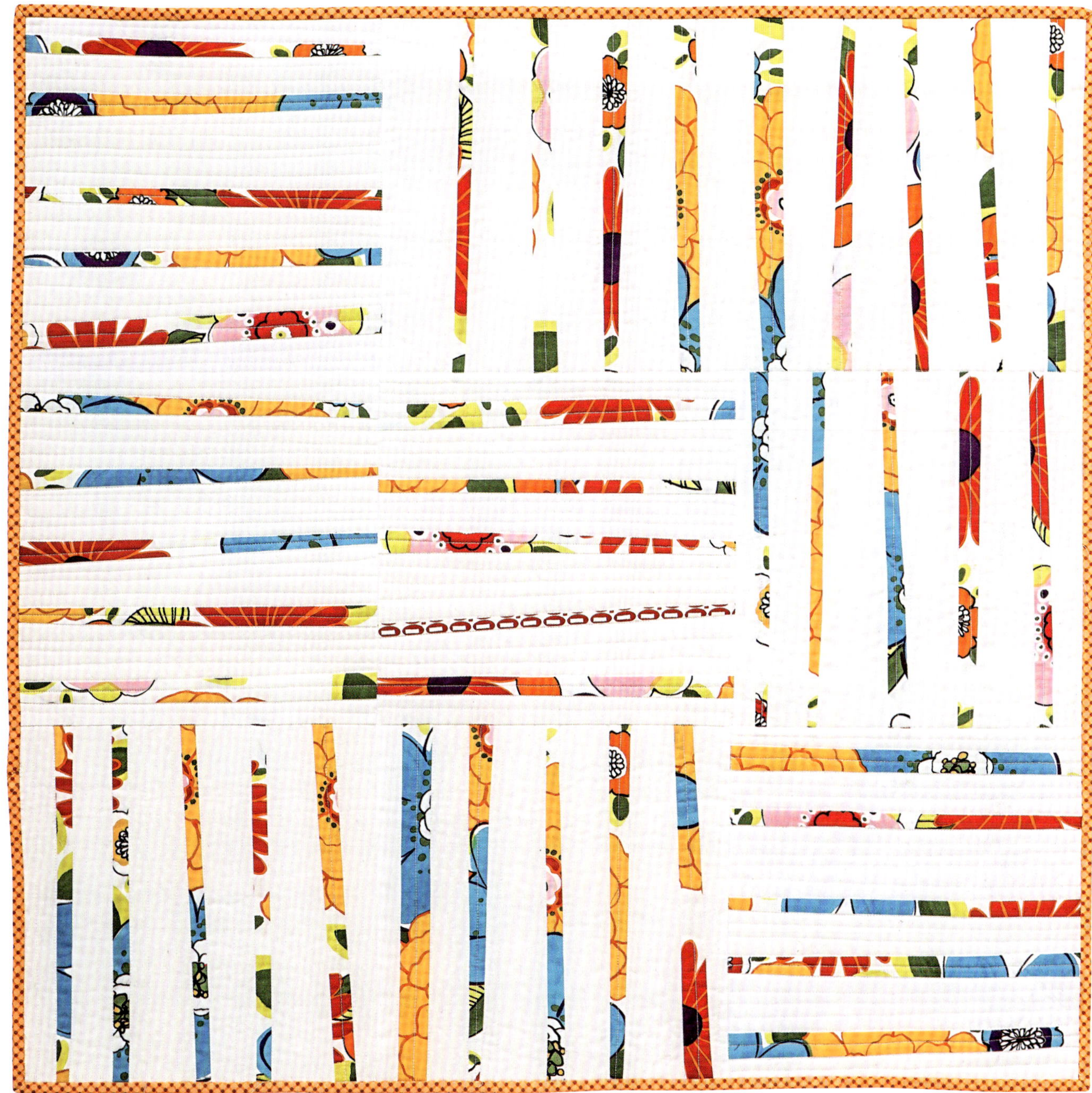

▶ *Needle in a Haystack* by Becky Goldsmith, 36″ × 36″, 2014
Strips cut from the big print shine against a white background.

TRY THEM—YOU'LL LIKE THEM

Big prints feel open and expansive, even when they are cut into small pieces. They add a particular kind of movement to a quilt. The scale of a big print especially stands out when combined with smaller scale prints or solids. I would encourage you to keep some in your stash. It will be even better if you remember to use them.

EASIER-TO-USE BIG PRINTS

Some big prints are more predictable than others. Look for big prints where the colors are mixed together well across the face of the print. This fabric, designed by Philip Jacobs for Rowan Westminster Fabrics, is a good example.

You can cut a variety of shapes from this fabric. Each shape will retain the look of the fabric it was cut from, and that look will be distinctly different from smaller, tighter, more predictable prints.

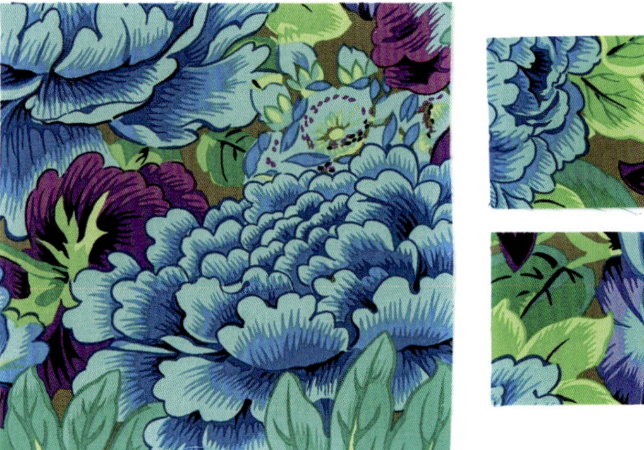

These smaller squares are obviously cut from the same big print.

Big prints with colors that are mixed together well across the face of the print are more predictable.

BIG-PRINT QUILT BACKS

Another way to use big prints is to put them on the back of a quilt. Big prints make great quilt backs, especially if you want to hide the quilting stitches on the back of your quilt.

I often sew different big prints together, in no particular pattern, until I have constructed a quilt back of the correct size.

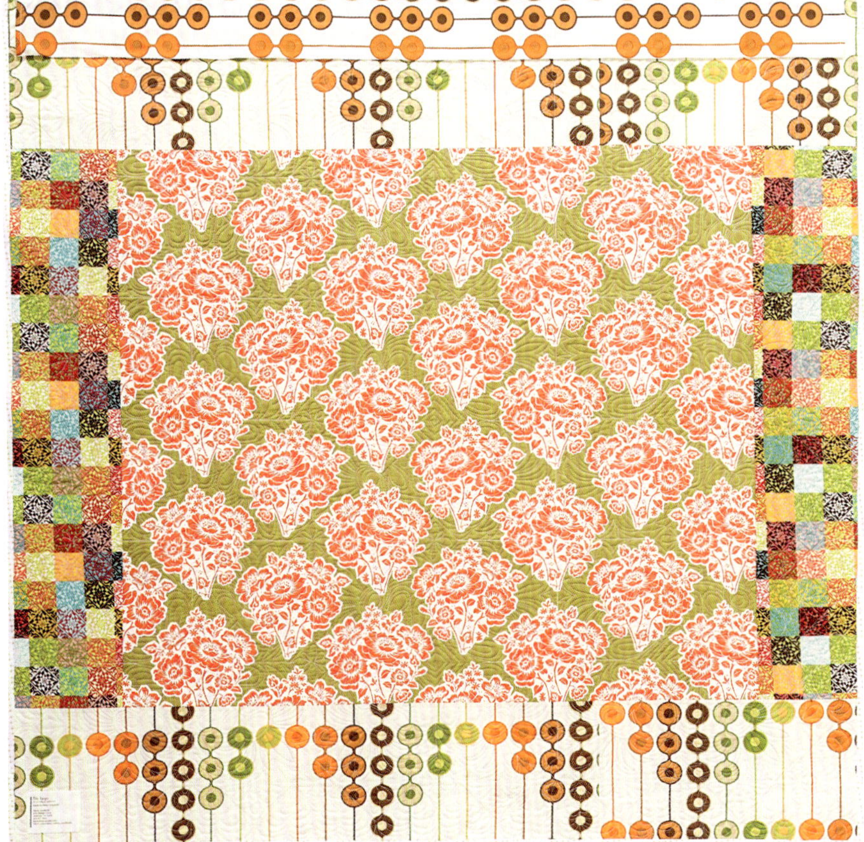

The back of *Tile Tango* is made from a combination of big prints.

UNPREDICTABLE HAND-DYES

Hand-dyed fabric that has widely spaced areas of dense color falls into the "unpredictable" category.

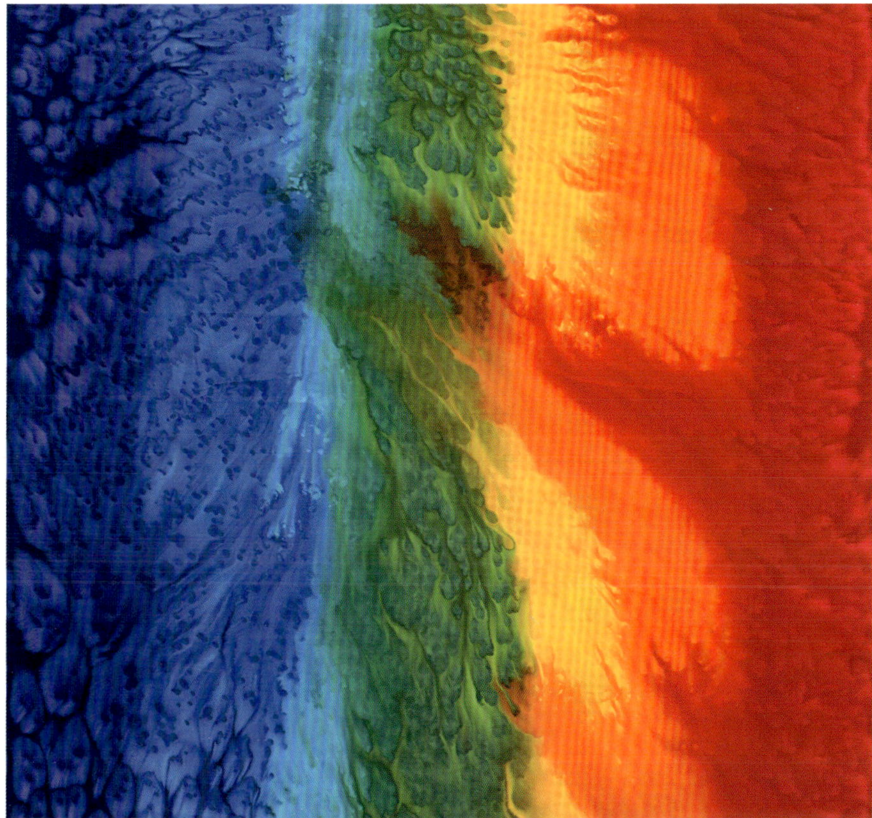

Multicolored hand-dyes can have bold areas of color that are widely dispersed.

Small squares cut from this fabric have nothing in common among them. They look as if they came from several different fabrics. That's great if you are fussy cutting, but this kind of fabric can be harder to use in rotary-cut piecing projects.

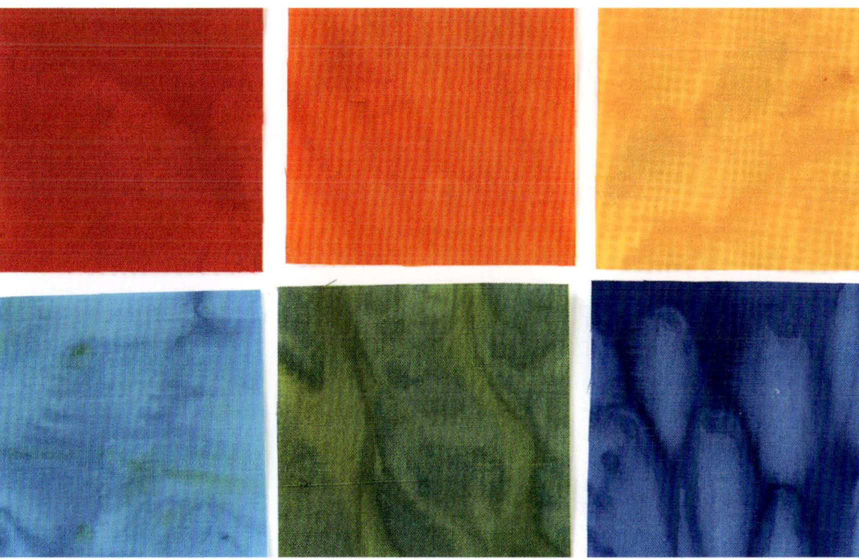

These 2½˝ squares cut from a multicolored hand-dyed fabric look as if they came from several different fabrics.

COLOR AND SCRAP QUILTS

By Judy Gauthier

Organizing Your Fabrics by Color

Organizing your fabrics will make it a million times easier to choose fabrics for the best possible scrap quilts. There are many ways to organize your fabrics. My personal preference is by color.

MORE ORGANIZATION

When I am actually in the selection process for a quilt, I also divide fabrics into light and dark, and warm and cool.

Find a space that will accommodate shelving, ideally with cubbies, so each color can have a separate spot. If you can't build cubbies, you can also use baskets or boxes. Make sure they are stored out of direct sunlight, because sunlight will damage your fabric considerably.

Fabric on Display

Having your fabrics out where you can see them is a good way to save money. I don't know about you, but with me it's "out of sight, out of mind." If I don't see a fabric, I will forget I have it—so it won't get used, and I'll buy more.

CUBBY RULE

In order to be put into a cubby, a piece of fabric must be ½ yard or larger in size.

I separate my fabrics first by color: red, orange, yellow, gold, brown, green, turquoise/aqua, blue, pink, purple, white, black, and tan (which is good for backgrounds and is understated). Halloween and Christmas have their own cubbies.

If you are uncertain about how to classify a fabric because of the multitude of colors in it, look at the background color. If this doesn't help, then create a cubby for fabrics that have such a multitude of colors that they cannot be defined. These fabrics are called the "I don't know what you are, but I love you anyway" fabrics. I think this is a good metaphor for life!

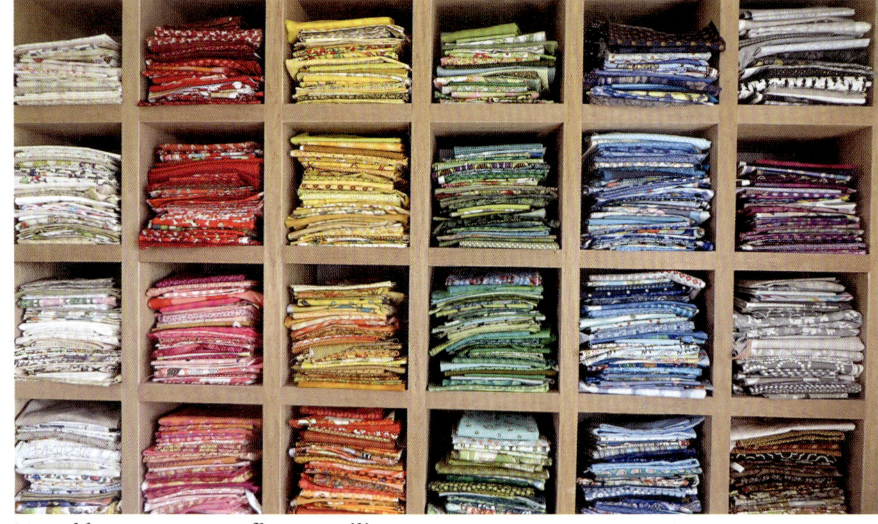

My cubby system spans floor to ceiling.

Photo by Judy Gauthier

CAREFUL FOLDING

If a fabric is larger than ½ yard and has a little bit cut from it, I will try to fold it so there aren't any selvage pieces or other stray pieces hanging from it. The cubby system is much more aesthetically pleasing that way. But as long as a fabric piece is larger than ½ yard, it stays on the shelf.

I have a wire drawer system for fat quarters. Wire drawers may be purchased at big-box do-it-yourself stores. You can see your fabric, and each drawer is sorted by color.

Next come the scraps. They're the ones we loved before we used them, loved as we used them, and still love even though they're not perfect.

I store my fun, less-than-perfectly shaped scraps (leftover strips from jelly rolls, pieces from charm packs, and scraps) in tubs. Yes, tubs. I use transparent ones so I can see what is in them. I have a tub for each of the colors for which I have a cubby.

If you follow my system, you probably won't have a lot of room left at this stage. We've talked about cubbies, wire drawers, and now tubs. And you still need to have room for your sewing machine! So you are going to need to stack those tubs, and they can get heavy.

Here is the last step in the organizational system. Tape bags to the edge of your sewing table or cutting table. Why would you ever do that? Well, if you're like me, you won't want to stop every time you create a scrap. You will pile them up on your cutting table until you're good and ready to throw them into the correct bin. Instead, tape a couple of bags to your cutting table or sewing table. When you have a scrap, throw it into one of the bags. Then, once a week, put the scraps in the correct bins.

Whew! That was a lot of information, but now you can have some fun choosing fabrics!

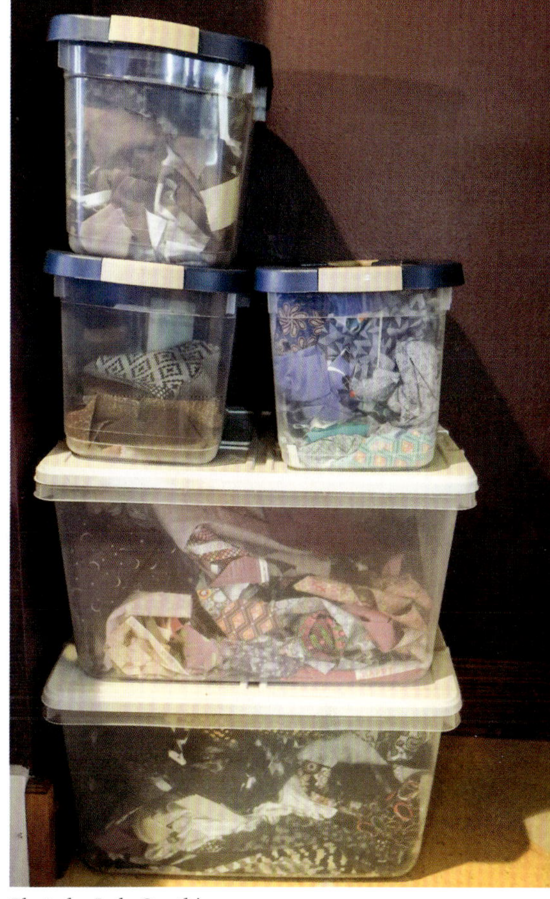

Photo by Judy Gauthier

Choosing Fabrics

Many people think that to make a scrap quilt you must use an assortment of all the scraps you own. Not true! You can decide on a theme or color scheme beforehand, and then pick your fabrics accordingly. Just because it's a scrap quilt doesn't mean that it has to be devoid of a theme.

For the most part, you are going to be picking from your bins. The entire premise of a scrap quilt is to help you use up your odd scraps—but that doesn't mean that you can't add a few new fabric pieces here and there if they are a good fit.

Decide what feeling you want your quilt to convey. Do you want a scrappy holiday feeling?

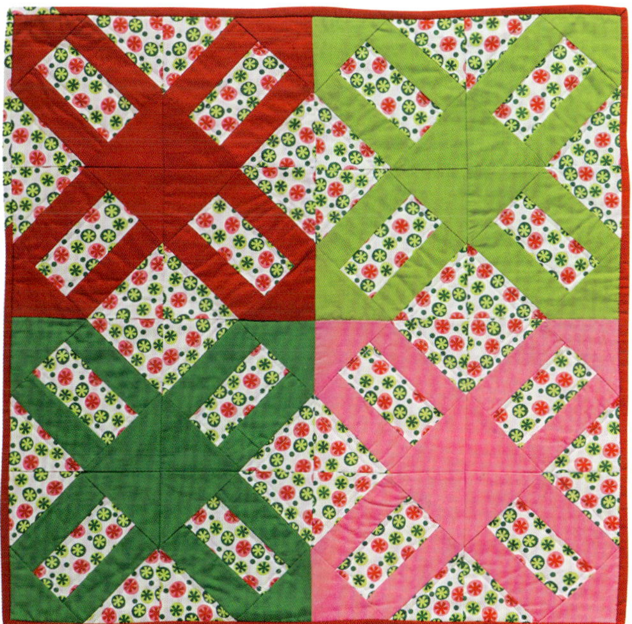

▶ *Holiday Scrap Crackers* features a pattern from my book *Quilts for Scrap Lovers* (by C&T Publishing). The tabletop quilt's candy motif and solids were left over from making Christmas pajamas.

Color and Scrap Quilts **51**

Perhaps you are trying to convey a summery look. Will it be reflective of the greenery of summer foliage or have a beachy or citrusy feeling?

A summer theme of new shoots and blossoms

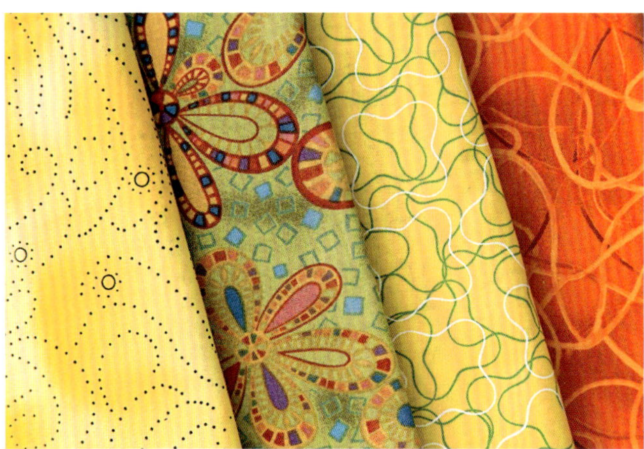

A more citrusy, summery feeling

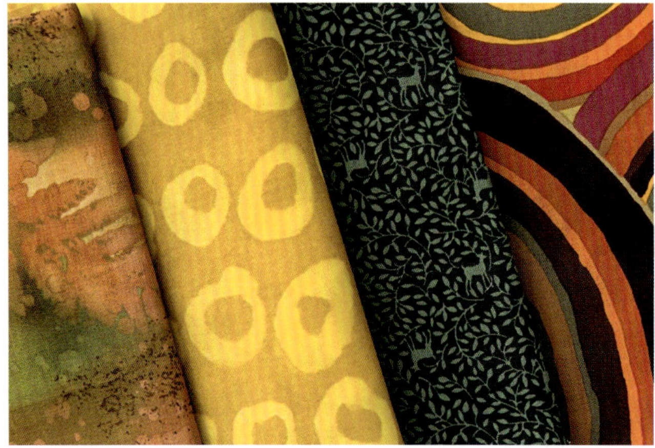

A woodsy feeling

WARM AND COOL COLORS

Although many people equate warm and cool colors with intensity, this is not an accurate association. Warm and cool colors have less to do with intensity than they do with mood. If you look at the color wheel, you will see that the warm colors tend to be on one side of the color wheel and the cool colors on the other.

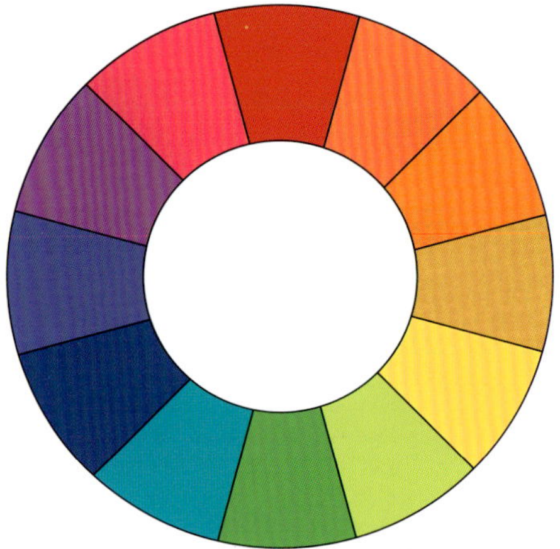

When I am referencing warm colors, I am talking about anything from yellow over to red. The cool colors are on the other side of the color wheel, and I am speaking now of green through blue.

There are a couple of colors that are generally in between, and these are purples that lean more toward the red end of the spectrum and greens that lean more toward the yellow end of the spectrum.

The effects of color may be simplified by saying that the warm colors charge our emotions. They make us feel comfortable, and well, warm. Red is a great color for marketing: It tends to make us feel good even though it may not be our favorite color. Cool tones are calming and restful. Most people think these are the colors that should be found in bedrooms or in quiet, restful spots.

So what does all this have to do with quilting?

Warm and cool tones evoke certain feelings. Your choice will depend on what your quilt is trying to convey. Look at the pile of fabric shown below. The fabrics all have warm tones, with an ambiguous one thrown in. How does it look to you? Playful? Bold? Youthful?

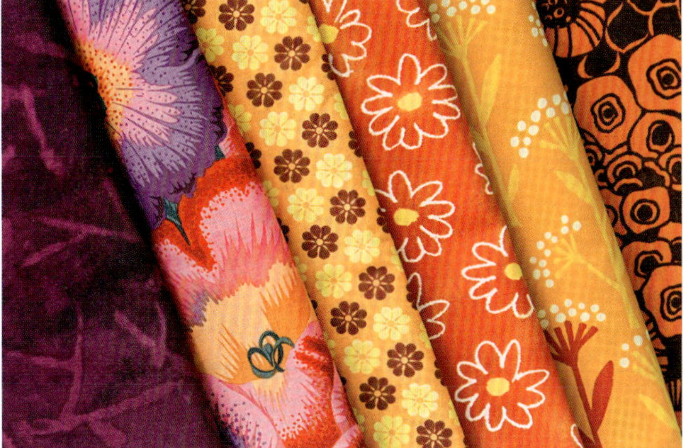

This fabric grouping has a definite look and feel to it.

Now look at this next grouping. It certainly feels different than the previous one.

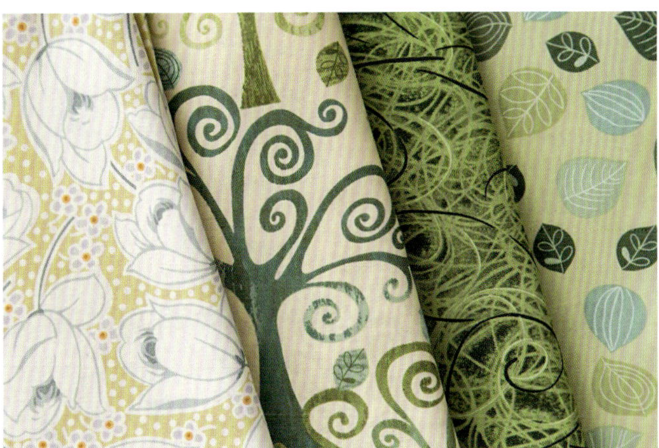

This colorway may be more appropriate in a room that feels restful.

Remember, not all quilts are made as bed quilts. Many are wall art, and art is definitely meant to convey certain feelings.

Now, having said that, I have to mention one little thing: Unless you are definitely trying to convey a sentiment with the color scheme or are doing it as a request, don't make a quilt to match a paint color or the color scheme of a room. *What?* I can hear all the commotion coming from readers! Think about this. All quilts are art. When you purchase a work of art, do you buy it because it matches the room? Not usually. Most people purchase art because it moves them.

I tell you this because it will free up your spirit to take a chance. Use that fabric you love. Use a fabric that moves you. Being a quilt shop owner, I often see people buy a piece of fabric and say, "I don't know what I am going to do with it, but I just love it!" Those are the greatest words a shop owner can hear, because you know you have reached someone with a piece of your fabric. You have made a connection.

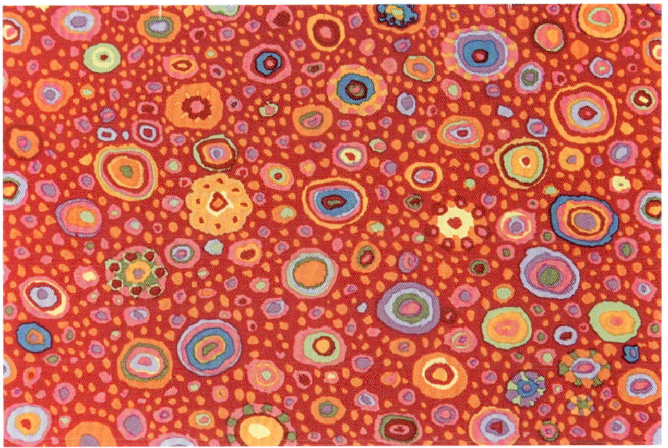

This is one of my most beloved pieces of fabric. I have cut it up and used it in many of my scrap quilts.

So put that fabric in—but help it to fit according to the rules of color, intensity, spacing, and possibly, theme.

UNDERSTANDING INTENSITY CREATES GREAT RESULTS

I think intensity (or *value*: light, medium, and dark) is more important than color.

Many quilters are very anxious when it comes to color selection. For most of my quilts, I have not agonized too much about color selection. That's because in order to use up as many scraps as possible, you can't worry as much about color. You want to use as many scraps as you can, so you are mainly going to be looking at the degree of contrast among your scraps. A good scrap quilt will have a balance of lights, mediums, and darks.

My best piece of advice with regard to intensity is to take a photo of your scraps using the black-and-white feature on your camera. (Most cameras have this feature, and all smart phones do.) When you look at a photo of a stack of scraps, you should see a variety of lights, mediums, and darks. If you don't, you will need to adjust your scrap selection to achieve the most successful results.

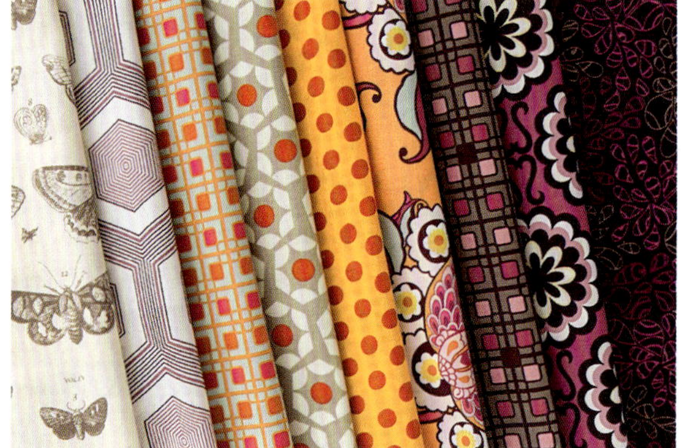

This stack of fabrics has a good combination of lights, mediums, and darks.

Color is almost secondary to light, medium, and dark intensity. See how well these work together when the color is hidden?

FINDING INSPIRATION IN UNUSUAL PLACES

Many people forget to look at the world as a color palette. I like to do this because it brings me fresh inspiration for how to put fabrics together. Almost everyone has a cell phone with them at all times these days. So put yours to work for you. Create a folder for pictures you take that may give you color inspiration for your next quilt.

Take some trees with bright red berries, for example. The berries are juxtaposed with lovely brownish-gray branches. Take a picture! How about cereal boxes? The companies that make cereal have entire art departments devoted to the science of making things look good. Take advantage of this and take a picture. Or what about washing dishes? (A mundane task for certain.) I have Fiesta Dinnerware. While washing these bowls, it struck me: Look at what a great color combination this is! For decades Homer Laughlin (the producer of Fiesta Dinnerware) has been committed to the science of color.

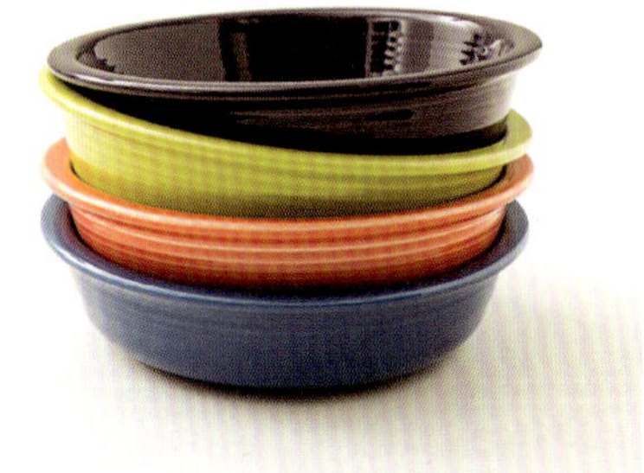

Finding color inspiration everywhere

Have fun playing with the fabric selections for each quilt. Many of them are monochromatic within an area, and this makes for easy decision making.

TAKING PRINT SCALE INTO CONSIDERATION

I am one of those rare people who is totally undaunted by large-scale prints. Often people come into the shop, look at large-scale prints, and become terrified. We have had so many years of small little ditzy prints that large prints scare some quilters. If there's one bit of advice I usually give to people, it's not to be afraid to use the large-scale prints in the blocks of their quilts.

So many people look at a large-scale print and think that it can only be used in a border. Not so. I also hear the comment repeatedly, "I think that's too big to be used in that block. People won't know what it is." Well, let's challenge that theory.

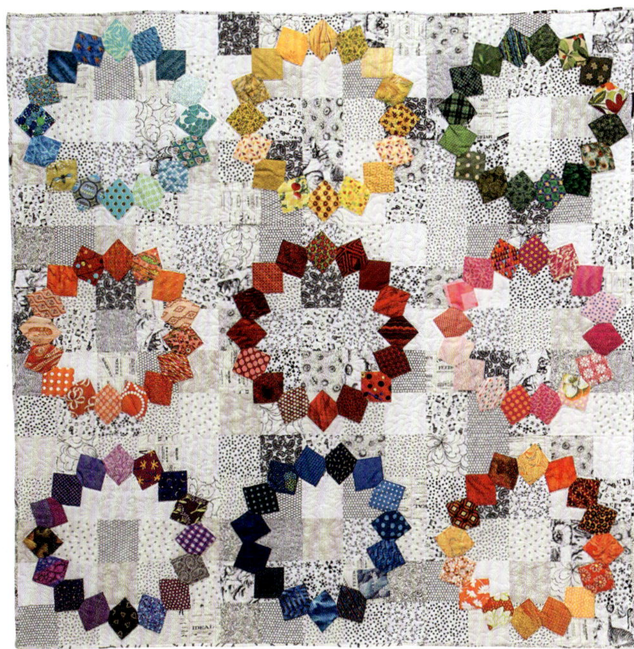

Aromatic Rings has a monochromatic theme within each individual block.

When a quilter looks at the piece of fabric shown below, it looks like a scary large-scale print. It was very popular in my shop, and it sold quickly, but most of the customers admitted that they didn't know what they would do with it. **A**

Most quilters might say that it would make a cute blouse, which it would. They might say that it would go well on the border of a quilt that had umbrellas in it. Yes, you could do that. But let's break this down.

Lay the 5½″ template from the fast2cut Simple Square Templates (by C&T Publishing) or your rotary cutting ruler over the motif. Don't center it so that the characters are right in the middle. Place it so there are portions of the motif included in the square but not precisely in the center. **B**

Now, if you cut out the square, look at the results. **C**

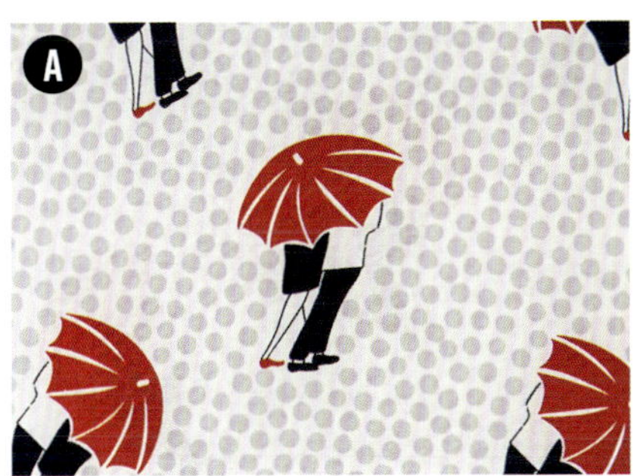

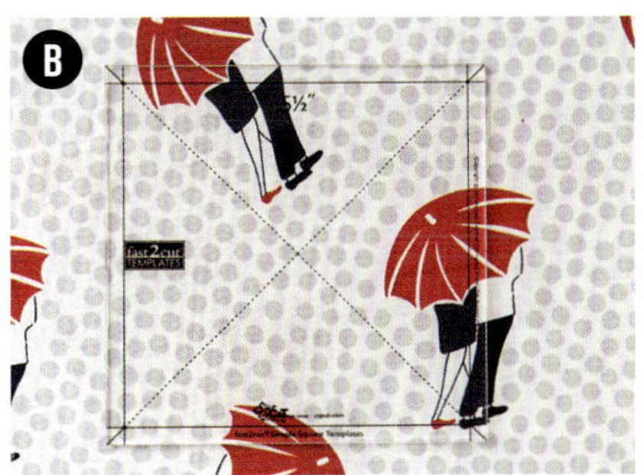

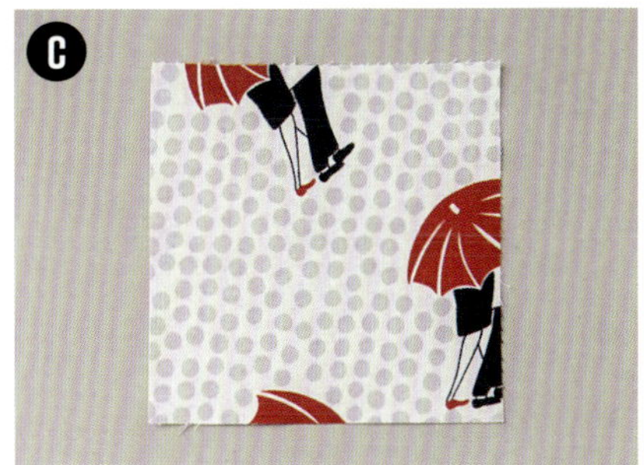

Is there any question that the motif shows a man and woman with an umbrella? No. There's no question. It's not hitting you in the face like the well-centered picture of something that a child would draw, but it definitely leaves the viewer looking at it for more than just a split second. It draws the viewer in.

You don't necessarily have to center the motifs. Because they're scraps, they should be used to their best advantage as scraps. The quilter should cut over to the edge so as not to waste fabric. I can still hear my mother's words: "Don't cut right in the middle of that scrap!"

Here's a photo of a baby that is taken slightly off center. This is the same concept. Even though you can't see the entire baby in the photo, there's no question that it's a baby.

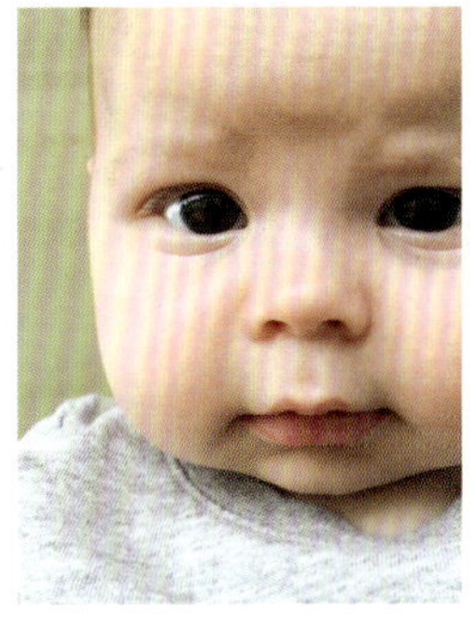

Photo by Judy Gauthier

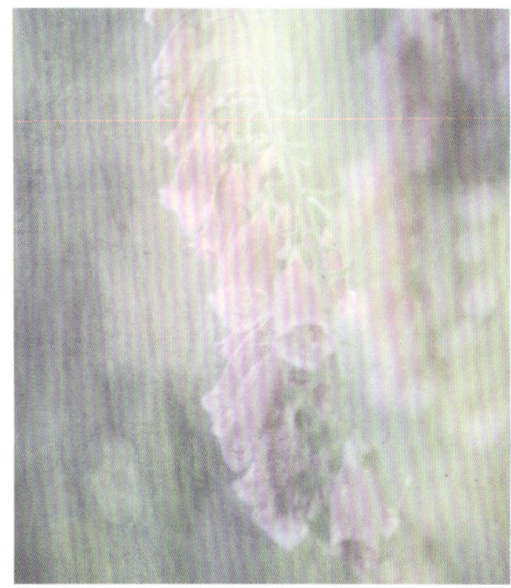

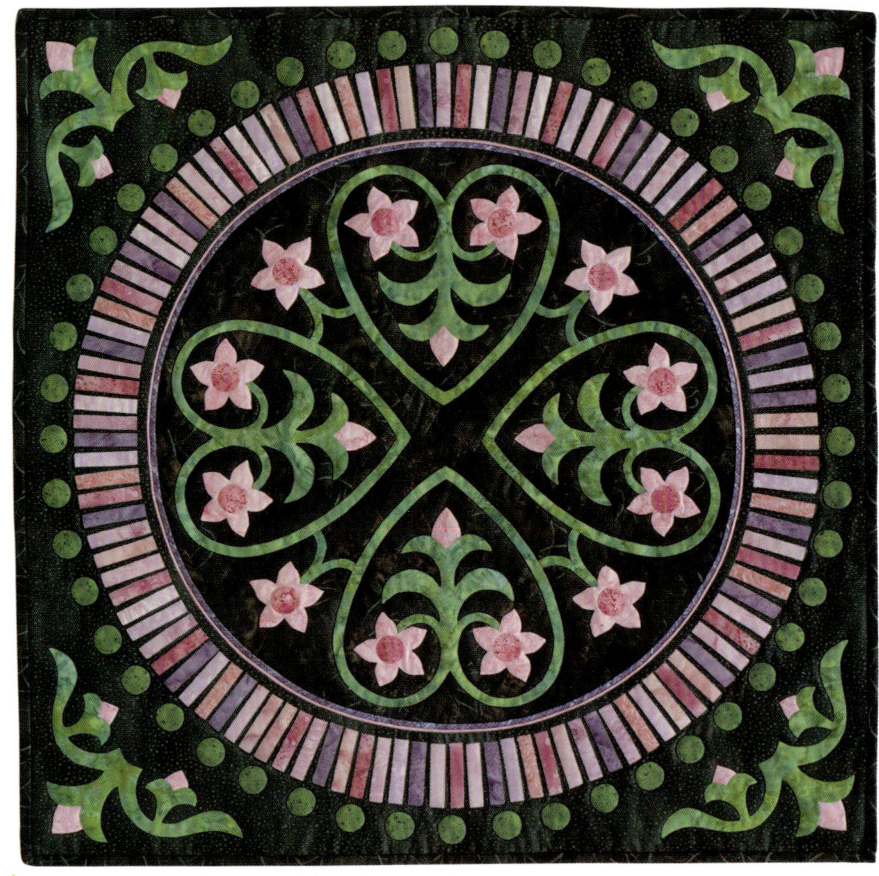

Star Flower Medallion made by Mickie Swall, Cranberry Township, Pennsylvania; 28″ × 28″

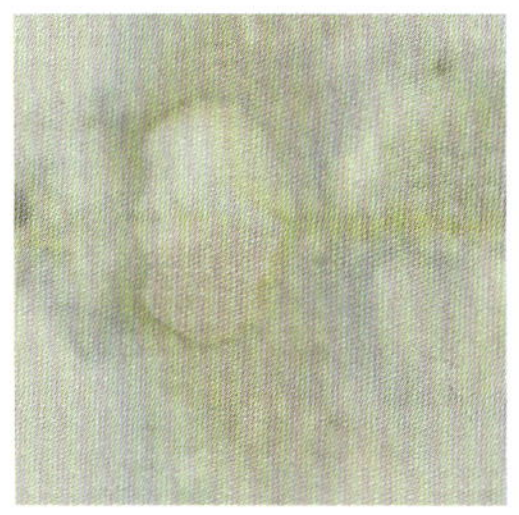
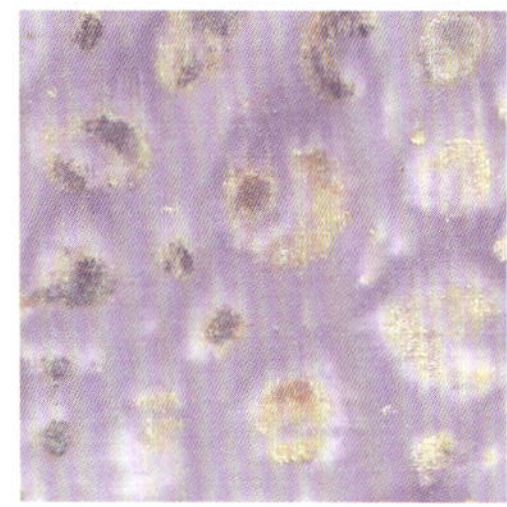
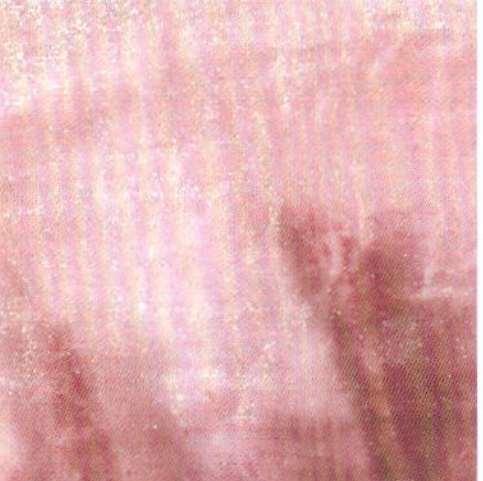
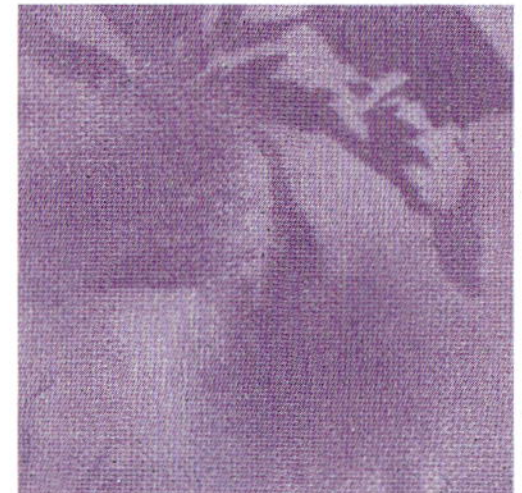
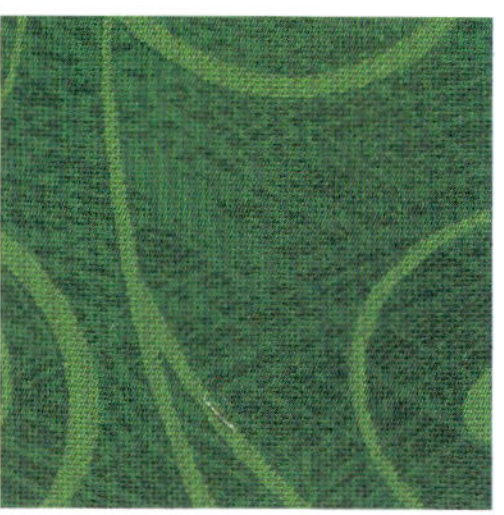

Can I make beautiful quilts without knowing any color theory?

YES

Is there a fun, fast, easy way to select colors for my quilts?

YES

Is there a way to pick my quilts' colors without being surprised at the end?

YES

The easiest way to select colors for your quilts is with a method I call visual coloring. It is fun and easy. It gives great results—and perhaps best of all—it takes very little time to learn. Join me in this wonderful adventure to unlock the keys to selecting colors and fabrics for your quilts. There's no risk, no anguish, and no pain. Instead, the time you spend choosing colors and fabrics will be filled with exciting realizations and fun exploration. Visual coloring is a simple step to color independence and—it could be the most important journey in your creative life!

I love color! I especially love beautifully colored quilts—quilts that are stunningly dramatic, visually exciting, richly autumnal, quietly subdued, and refreshingly cool. I find beauty in both quiet hues and brilliant colors. I have rarely met a color I didn't like! You may be like I am, or you may be more discerning about your color preferences. The big question for quilters isn't what colors do we like, but how can we use the colors we love to create the beautiful quilts we envision?

I pondered this question many years ago, which led me to devise a simple color-selection method. I have named this method visual coloring.

Visual coloring allows us to work with colors successfully in an almost foolproof manner. It trains our eyes to see the subtle nuances in nature's colors. The colors and fabrics incorporated in every quilt in this book were selected by using visual coloring. Before immersing ourselves in the idea of visual coloring, let's look at some of the most important aspects of our relationship with color.

Color Influences

No matter how old you are or how long you have been quilting, it's important that you get in tune with the colors you intuitively respond to in a positive way. Each of us responds to colors and color combinations positively or negatively, depending on our makeup and life experiences.

Many of our color responses have much to do with where we grew up, where we have spent most of our adult lives, and our life experiences. These influences are often so subtle that we aren't even aware of them. If we think back to our early experiences, we may find clues to many of our color loves and dislikes. It may be interesting to see how environment, geographic region, and culture play a role in the colors we intuitively love. Different regions provide their own unique natural colorings. Our color favorites are deeply rooted in the areas we know best and in those we feel most at home.

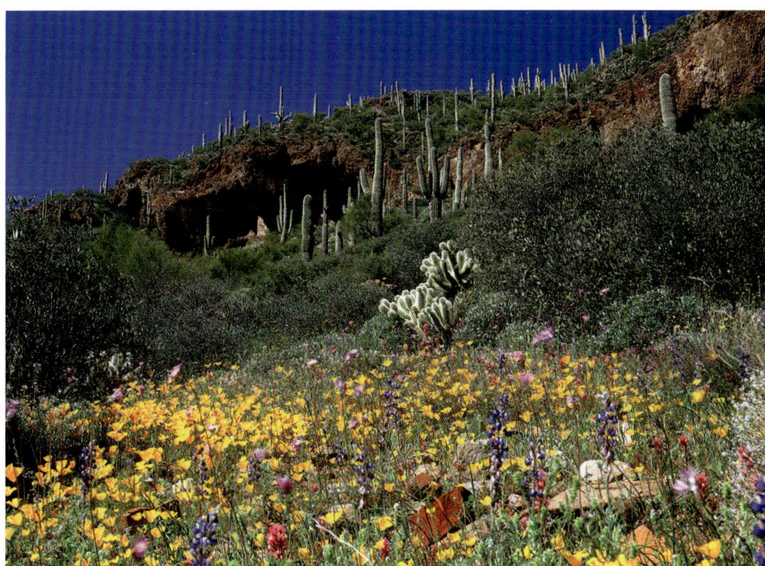

Ablaze with Color—The desert is in its glory with the vivid colors of the wildflowers.

Photo courtesy of Lonnie Brock, nature photographer.

If you grew up in or near a desert, you may have a natural affinity for the strong desert hues: the warm earth tones, the strong blue skies, and the brilliant hues of the wildflowers. If you are from the desert, you know how stunning the textures and colors of rock formations can be, particularly when highlights and shadows accentuate their beauty. No doubt your memory bank is filled with visions of the breathtaking desert hues of the sunrises and sunsets. The blend of earthy cacti colors, set against the desert sky, is second nature to you. It would be difficult to remove the desert colors from your subconscious mind.

Likewise, if you moved to the desert as an adult, or visit it often, then its color characteristics may have subtly become part of your color personality.

The tropical regions are rich in dramatic colors too. The flowers are exquisite in pure colors—the greens so very lush. Even the birds exude a brilliance that is rare in northern regions. I doubt that a person who lives in the natural brilliance of tropical colors could remain unaffected by their exuberance. People who live in these regions may have an affinity to strong, pure-spirited hues.

If you grew up in a land of mountains, evergreen forests, sparkling lakes, fjords, rivers, and other waterways, your love for green and blue hues may be substantial. These preferences could easily include the beautiful water hues that are so dazzling—aqua greens, aqua blues, teals, turquoises, deep blues, emerald greens, blue-violets (periwinkle), lavenders, yellow-greens, chartreuses, and deep olives. No doubt, the blues and soft violets of distant mountains are deep in your memory too.

At sunrise and sunset, you can see the wonderful play of colors in both the sky and the water. Violet, orange, lavender, gold, coral, pink, magenta—all can be seen in both subtle and stunning drama.

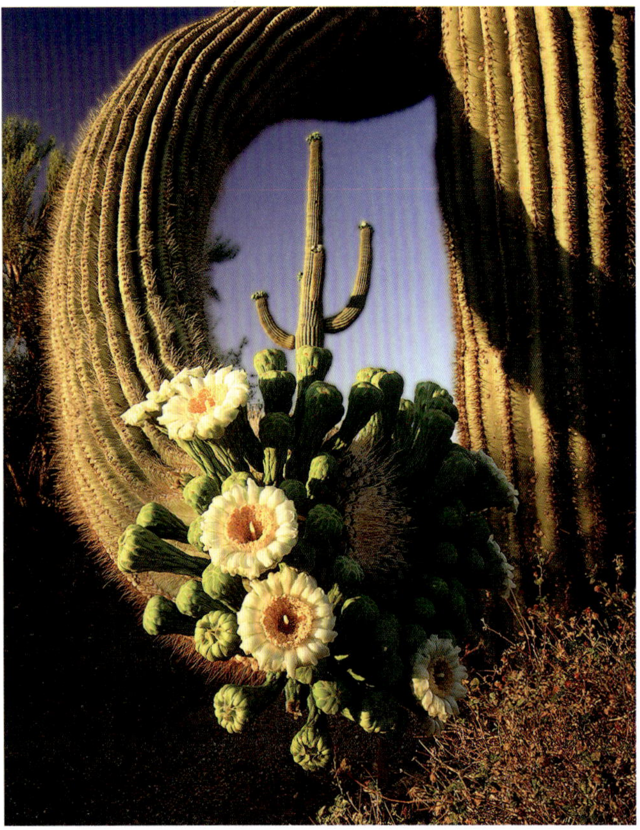

The Desert in Its Stunning Beauty—Desert vegetation is like no other. It's filled with magical color inspiration.

Photo courtesy of Lonnie Brock, nature photographer.

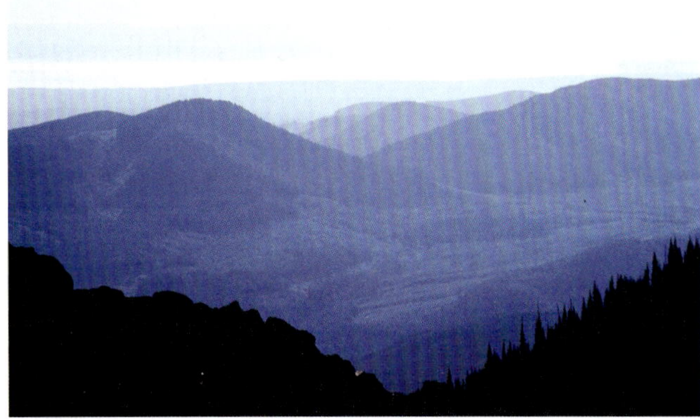

The Land of Forests and Mountains—The evergreen forests and mountain ranges are filled with green and blue hues, which are featured dramatically in areas such as America's Pacific Northwest.

The vast countryside has its own rich blend of colors, often varying greatly with the season. Fields may be ablaze with brilliant yellows, oranges, chartreuses, or other strong colorings as crops reach maturity. During much of the year, the subtle greens, browns, and rich earth tones are exhibited quietly. These understated colorings become deeply embedded in people who have lived in one of the many farming regions of our country.

In the countryside, the feeling of spaciousness is so apparent. The open land and huge sky seem to form a grand partnership that provides magnificent color combinations awaiting our interpretations.

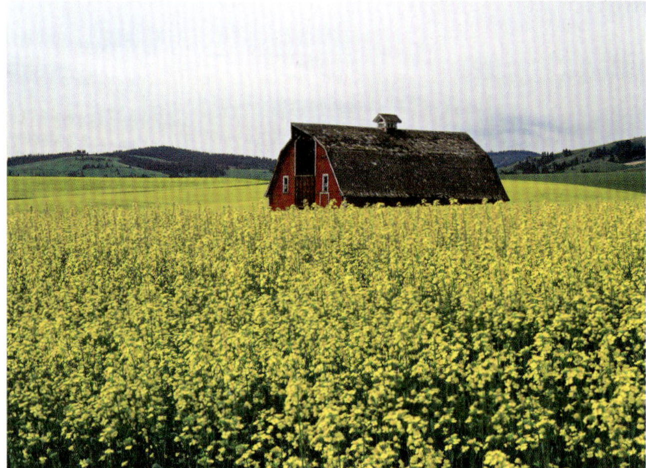

Fields Shimmer with Vivid Color—The beautiful colors you see in farming regions vary greatly with the seasons and the crops. Here, a field ablaze in the brilliant colors of the rape plant contrasts with the red of the barn and the deep green of the hills in the distance.

Photo courtesy of Lonnie Brock, nature photographer.

Think about the natural colors of the area where you grew up. How do you respond to these colors? If you are not certain, begin noticing your reactions to colors that are common to the region where you spent the most time in your childhood. If you moved from region to region as you grew up, your color personality may be more complex and more difficult to discern. Visualize the regions you loved best. What colors come to mind when you think of these regions? Your natural color inclinations may arise either from the region where you lived the longest or from the area where you were the happiest.

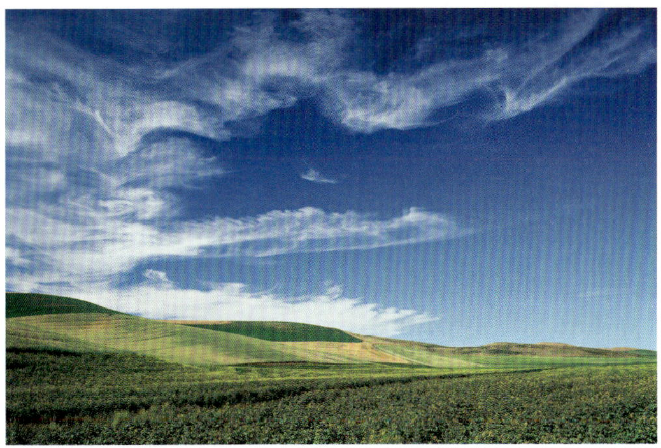

A Magnificent Partnership—The open fields and rangelands form a great color partnership with the sky. Their palette can be striking or quite mellow. Here, the sky provides wonderful hues to blend with the rich fields.

Photo courtesy of Lonnie Brock, nature photographer.

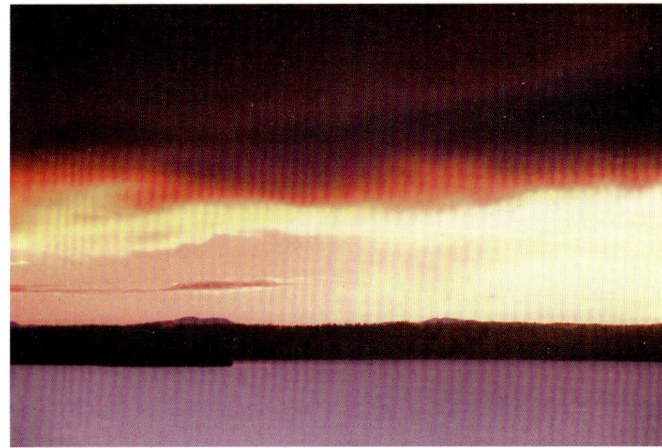

Drama at Day's End—Sunsets are filled with glorious colors that can elicit many emotive feelings. Each sunset is like an exquisite palette. It gives us the opportunity to reflect on another beautiful way to put colors together. Take advantage of these color inspirations by recording them with your camera.

The Blending of Cultural and Regional Influences

In the United States, we are a compilation of so many countries rich with traditions and cultures. Many regions of our country are microcosms of the cultures of far-off lands. For example, there is a strong northern European influence in the Pacific Northwest because so many of its early settlers came from the Scandinavian countries, where many geographical features are so similar.

This population's naturally reserved personality, combined with the area's natural resources, helps define this region's historical color use. Warm wood tones, neutrals, and the blue hues of sky and water have been the mainstay colors of the Pacific Northwest for generations.

The color use and color spirit of faraway lands, such as Italy, Turkey, South Africa, China, and Japan, are part of our country's color history, and the cultural and geographic features of these regions meld in our country's colors. Natural geographic influences, the origins of an area's settlers, and the influence of new residents blend together to set a regional color pattern.

Close your eyes and allow your mind to see the colors of your childhood region. Reflect on how these early influences have affected your color choices in both your home and your quilts. Do the same for the area where you currently live. Find and use the colors you are naturally drawn to as much as you can.

The Art of Seeing

When I was young, I believed that sky and water were blue, grass was green, sand was tan, stones were gray, tree trunks were brown, and apples were red. You could have asked me the color of almost anything, and I am quite certain that I would have been able to tell it to you in the blink of an eye. You probably would have given similar responses. As children, we knew

the color of any item without giving it a second thought.

One evening in my fourth decade of life, I had a color epiphany while observing a glorious sunset. That experience awoke in me the realization that I had never noticed how nature painted the world in colors. I had not really been aware of the colors my eyes saw.

It was a profound awakening for me to realize that knowing the colors and seeing the colors were two different concepts. I was startled to find that my mind had been working in color assumption mode for as long as I could remember. It was then that I decided to seriously train my eyes to really take note of the colors I saw and to stop making color assumptions that relied on color labeling, which is easy but not very accurate.

Soon after this experience, a simple idea for selecting colors for my quilts came to me. I experimented with the idea on quilts. It was easy and fun, and, best of all, it gave me the guidance I needed to select colors and fabrics. Thus was born the idea of visual coloring.

Visual coloring works for everyone, regardless of color experience. It doesn't matter whether you are a color theorist extraordinaire or you have never opened a color book. This method provides you with color confidence as you create beautiful quilts.

First Steps to Visual Coloring

The first step to visual coloring is finding out what colors and color combinations you are drawn to. Your intuitive color attractions are the foundation for visual coloring. To begin, set a date to have a relaxing day, listening to your favorite music, keeping your favorite beverage close at hand, and looking through magazines, calendars, date books, greeting cards, photos, and other similar material in search of color combinations that you absolutely love. Be certain to keep this date with yourself— it's an important first step in creating beautiful quilts in the colors you love. As you look through your selections, pull out all images that attract you deeply: those that take your breath away, those filled with unbelievable beauty, those that give you a sense of serenity, and those that bring you excitement or drama. Sort these images into visual groups (you can use file folders to organize the images), such as brightly colored hues; soft, quiet colorings; autumnal colorations; and perhaps wintry hues.

As you find new color-inspiration images you love, add them to your files. Once you begin, you'll find all sorts of color inspiration you will want to duplicate in your quilts. Subconsciously, your eyes will continue to search for the color combinations you love. Keep these color-inspiration files handy so you can thumb through the images frequently to get your subconscious mind to begin thinking about the colors for your next project. On these facing pages are samplings of color inspiration images I have placed into different files.

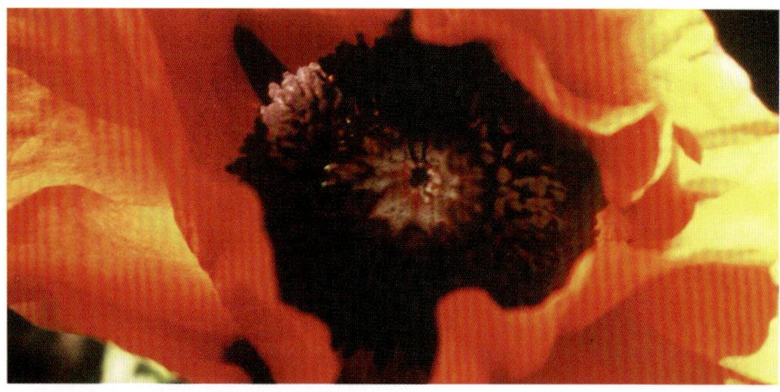

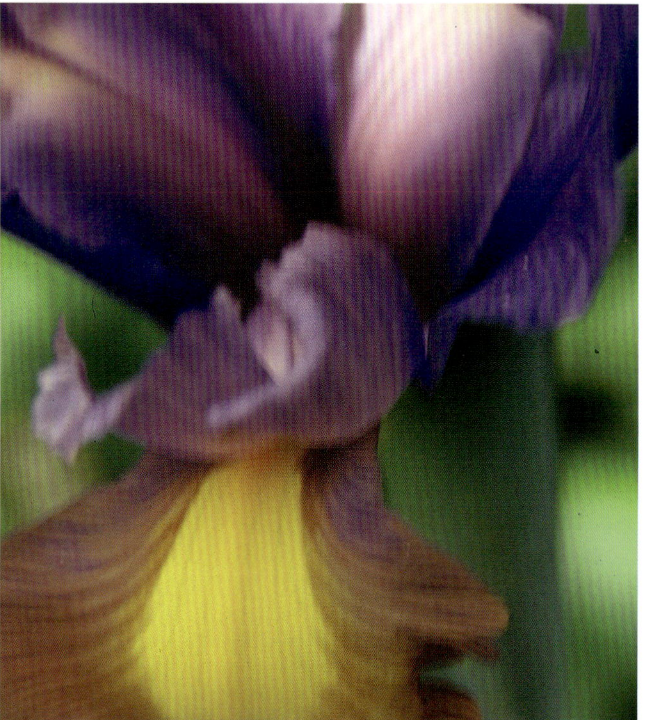

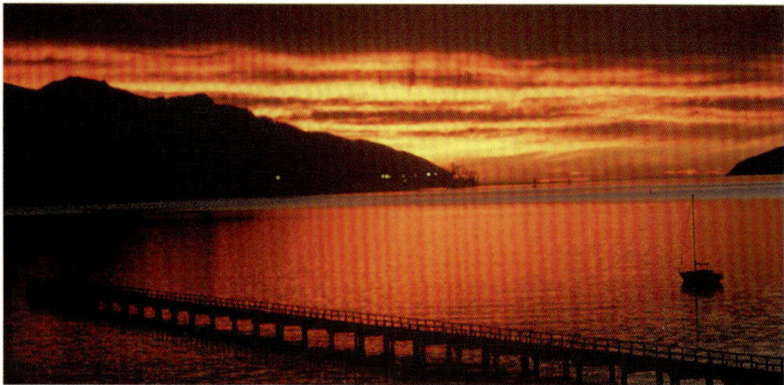

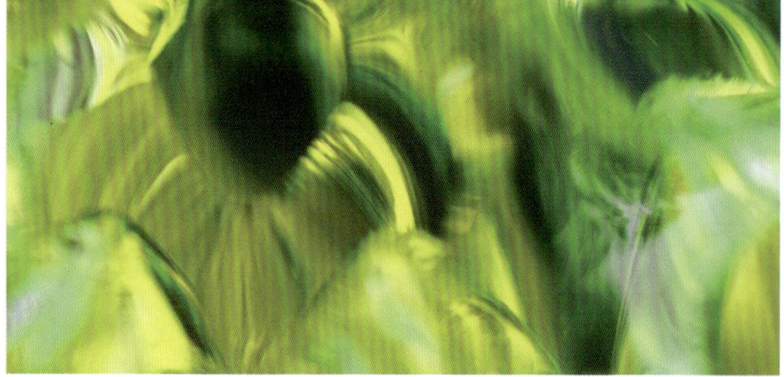

Dramatic Color-Inspiration File—I have dozens of bold color-inspiration images in this file because I love strong, clear colors. Flowers and sunsets are great for providing dramatic coloring. Not all images need to be from nature. The chartreuse image is a photo of a mixture of water and food coloring.

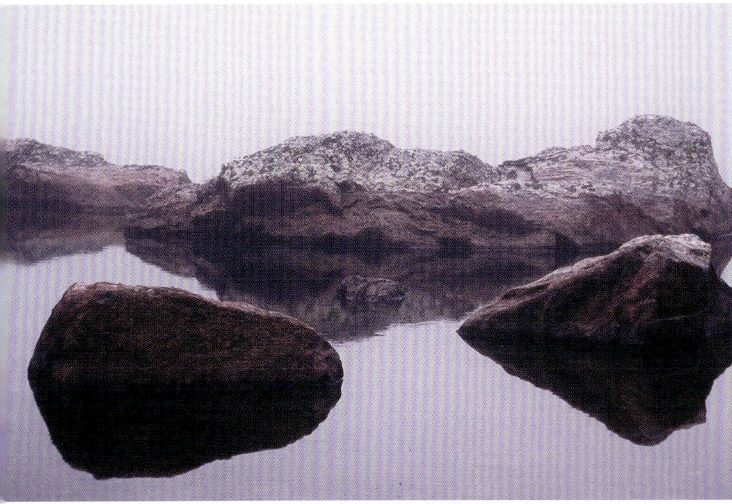

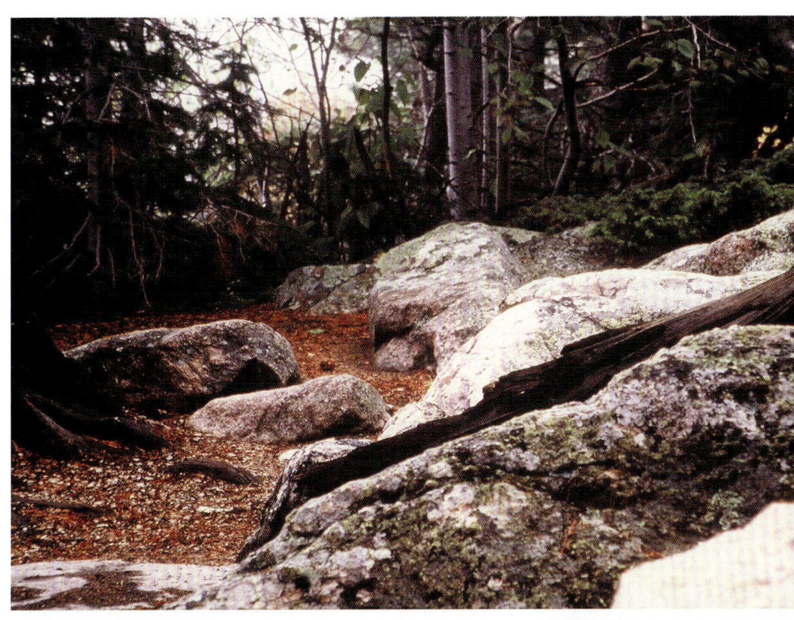

Quiet Color-Inspiration File—Winter scenes, quiet nature scenes, and grayed colors (tones) can all be part of this file. You can divide it further by color or the emotions the images evoke.

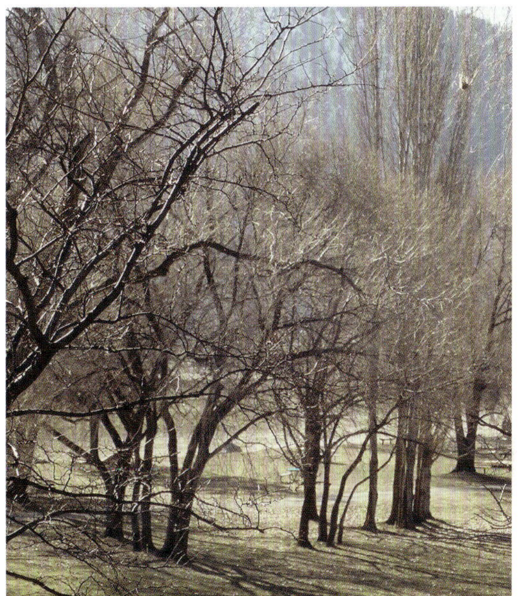

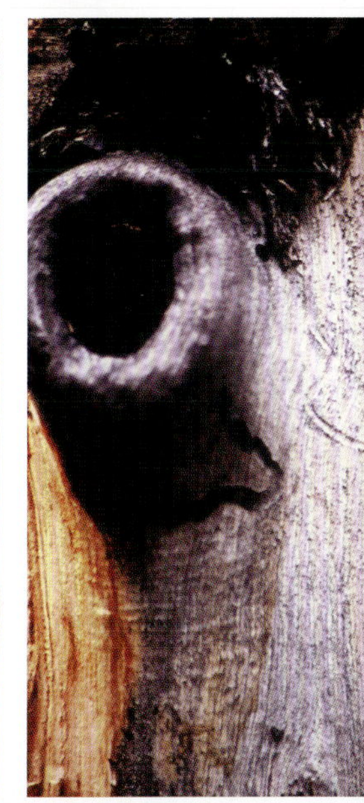

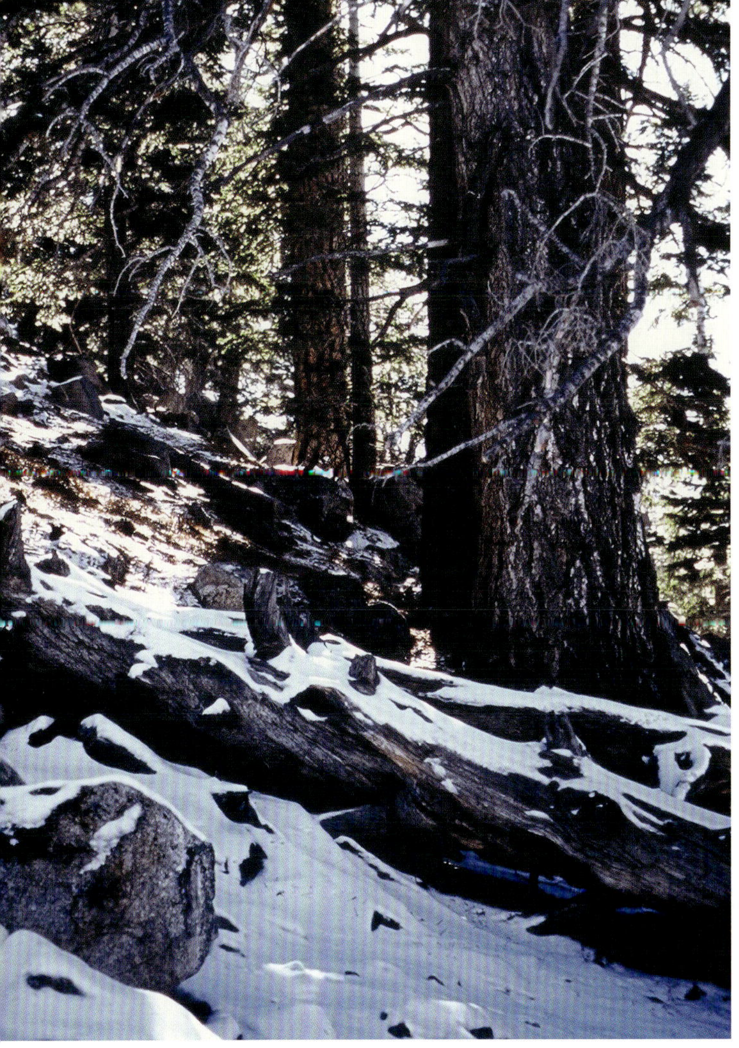

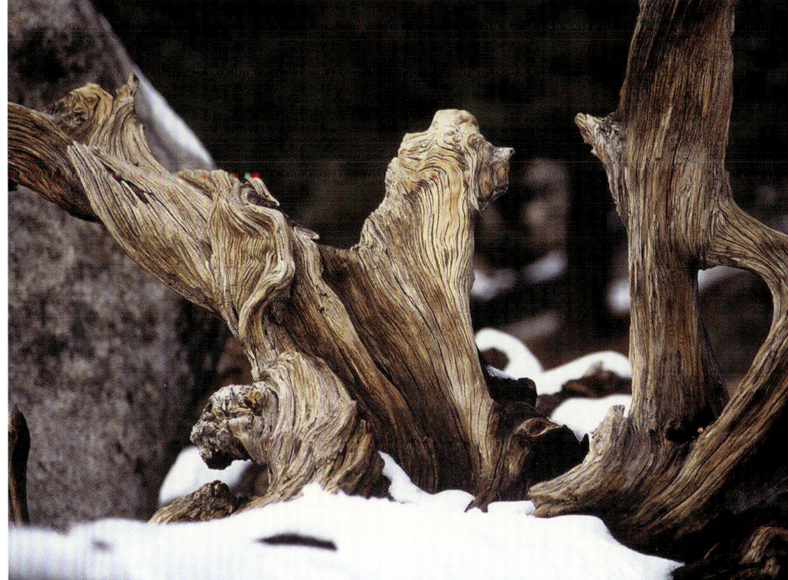

As you begin thinking about a new project, pull out your files and study your images. You will probably find yourself responding to the colors in one image more than any other. Those colors are the ones your creative spirit is most in tune with at that particular time.

You may notice that you respond differently to colors as the seasons come and go and as your mood changes. One image might appeal to you most at one time, and another might tug at your heart later. If you find yourself responding to two or more images equally, you will have to decide which one to use. Generally, the decision is based on which colors work best with the pattern you have selected or the fabrics you have available.

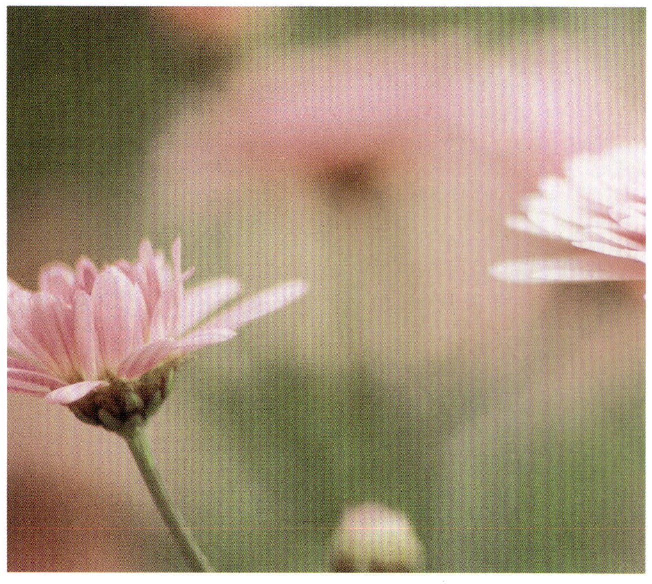

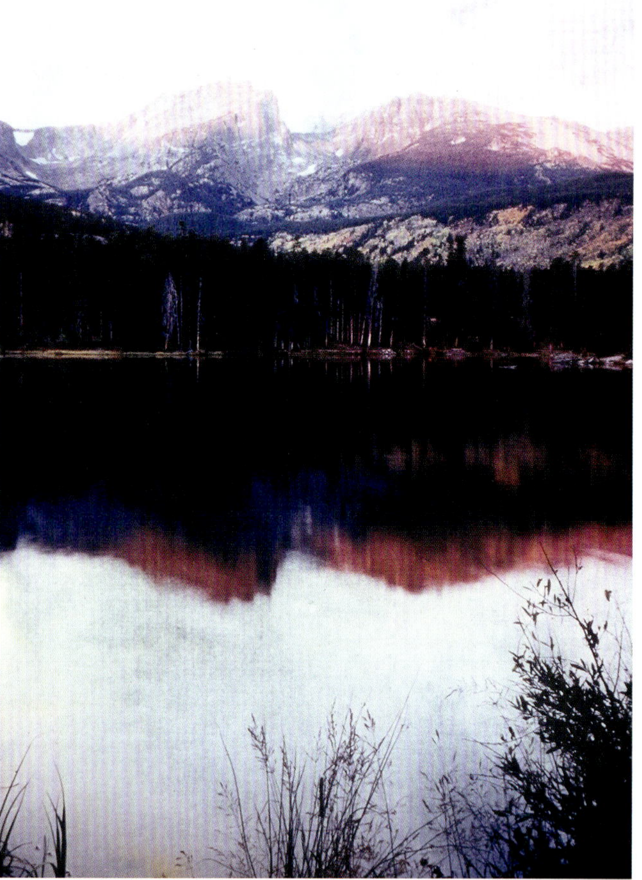

Serene Color-Inspiration File—I love serene color inspiration. The colors are so clear and striking even though they are reflective in nature. Here are a few photos from my file.

Selecting Colors and Fabrics with Visual Coloring

When using visual coloring, you are actually selecting your colors and fabrics simultaneously. Quite simply, you are choosing fabrics to use that visually read like the colors in the image. You are matching fabric colors with the image colors. After you have selected your image, I recommend that you enlarge it to fit on an 8½″ × 11″ sheet of paper (or other similar size). Enlarging the image allows you to see the colors more easily than if you were working with a small image. Unexpected colors are more readily seen in enlarged images. I have included a visual coloring example to illustrate the concept of pulling colors from the color-inspiration image and fabrics from your stash.

SAMPLE: DANCE, IRIS, DANCE

This image presents a strong emotive feeling with irises in dramatic colorings. I began choosing fabrics from the most pronounced iris colors first. As I worked, my eyes began seeing many more hues. These

unexpected colors can be very important additions, bringing depth or richness to the overall color plan. I absolutely love the fabrics I chose from this visual coloring, and I am eager to begin designing a quilt with them. These fabrics exude a contemporary feeling for me. Therefore, my design thoughts lean toward an impressionistic garden or a contemporary design.

If more fabrics were needed to create my quilt design, I would head for my local quilt store with my image in hand. In the store, choosing the fabrics that match the colors in my selected image would take only a few minutes.

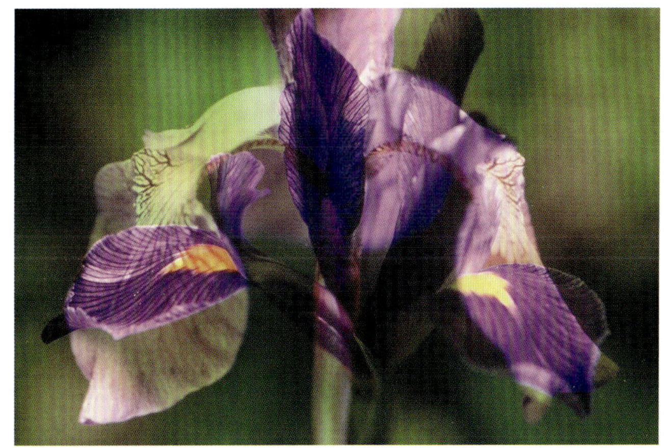

Dance, Iris, Dance

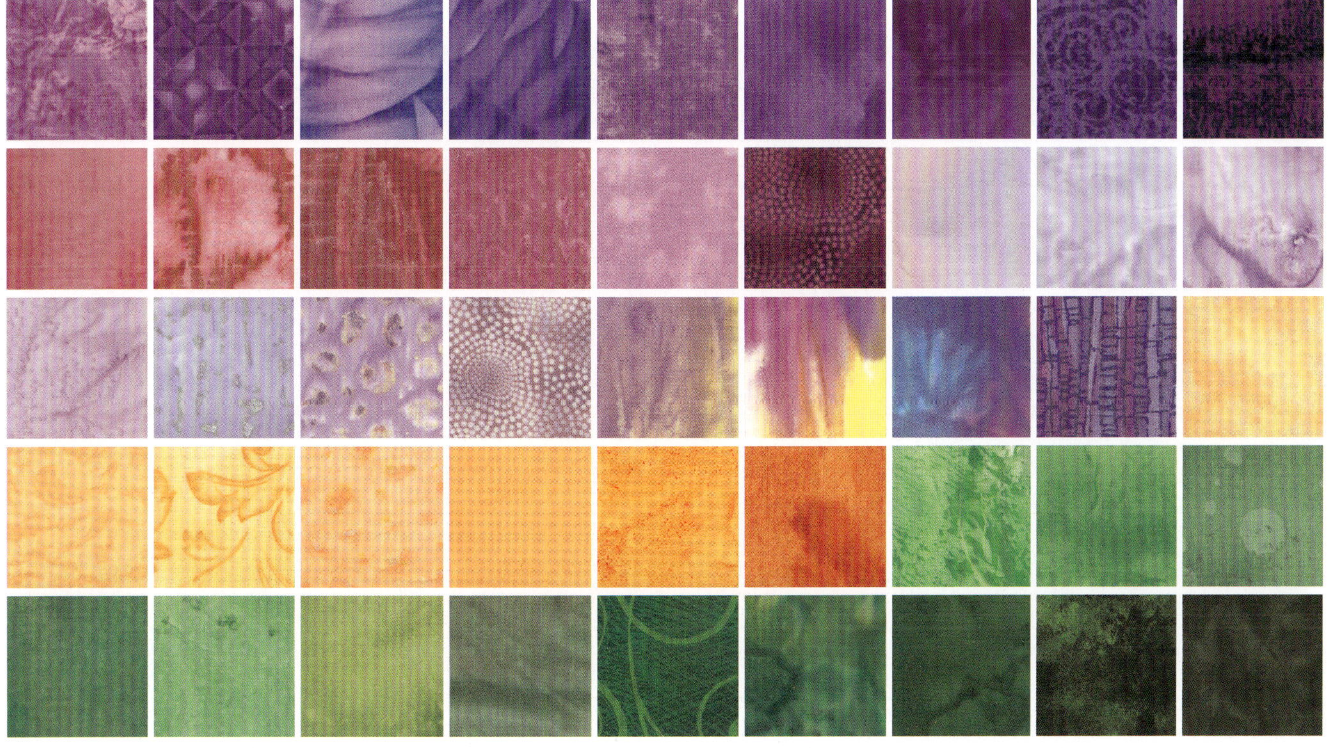

Visual Color Options

If you love all the colors in your selected image, and if your design can accommodate it, use all the colors in your quilt. Then your quilt will give you the same feeling as the color image. Unexpected colors often accentuate the overall beauty by adding a rich, unanticipated quality. These hues can cause visual vibration, which gives great excitement or drama to a design. Most often, the surprise colorations in an image are given the role of accent colors. You can give them a larger role if you want to make a more vivid design statement.

Visual coloring is not meant to be rigid. Options may present themselves, giving you slightly different visual paths to consider. Some of the most obvious options are discussed below.

SHARPENING YOUR COLOR SELECTION

If you think one color may be too strong, too intense, too light, too dark, or too distracting, eliminate it from your quilt project. For instance, I love the Sunrise in the Rockies image, but I felt that the dark hues of the rocks and grasses were too strong for my quilt's design. I chose to use only the water colors. Some of the colors in Canadian Sunrise felt too strong for the design I wanted to use, so I omitted the stronger colors here too.

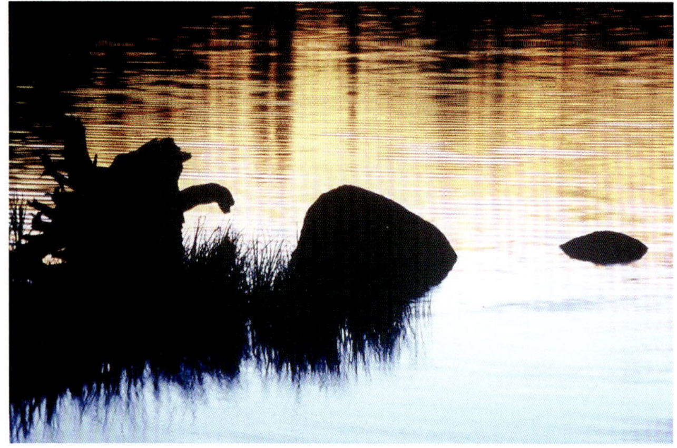

Color Inspiration: Sunrise in the Rockies

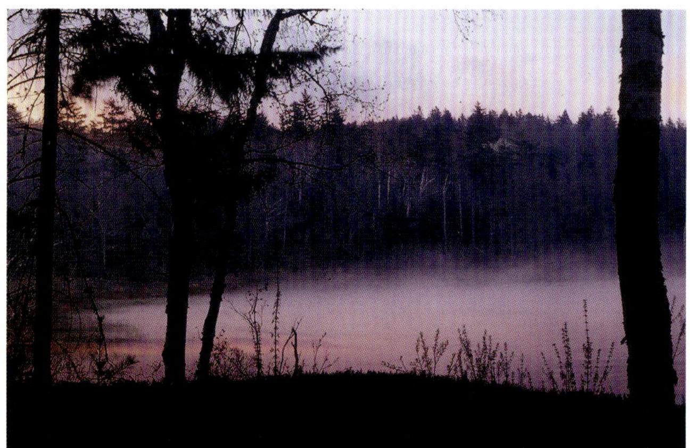

Color Inspiration: Canadian Sunrise

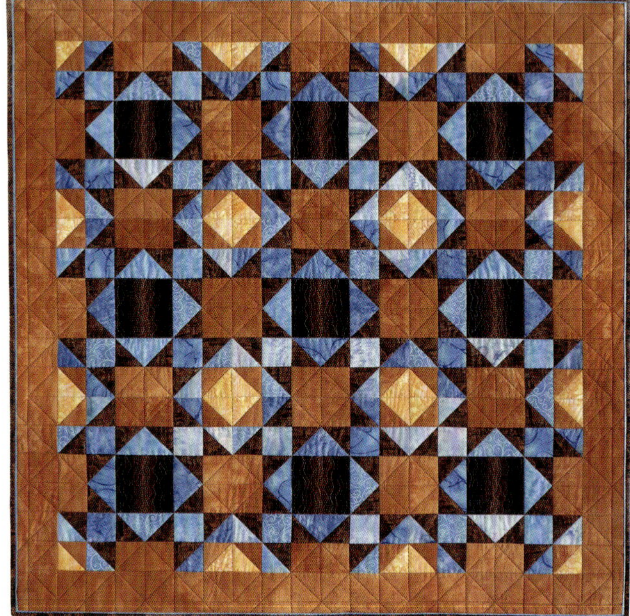

Sunrise Lattice Stars

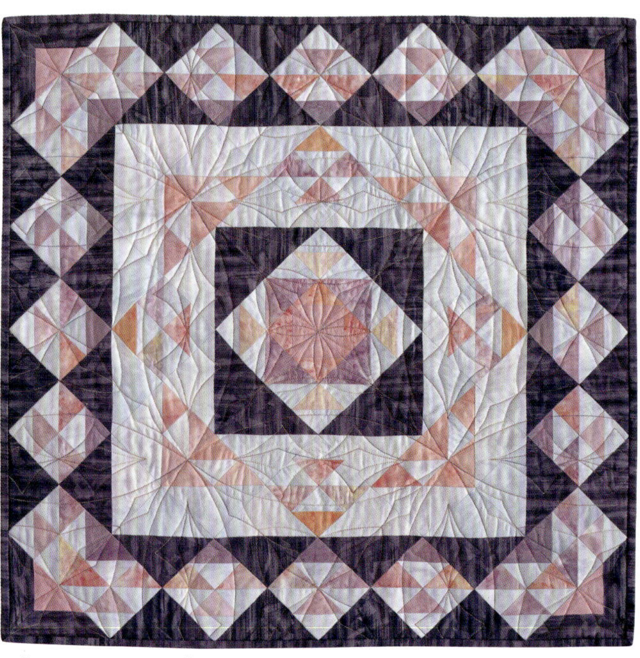

Misty Morn at Sunrise

You may want to focus only on the foreground colors or on the colors of the main focal point of the picture, choosing to ignore the background colors. For instance, I absolutely love the autumn colors in Impressions of Autumn. However, I felt that the soft blue of the background sky would be distracting, even though it was not very noticeable in the image. I eliminated the sky hues from my quilt.

There are numerous reasons to omit one or more colors from your selected color-inspiration image. If you don't like a color, omit it. If you can't find fabrics to match certain colors, leave them out. If your design can't accommodate all of the colors, you may have to eliminate a few or combine them within certain fabric placements.

COLOR PROPORTION

More often than not, you will choose to keep the colors in your quilt in approximately the same proportions as in your color-inspiration image. However, you can change the proportions. You may decide to give another color the lead role. If you change the color proportions, the resulting quilt may elicit quite a different effect than the original imagery, but the quilt will appear related.

An example of changed color proportions is *Star Bright, Snow White,* which uses far more white in its design than the original photo shows.

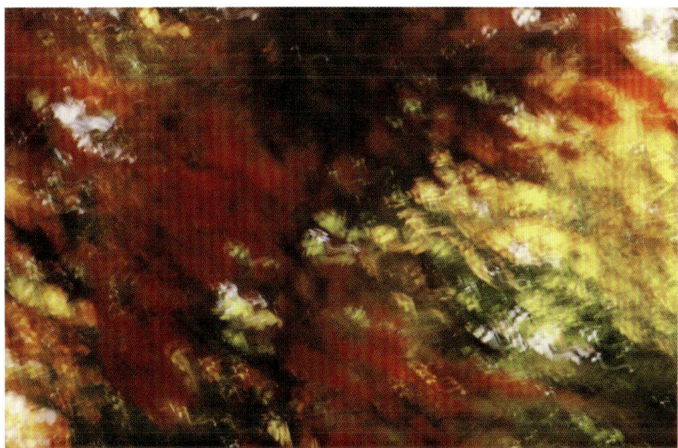

Color Inspiration: **Impressions of Autumn**

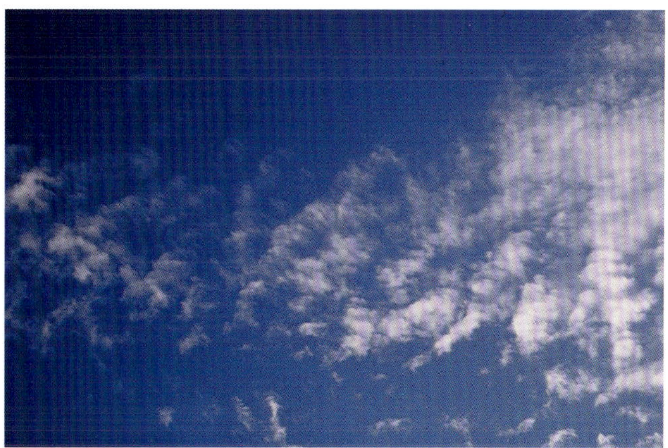

Color Inspiration: **The Sky's the Limit**

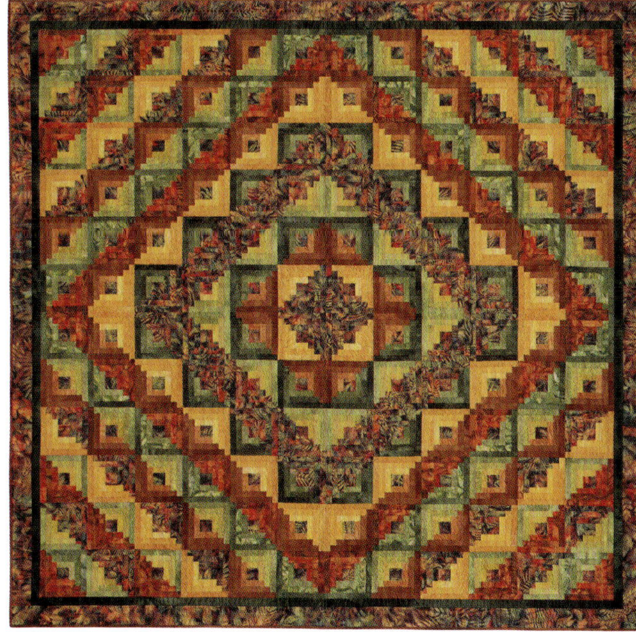

Autumn Log Cabin

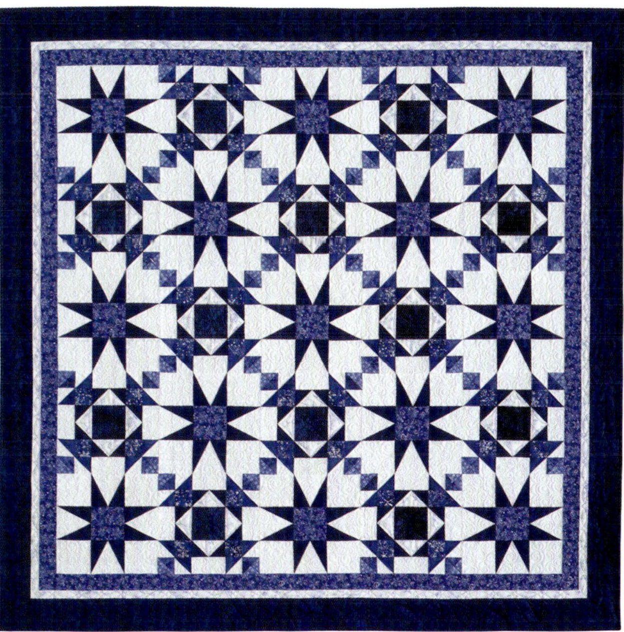

Star Bright, Snow White

Hybrid Lily (inspired by the colors in Waltz of the Bleeding Heart) and *Pandora's Box* (inspired by Hanging On) used much more plum than the small amount in their respective color inspiration images.

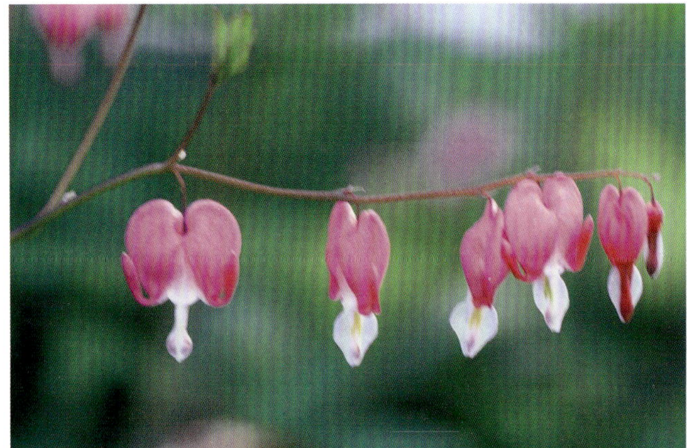

Color Inspiration: Waltz of the Bleeding Heart

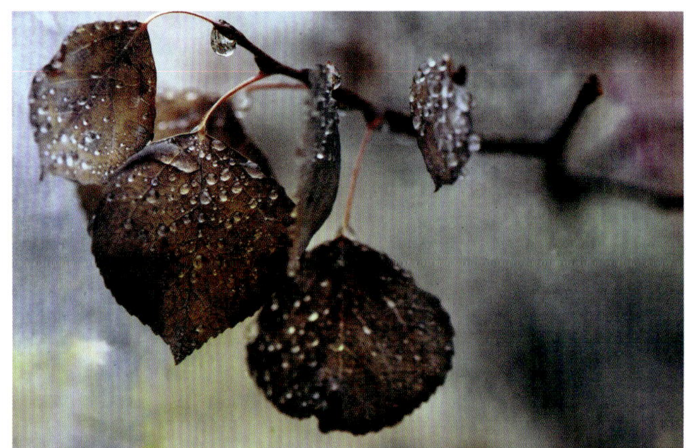

Color Inspiration: Hanging On

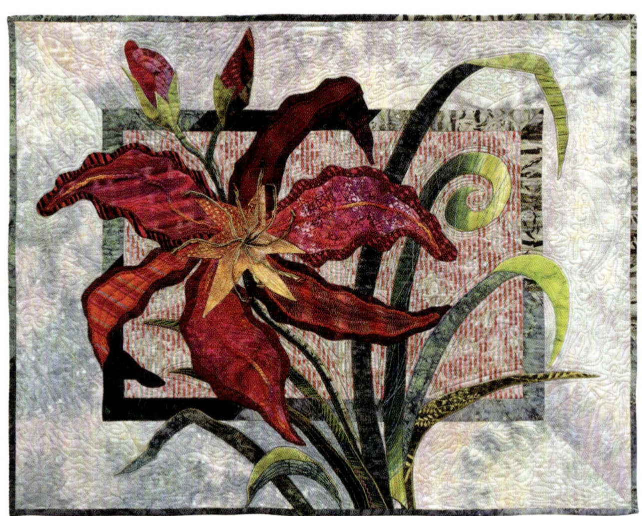

Hybrid Lily

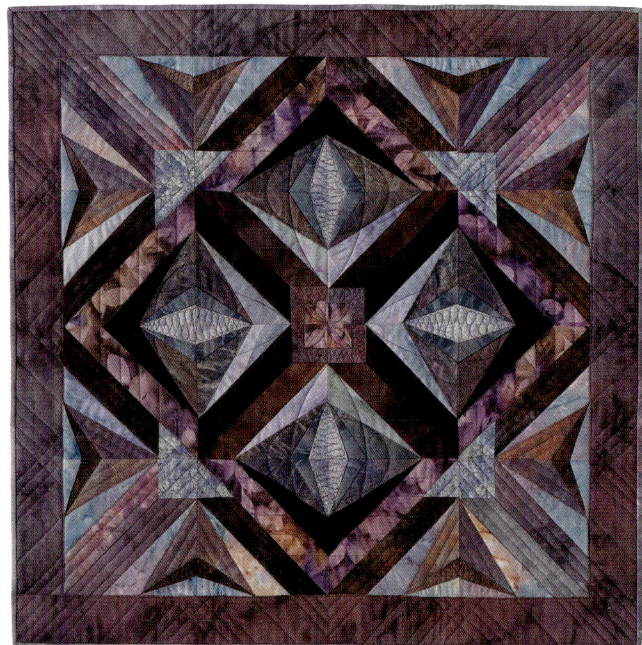

Pandora's Box

CHANGING OR EXPANDING VALUES

If you love the colors in your image but want to use lighter hues, do so. Feel free to expand your options by including lighter versions of the colors in your image. For instance, if you are working with orange, you may want to add a soft apricot. If you are working with blue, you may want to include a light blue. Patrice Creswell expanded the values in her quilts Made in the Shade and Fire Bowls. If you want to add darker hues in your quilt, consider including darkened versions of the colors in your image. Again, if you are working with orange, you may use a darker version, which might be rust or brown. If you are working with blue, consider adding a darker version of that blue, such as dark blue or navy blue.

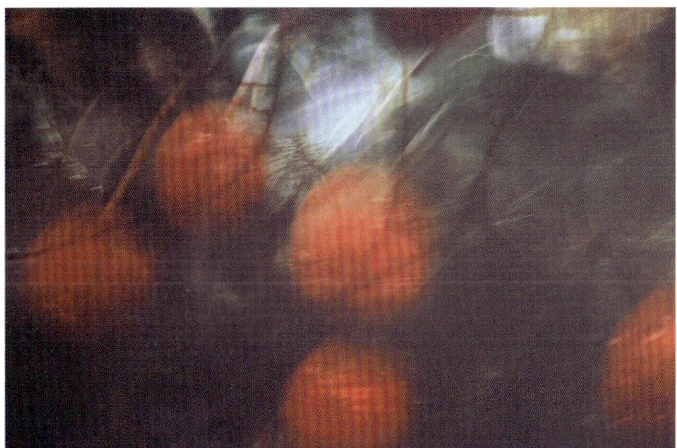

Color Inspiration: Dogwood Berries in Wind

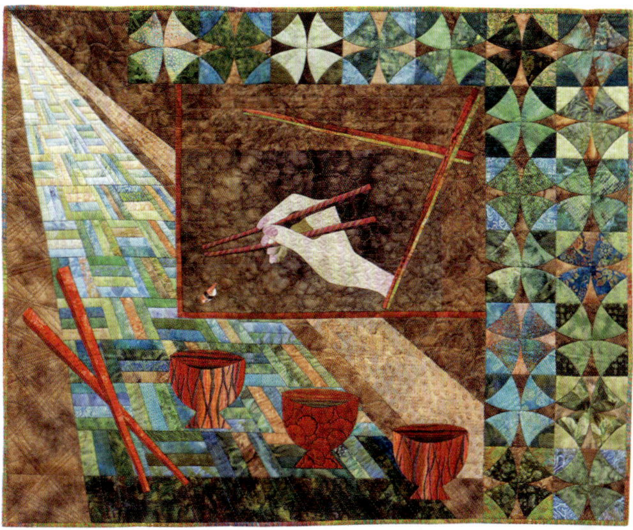

Fire Bowls

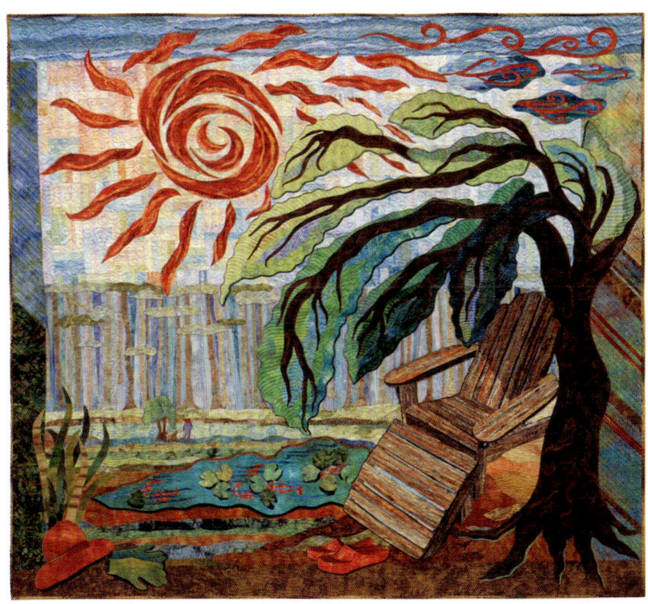

Made in the Shade

If you wish to calm down one or more colors, do so. Simply use fabrics in colors that appear grayer than the colors in the image. The more grayed the colors, the more subdued the results. As hues become grayer, they appear to recede into the design. Instead of using a clear blue, you might add a dusty blue from the same color family. Perhaps you could use a salmon or a grayed apricot instead of a bright orange. Pieceful Garden is an example of this option, as more toned fabrics are in its background than its color-inspiration image exhibits.

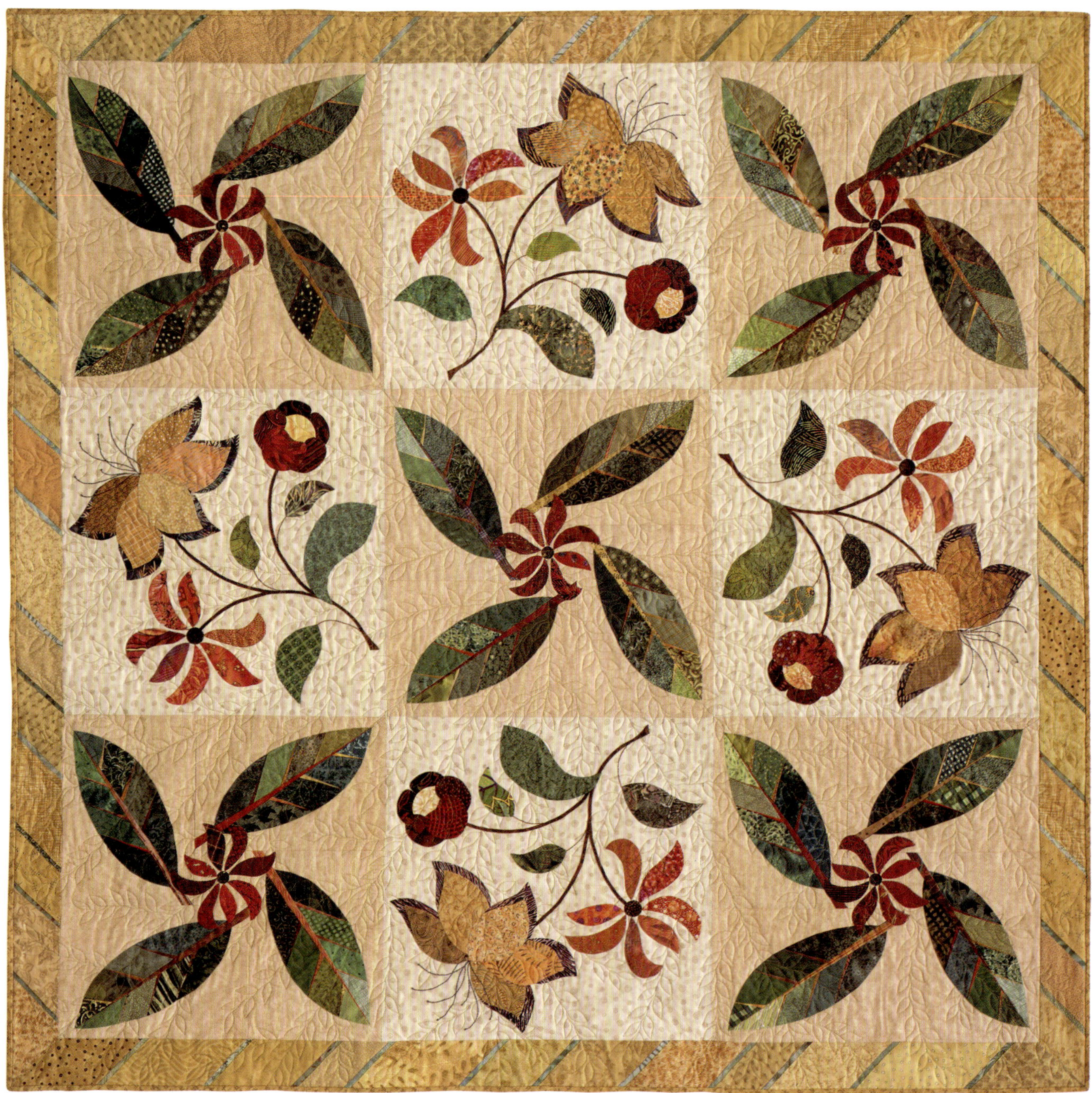

▶ *Pieceful Garden* made by Mary Sorensen, Longwood, Florida, and Jan Wildman, Orlando, Florida; 56″ × 56″, hand appliquéd, machine pieced, machine quilted.

Exercises: Visual Coloring

1. With your camera in hand, begin taking pictures of things that you respond to because of the colors—flowers, plants, hillsides, meadows, farmlands, mountains, sunrises, sunsets, water, waterfalls. Get in the habit of taking pictures throughout the year, so you can see the nuances in the hues from one season to another. It's important that you photograph what you like—what you visually respond to.

2. If you are not comfortable with a camera or feel that photography is not an activity you would enjoy, then find another way to collect scenes or items that you find beautiful. Collect images incorporating colors you love from magazines, calendars, brochures, and advertisements. You are using these photos not for their imagery but for their colors.

3. Categorize your photos into color files. It's up to you to choose the categories. I find that the color choices that pull at my heart usually come from images containing these types of features: autumn scenes, closely related warm colors, closely related cool colors, sunrises and sunsets, subtle colorations of flowers, dramatic colorations in flowers, water, and reflections. The images you respond to may be quite different from mine.

4. Select the color image that most appeals to you in your collection. Begin collecting fabrics that match the colors in this image. Also, plan the design you wish to create. Once all is in place, begin your quilt. You may want to read over visual coloring options (pages 64–68) as you plan your quilt.

5. Enjoy creating quilts filled with colors you love.

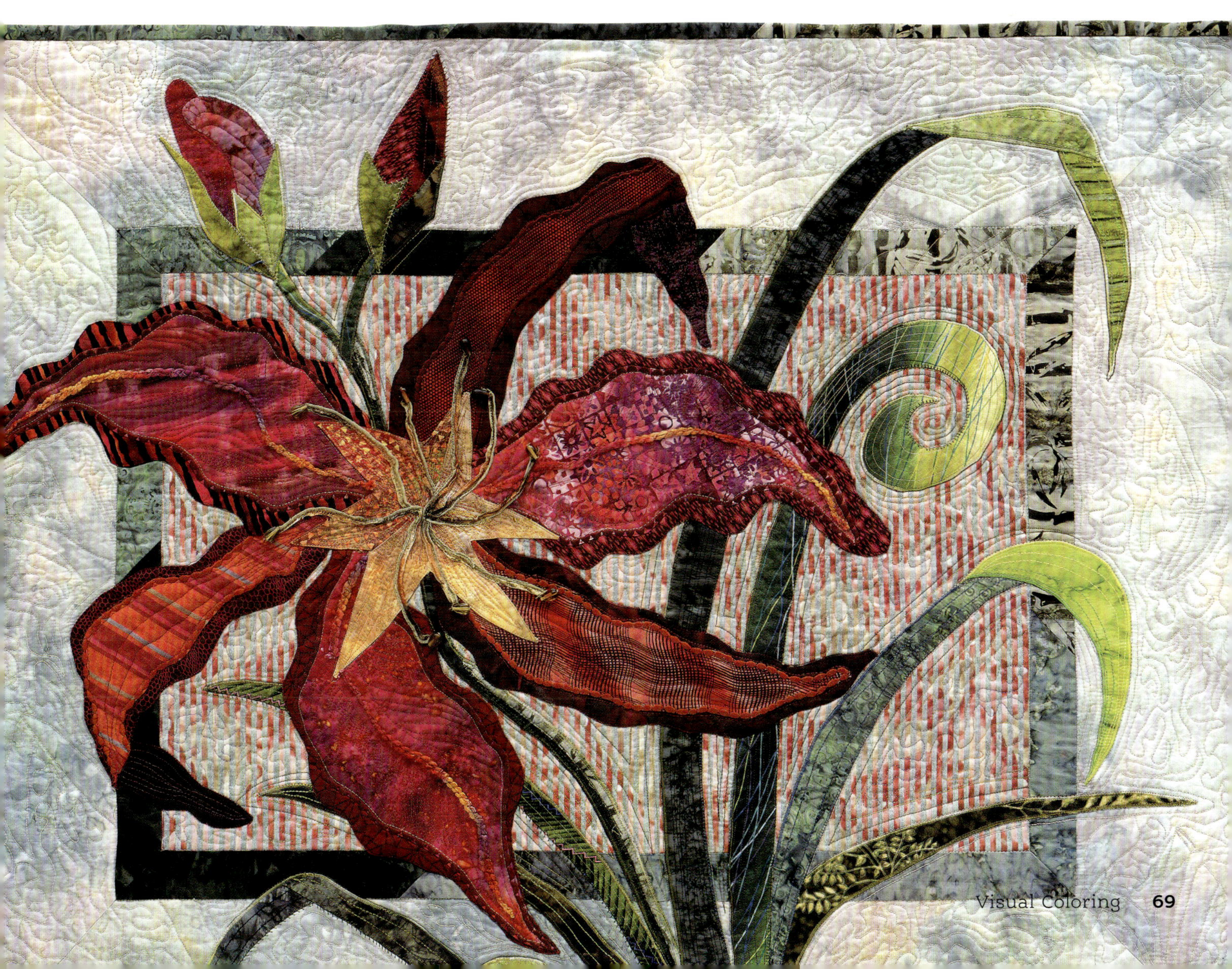

THREAD SELECTION AND THE IMPRACTICAL COLOR WHEEL

By Teri Lucas

A color wheel gives us the "rules" for choosing colors of thread. Once we have a basic understanding of those rules, it's time to break them.

Let's consider the complementary colors of orange and blue. Quilting blue on orange or orange on blue is rather dynamic by itself. Let's break that rule by pairing purple and orange. Our color wheel is now impractical by our very pairing.

That impracticality is ours—our rules, our preferences, our designs, our stitching, our color choices. The color wheel you make is the one that honors your own color preference, your own design.

Making impractical color wheel after impractical color wheel gives us a personal understanding of how color works, what we like, what we don't like.

Here are some examples of impractical color wheels I've made by stitching onto different colors. In these photos, you can see how thread color and weight, fabric color, and quilting motifs intersect to create different visual effects in a quilt.

The color wheels shown are intentionally unfinished pieces. These pieces do not need finishing as they are pieces I intended to learn and teach from, and in the words of Melanie Testa, "… sometimes they have taught us all they need to."

Exercise: Make Your Own Impractical Color Wheel

Making your own impractical color wheels allow you to play with different color combinations. It also allows you to see how different colors of thread interact with different background colors. To make your own impractical color wheel quilts, use different colors of scrap pieces of background fabric and batting and backing. Collect five shades/tones each of red, orange, yellow, green, blue, and purple thread in different weights. Stitch a variety of designs of your own choosing. Here are my impractical color wheels that show how different colors of thread read on white, gray, and black backgrounds.

WHITE

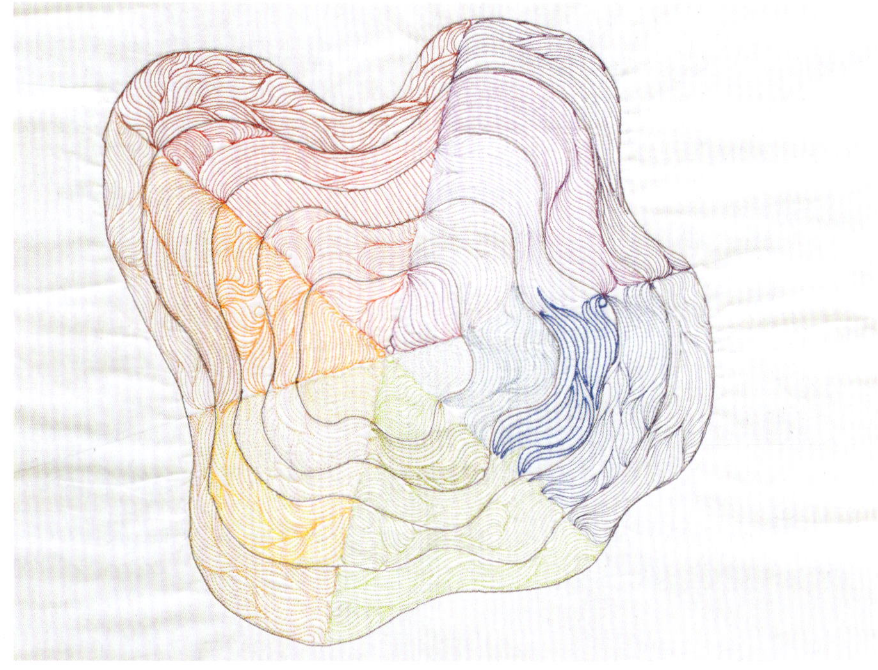

Quilters have strong opinions regarding which white they will use and when—even with white tone-on-tone prints, it's got to be just the right one. Some of this has to do with what we might wear: Bright white tends to be winter/summer and less bright whites tend toward spring/fall.

A white background lists the colors of the quilting threads shine.

GRAY

Gray is a fascinating color, with a range from nearly black to barely there. Red, orange, and yellow pop off gray backgrounds and cool colors—blue, green, and purple—can be toned down by gray. Gray thread is quite neutral, making it great for piecing.

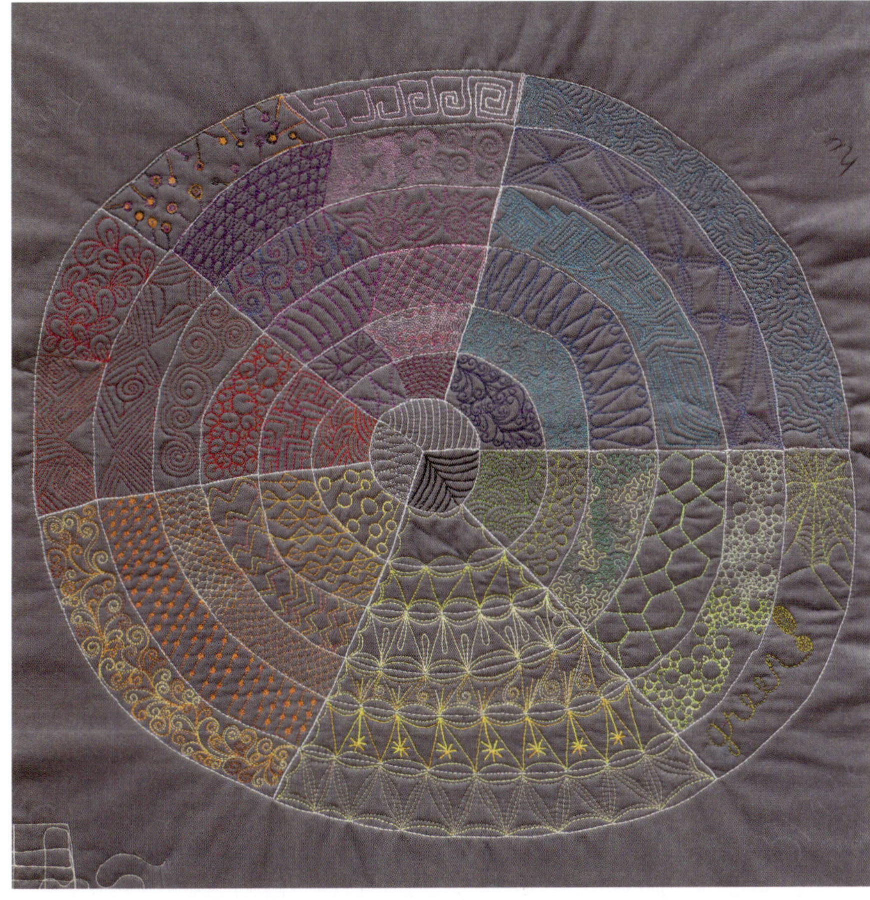

BLACK

This color wheel didn't surprise me one bit. The darker colors (think *tone*) are there adding a rather fascinating subtlety. The brighter colors (think *tint*) really pop.

Take note of the different stitch densities that effectively draw your eye to them. This helps you see the color itself rather than the black background. The background is much more present in the more open motifs; the color is a highlight. This piece also shows that while we want consistent stitching across the surface of a quilt, leaving open space can be rather dynamic.

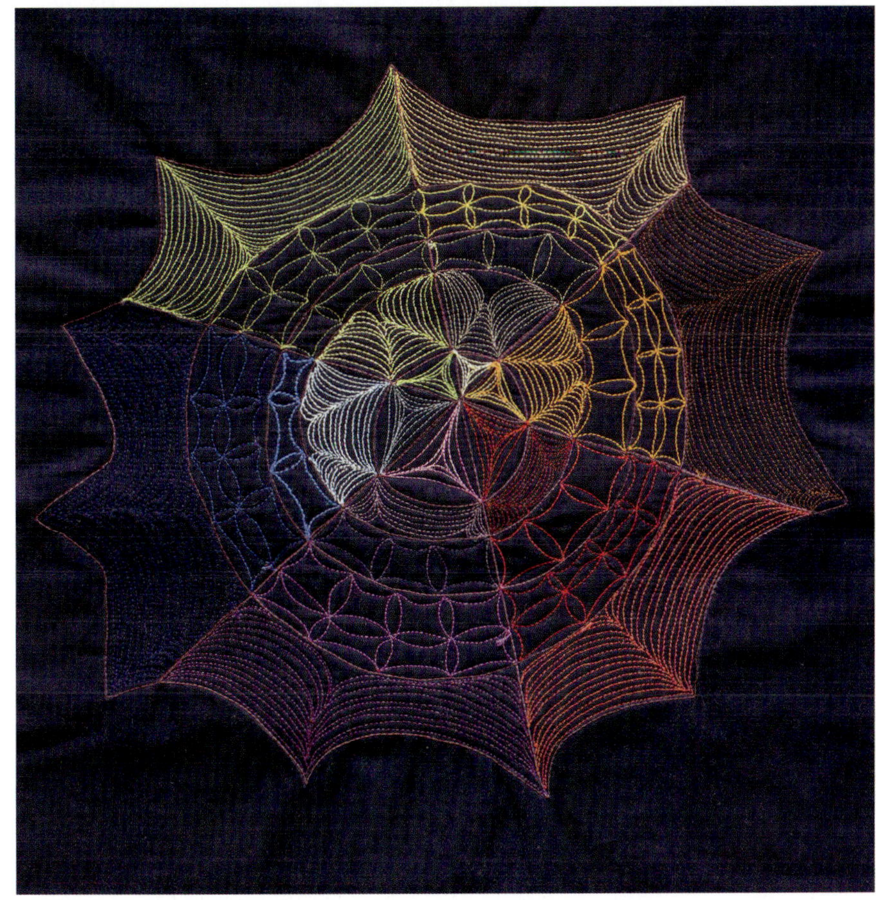

Over the years, I have probably made a dozen quilts using only white, beige, tan, gray, and other "non colored" prints. After months of making quilts in a wide variety of colored fabrics, I welcome the opportunity to clear my visual palette by creating a quilt entirely with neutrals. I think of these quilts as the intermezzo course in my usual brightly colored fabric diet.

Invariably, I love the results, and before long, I find myself reaching once again for my ever growing stash of these subtle—but oh-so inspiring!—fabrics.

Making a quilt entirely from neutral fabrics is not much different from making a quilt in any other color scheme. Just keep a few simple "rules" in mind, and I guarantee you'll be making smashing neutral quilts in no time flat!

What is a neutral?

Webster's *New World Dictionary* defines "neutral" as "having little or no decided color; not vivid" and "free from mixture of other colors." You'll find this definition—or one much like it—in just about any English-language dictionary, and the definition translates perfectly to the neutral fabrics you'll find in your favorite quilt shop. Neutrals include a wide range of white, off-white, cream, ecru, beige, tan, and even gray fabrics. Within this range, you'll find a sizable variety in character of print, from tiny florals to bold stripes to large-scale paisleys. I was lucky to be introduced to neutrals early in my quiltmaking experience and to be trained to check them out whenever the opportunity presented itself. That's the secret: recognizing the versatility of these wonderful fabrics and buying them when you see them.

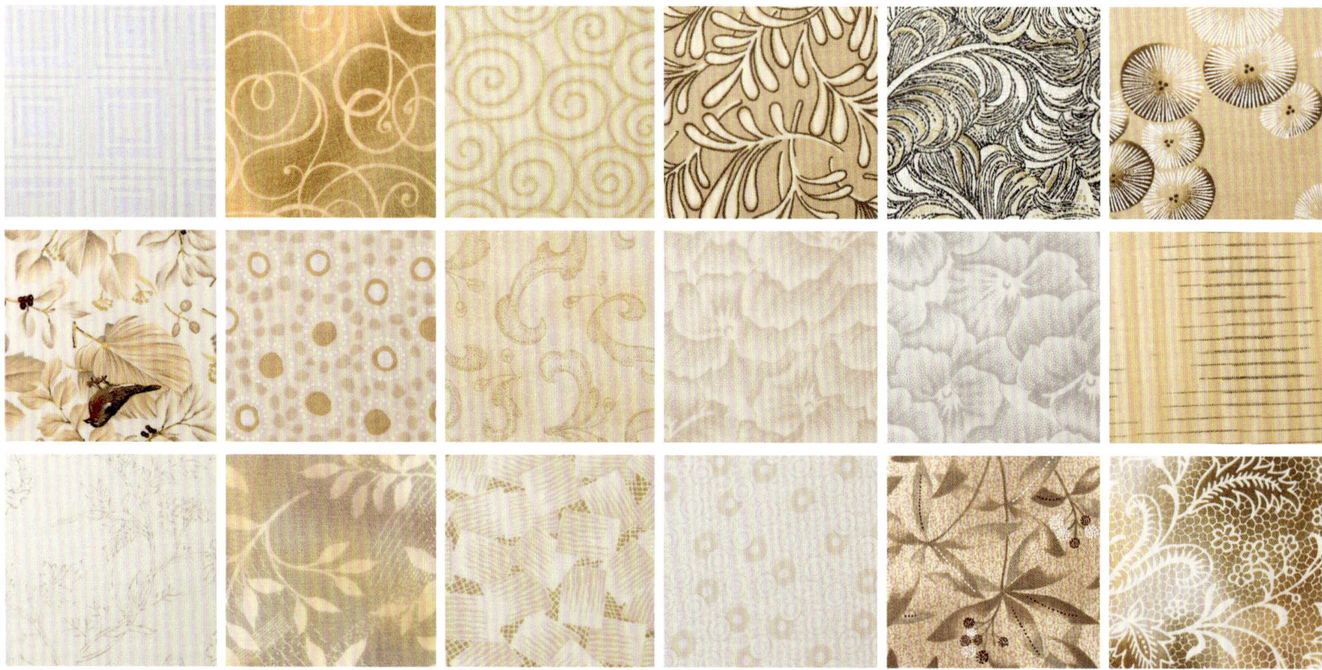

A collection of neutral fabrics—large pieces or fat quarters—in a range of "colors," values, and prints

The Three Keys To Success

There are three key elements to consider in choosing fabrics for quilts: color, value, and character of print. Let's look at these elements one at a time and see how neutrals play into this formula.

COLOR

Do you know a single quilter who is not drawn to the rows of colorful bolts that call from the shelves of quilt shops and the booths of quilt show vendors? Let's face it, we're like little kids attracted to the vibrant colors in the candy shop window. The subtle neutral fabrics are easy to overlook in this dizzying display.

Big mistake! Those neutral fabrics can be lifesavers in a traditional, multicolored quilt, but that's only half the story. Quilts made *entirely* with neutral fabrics can be stop-in-your-tracks gorgeous. Furthermore, I've never known anyone who didn't love quilts made in this style, which makes neutral quilts ideal for gifts.

There are a couple things to remember when choosing the fabrics for a fabulous neutral quilt.

- Always include a touch of white for sparkle. If you don't, the quilt will look muddy.

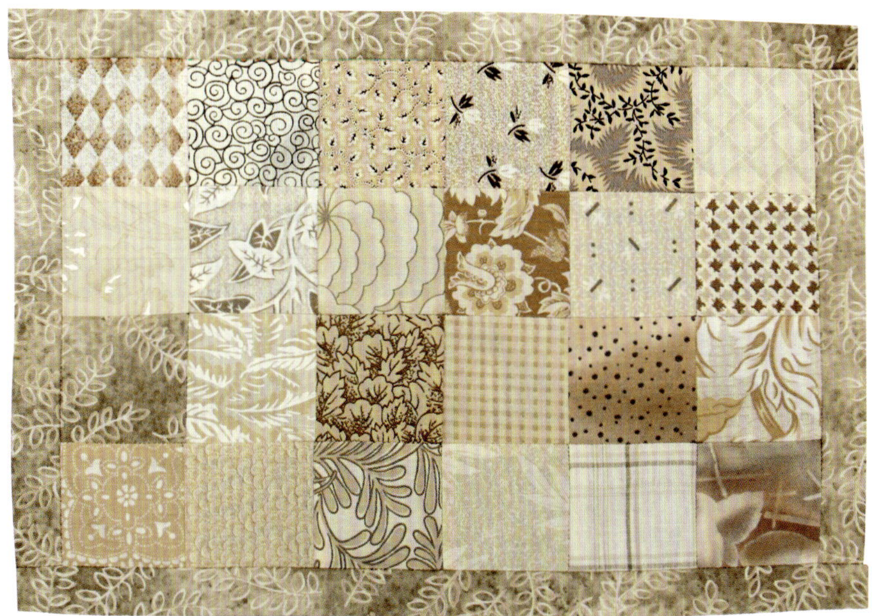

Muddy

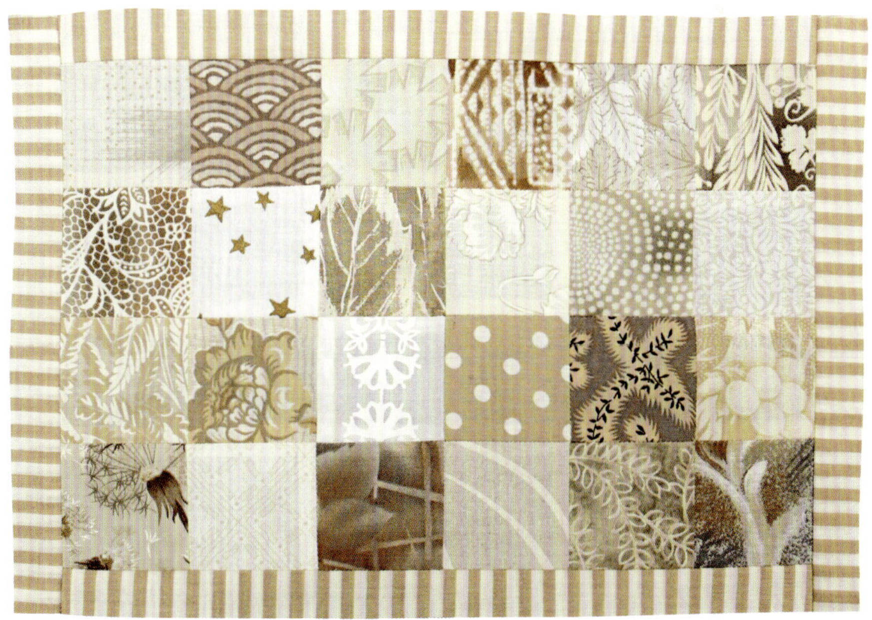

Sparkle

- Variety adds spice. Avoiding the tendency to be matchy-matchy is more important than ever in a neutral quilt. Mix white, cream, ecru, beige, tan, and even gray—the more the merrier. The neutral family is surprisingly large, and the element of mix and match will give your quilt richness and depth.

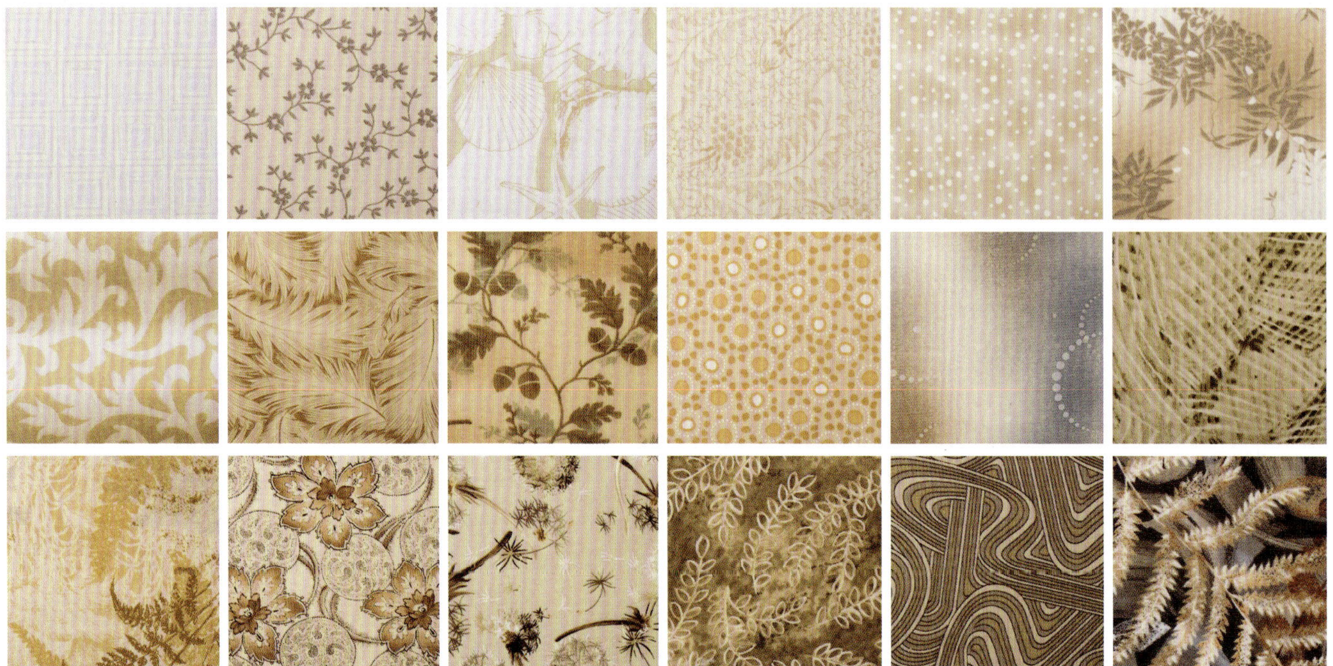

Swatches illustrating the large neutral family: white, ecru, beige, and so on

- Call on bridge fabrics to help the various neutrals blend. A bridge fabric incorporates several members of a single color family—in this case, the neutral family—in one print.

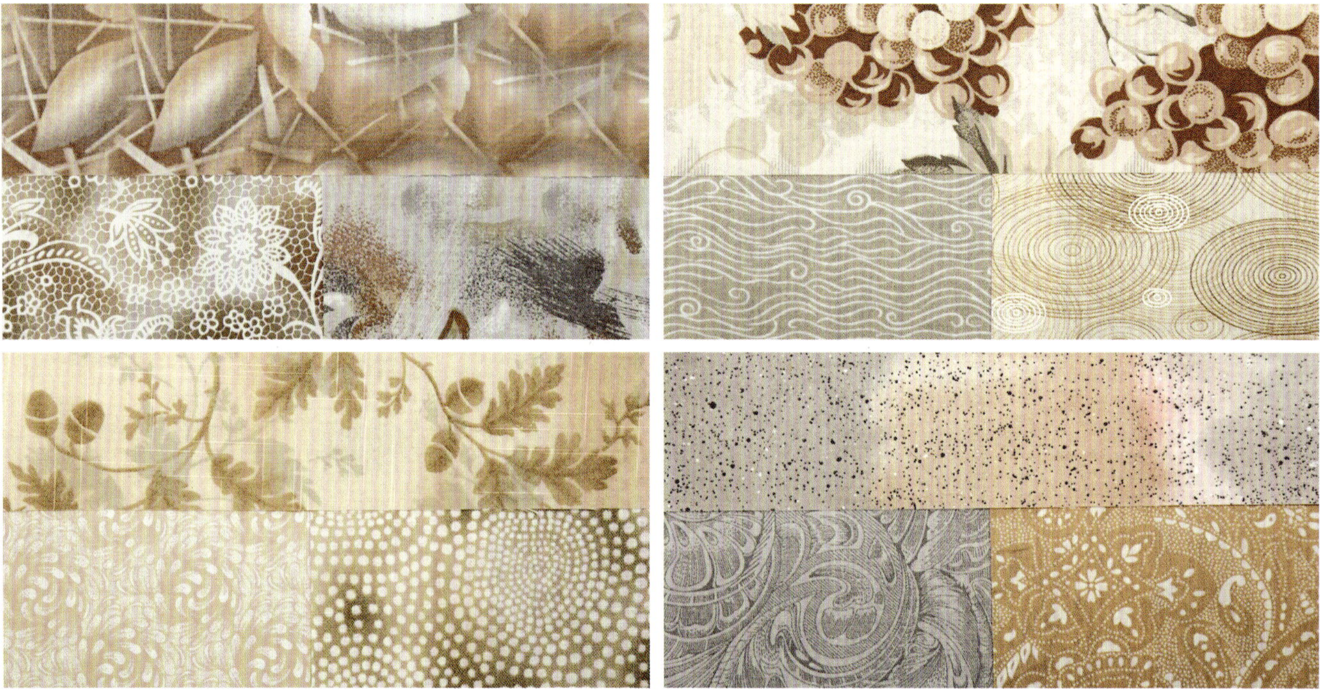

Several examples of varied neutrals and the bridge fabric that pulls them together

VALUE

Value refers to the degree of lightness or darkness of the color in a particular fabric. Because the element of contrasting color is removed—or at least drastically minimized—when you are working with neutrals, value becomes even more important in helping you establish the design of your quilt. In fact, working exclusively with neutrals is an excellent way to learn and master the concept of light, medium, and dark. Keep in mind that the value of a fabric is relative; that is, the value of a fabric depends upon the fabrics you surround it with. A fabric that reads as a light compared to one fabric may read as a dark when placed side-by-side with a lighter piece.

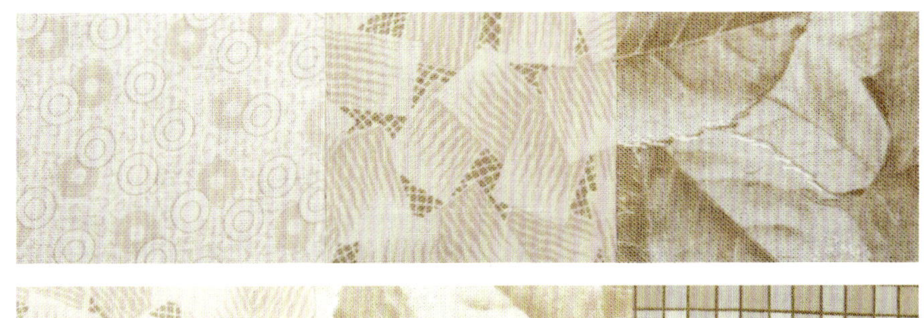

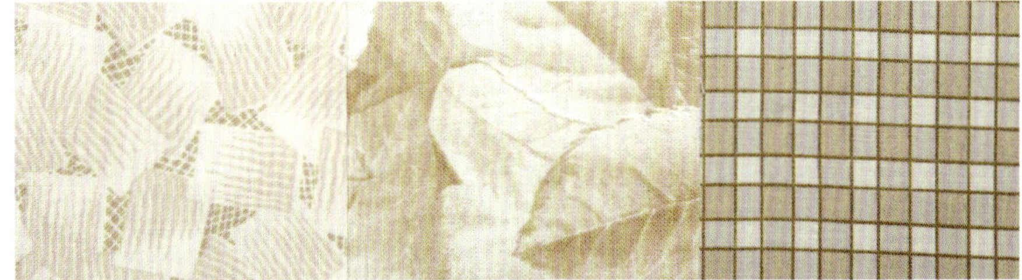

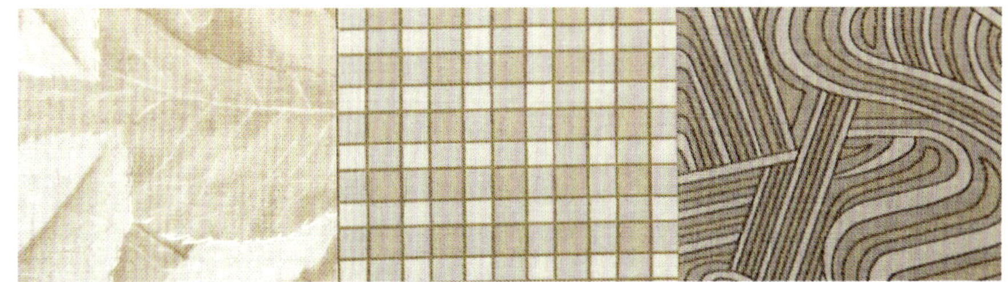

Three groups of three swatches each; one fabric appears progressively as the dark, the medium, and the light.

Differences in value—whether subtle or more pronounced—help create the contrast that defines the design of your quilt. The degree of contrast can give your quilt a distinctive look or feel.

For example, low contrast between the backgrounds and the pieced or appliquéd patterns can give your quilt an elegant and dreamy flavor. I used this look in my quilts Stars and Pinwheels (below) and LeMoyne Star Appliqué Medallion (below). To duplicate this look, limit the fabrics to the range from white to medium-value neutrals.

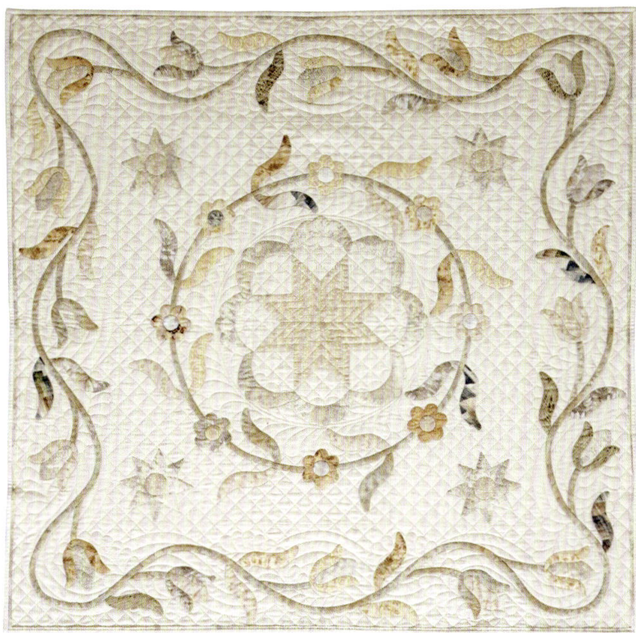

▶ *LeMoyne Star Appliqué Medallion* Pieced and machine appliquéd by Alex Anderson and machine quilted by Paula Reid, 2006

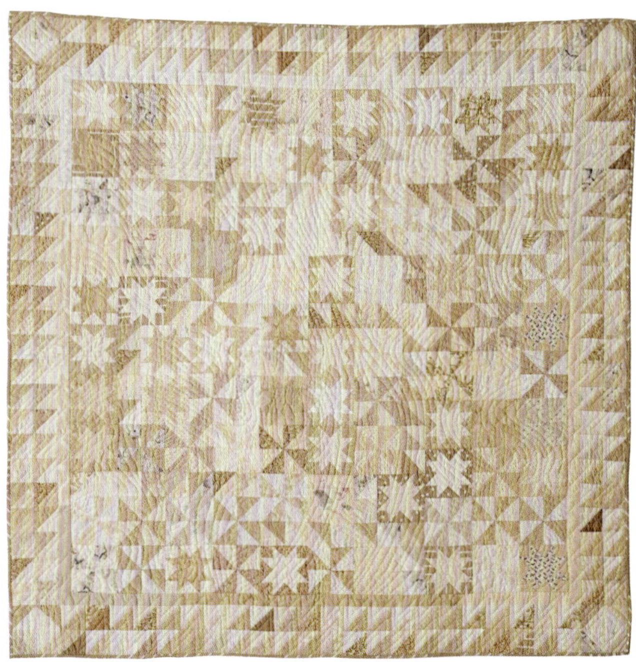

▶ *Stars and Pinwheels* pieced and hand quilted by Alex Anderson, 1987

Working with Neutrals **75**

For a little more punch, push the medium-value neutrals darker, perhaps even into the lighter browns, as Cheryl Uribe did in her quilt *Paradox*. This quilt projects a dramatic, contemporary image due to the greater degree of contrast in the value of the fabrics. Cheryl enhanced this bolder look by using large blocks with simple shapes that create the illusion of secondary patterns.

SPEAKING OF APPLIQUÉ

Although neutrals are traditionally viewed as the ideal background for classic appliqué, don't feel confined to a single neutral background. Many years ago, I met a woman who had made a classic, Elly Sienkiewicz-inspired Baltimore Album quilt. Rather than using a single white or off-white solid or subtle print for the background, this quilter created a pieced background of neutral fabrics as the backdrop for her intricate Appliqué.

The subtly shifting values gave the quilt a shimmering effect, and the quilt was an absolute knockout.

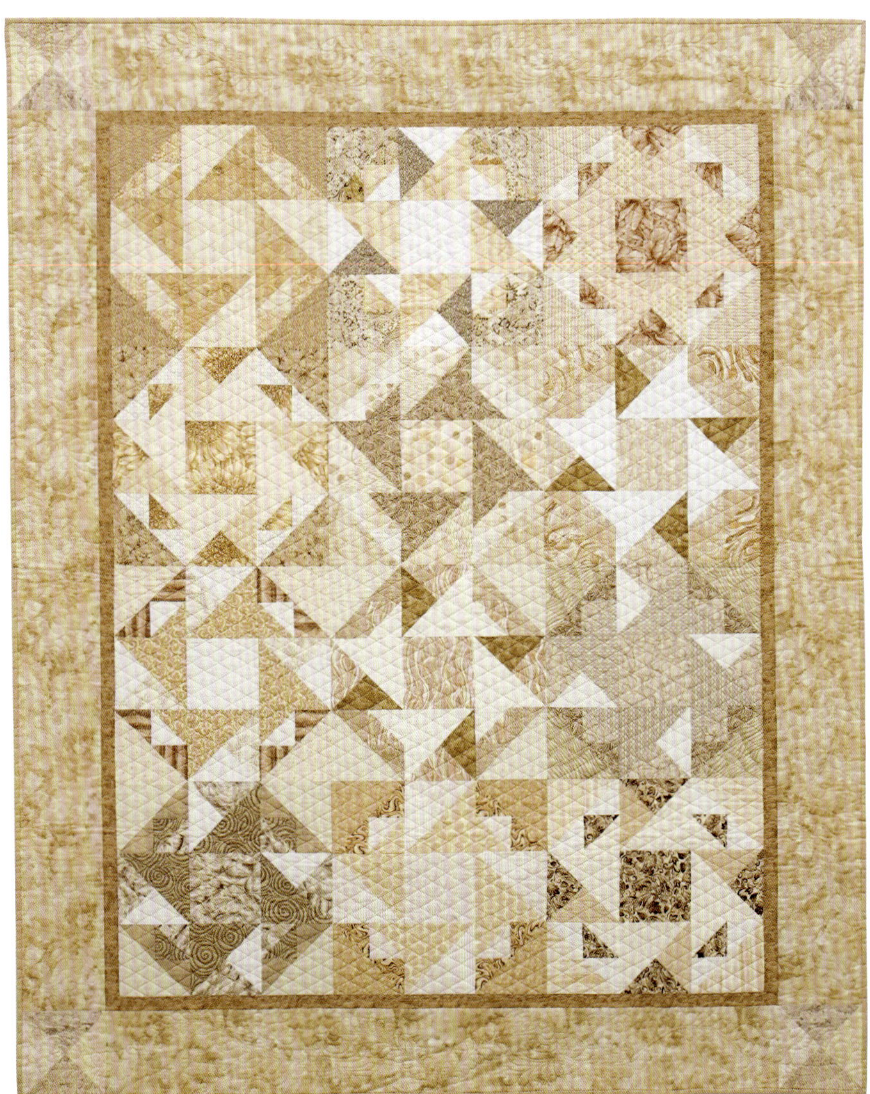

Paradox pieced and machine quilted by Cheryl Uribe, 2006

CHARACTER OF PRINT

Character of print—sometimes called visual texture—refers to the type, size, and scale of the printed motif on a particular fabric.

This is the element we quilters most often overlook as we aim to create a distinctive pattern in our quilts. Not good! Variety in character of print creates contrast just as variety in color and value can. The results may be a bit more subtle, but the distinction between the pattern and the background—or, say, between star points and star center—should be there. (If you squint and can't see contrast between the shapes, perhaps because a large flower at the tip of a star point is the same color as and blends into the background, try cutting the star point from a different part of the print, or switch to a different print altogether.)

Sawtooth Star block with little contrast in character of print

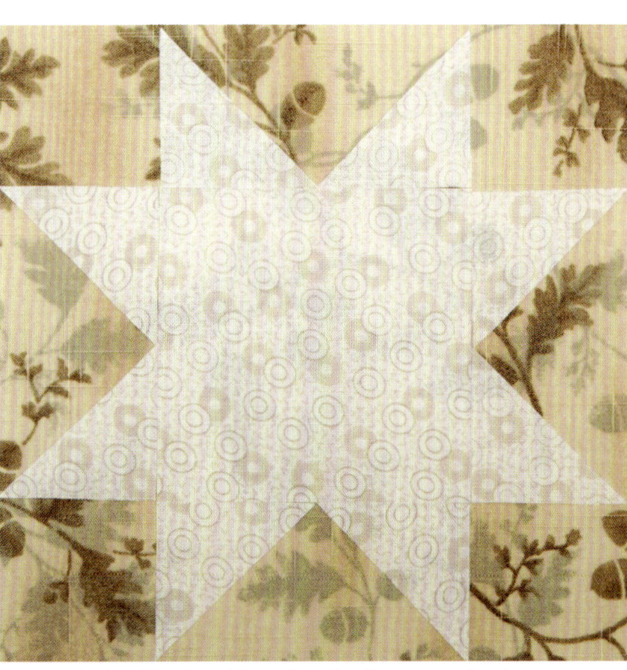

Sawtooth Star blocks with variety in character of print

When collecting neutrals—as with any other fabrics—look for variety in character and scale of print. Here are some examples of prints to look for:

- Florals, vines, and other growing things

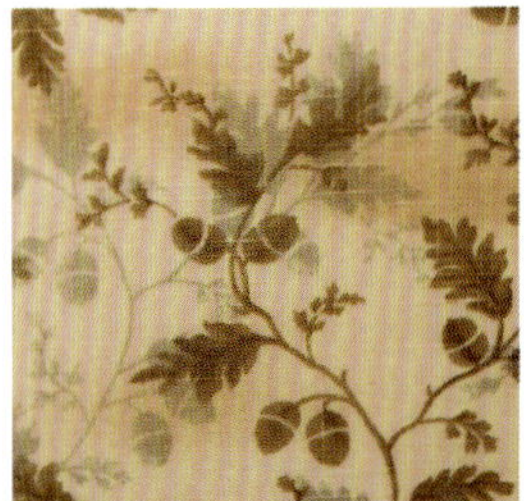 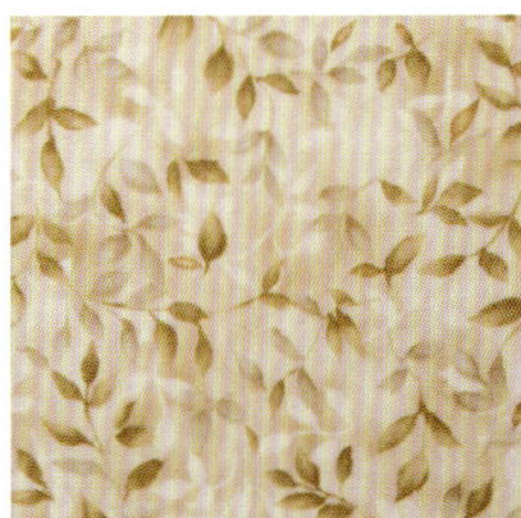  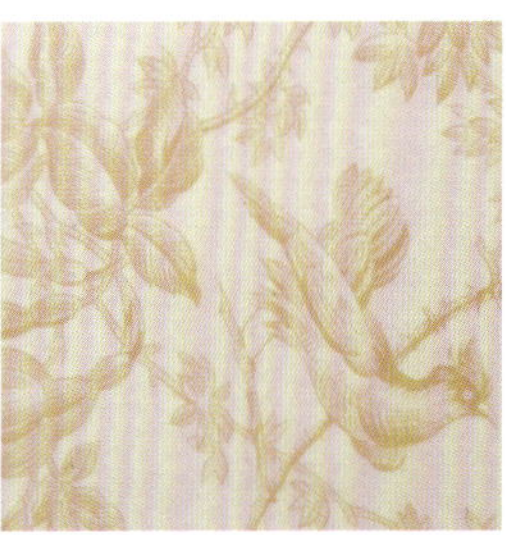 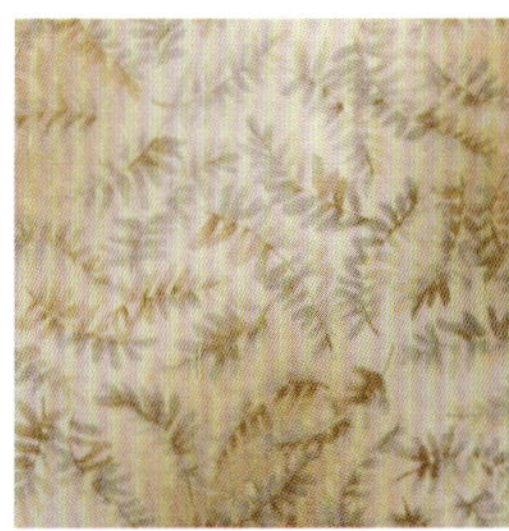

- True geometrics, including plaids, stripes, and checks

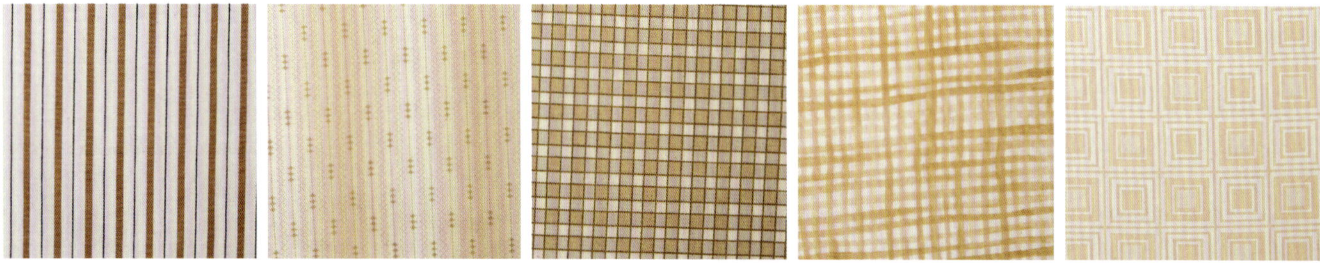

- Directionals (fabrics with motifs printed in a repeating, predictable one-way fashion)

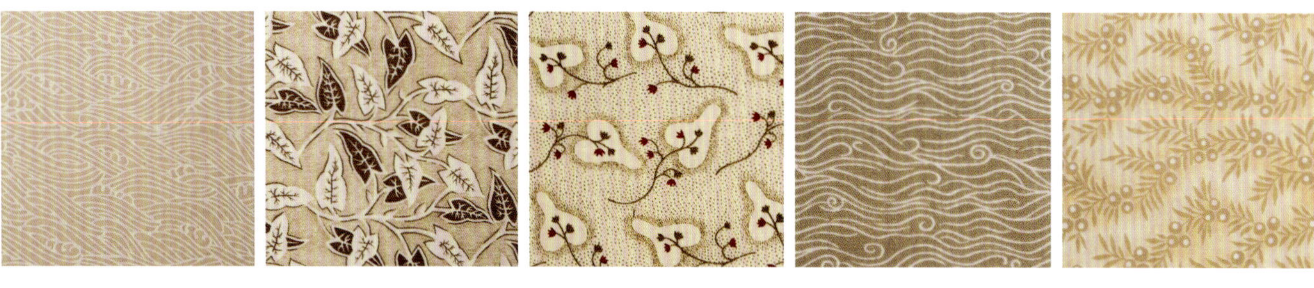

- Dots and circles

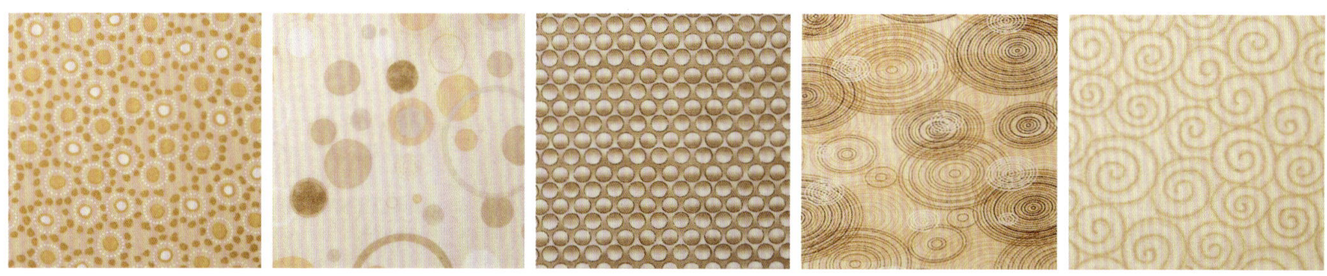

- Paisleys and feathers

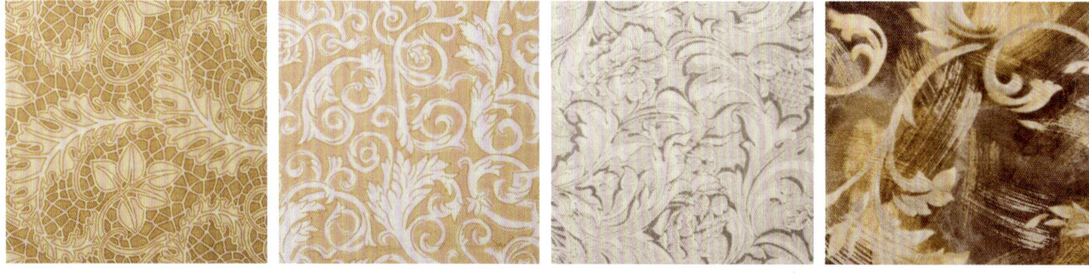

- Tone-on-tone or other subtle prints

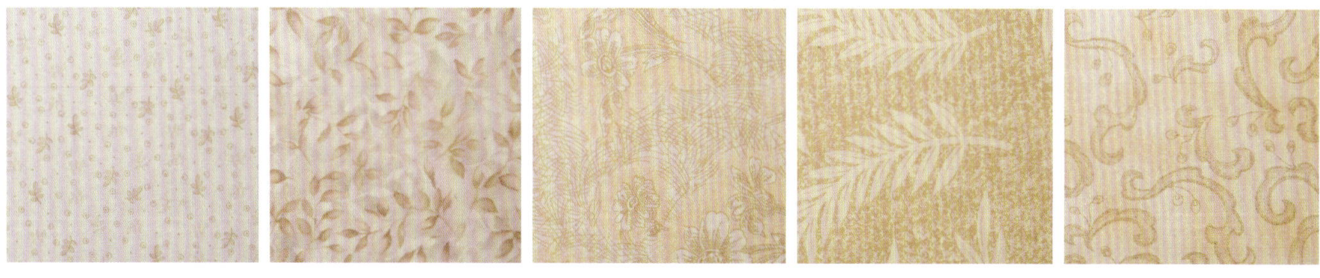

- Prints with white (for sparkle)

 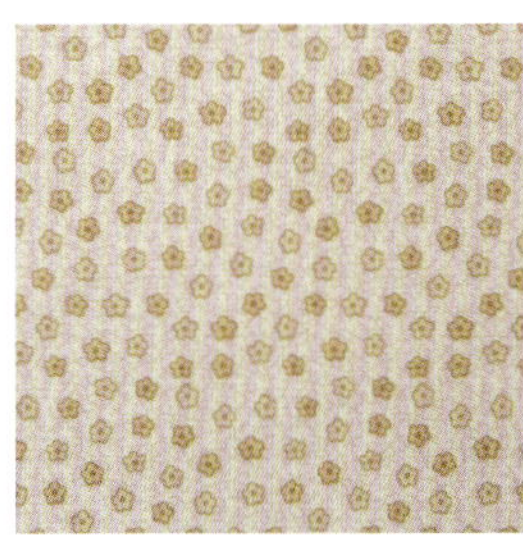 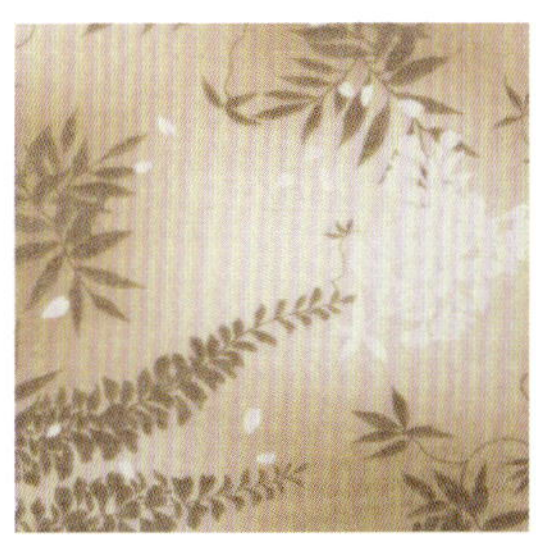  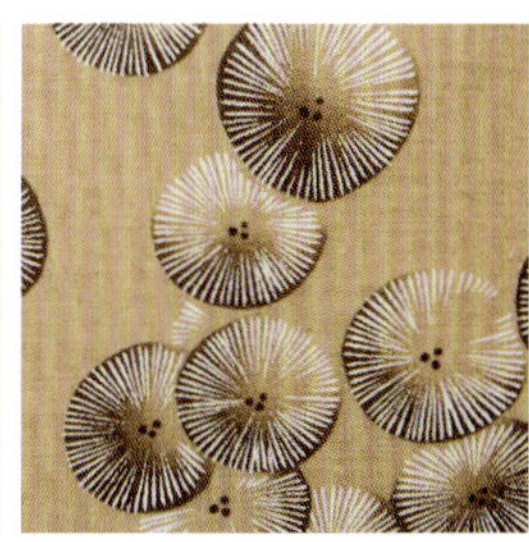

Create a Window

If you have a hard time determining the potential of a fabric with respect to character of print, cut a 2″ square opening in the center of a 3″ × 5″ index card and place the opening over various places on the print. This technique will give you a good idea of how the fabric will read when cut up and pieced or appliquéd in your quilt.

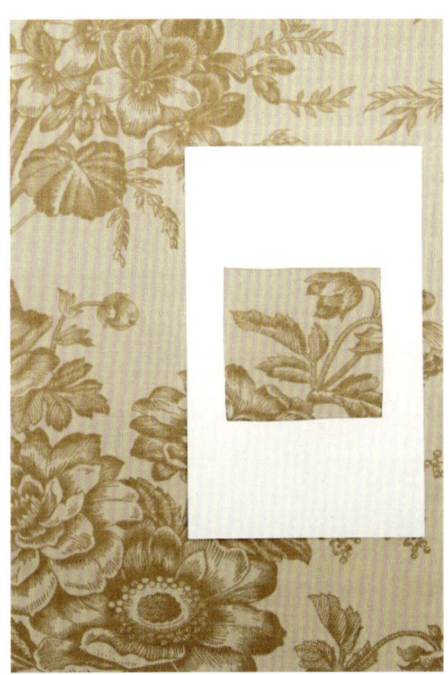

You don't need to be in love with every fabric in your quilt. Because neutrals tend to be subtle by nature, they offer a great opportunity to use quirky—or even questionable—prints you might never touch otherwise. One time, about twenty years ago, my eyes locked on what at the time seemed like a hideous, what-could-I-bethinking neutral print. The beige background was printed with a combination of chunky white polka dots and clunky white stripes. For some reason, I brought it home. (As I recall, my friend Diana McClun made me buy it.) To my surprise, this ugly duckling turned out to be the most wonderful piece of fabric! I used it over and over in my scrappy neutral quilts, hoarding the tiniest pieces as I watched the yardage shrink. I think I actually cried—or at least whined loudly—when the last scrap was gone.

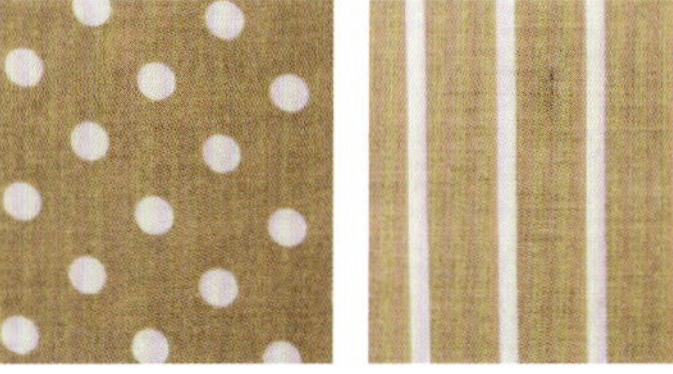

Postscript: In preparing the fabric sample for this chapter, guess what I found? Yippee!

Once you've got a good variety of prints to work with, mix them up in your quilt. Place stripes beside florals and polka dots beside paisleys. You'll be amazed at the richness this variety adds to the finished quilt, even when all the fabrics are from the same color family.

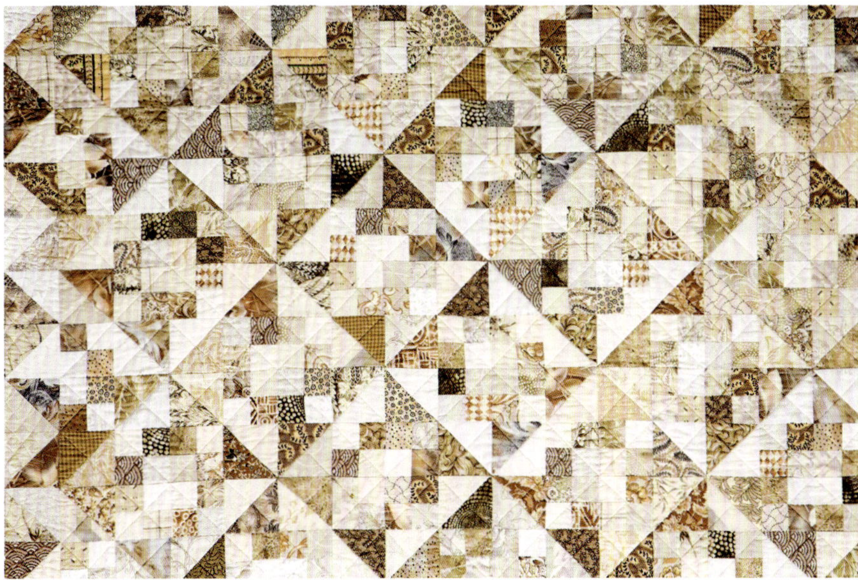

STARTING A COLOR CLUB
By Christine Barnes

Quilters need a casual, creative setting where they can explore color concepts one at a time and give each other feedback. Quilters need a club devoted to color! It's easy, really. All you need is a place to meet and a group of motivated, like-minded quilters. Following are a few guidelines for success.

WORKING ON YOUR OWN

You can embark on this adventure with a merry band of friends or pursue color independently. As a "color club of one," your color sense will develop by leaps and bounds if you work your way through the book and apply what you learn in the exercises and projects. Follow the suggestions in Ways to Work (page 81); most apply to one person as much as to ten people. And remember, even if you're on your own, you belong to the Color Club!

Logistics

- A small group of six to ten members is best. Any larger and you may have trouble with an abundance of enthusiasm and "crowd control."

- Plan to meet monthly to keep the ideas fresh and the momentum going. Every other week is even better—just think how much more you'll accomplish.

- Find a meeting place with good light; it makes all the difference.

- A design wall is essential, although several 32″ × 40″ foam-core boards covered in flannel are just as good. They have the advantage of being portable.

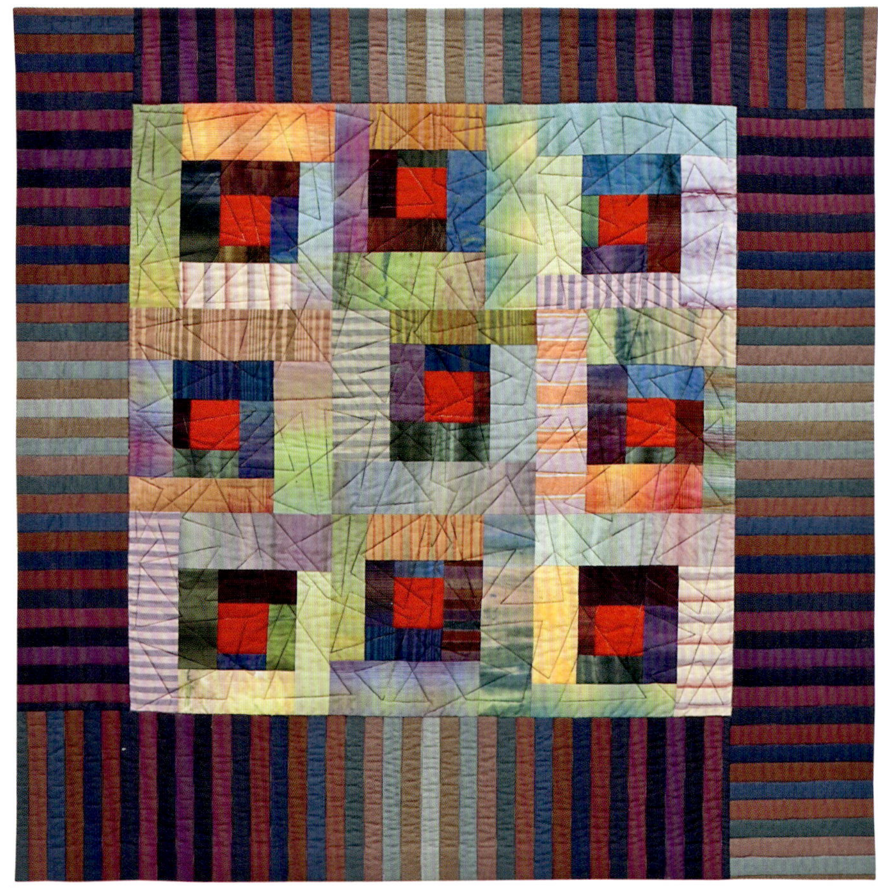

Squares and Stripes by Christine E. Barnes, machine quilted by Sharon Cook, 2009

Ways To Work

Gather a wide variety of fabric, and if that means buying more fabric, you have my permission. I suggest at least one light, medium, and dark value (pages 28–29) of every color on the color wheel. In reality, you'll want many more than 36 pieces. Quarter-yard cuts or fat quarters are plenty.

- Bring your best fabrics, not your so-so ones. This is not the time to use up your ugly fabrics.

- Look for magic fabrics (pages 86–87). They bring life to a quilt.

- Be willing to swap fabrics; you'll get so much more out of the experience if you have access to other fabrics, and your fellow Color Club members will love you for sharing.

- Strive to truly understand value, temperature, and intensity. On your own, read the text and look at the examples, then read and look again. It takes time and repetition for these concepts to sink in, but the more fluent you are in the language of color, the more fun you'll have.

- Don't rush. I suggest working with one concept, such as value or temperature, per session. You'll probably want to stretch out your study of color combinations for several meetings, and I guarantee you'll want to spend several sessions on transparency.

- Feedback is everything in the learning process. Be honest when you critique each other's work, especially when you're making sample blocks, which are so easy to change.

- When you're ready to start one of the projects, commit to making sample blocks and critiquing them before you begin your quilt. This is the time to get the group's input.

- Persevere! It's human nature to quit when you're almost there, but that's the time to push ahead.

Finally, I can tell you from my work as a quilter and a teacher that color is accessible to all quilters, no matter what their experience. And the best-kept color secret is this: *It's more about practice than talent.* I've seen so many quilters grow in their work, and the pleasure they get from making quilts they love is beyond measure. You can grow, too. Come on—join the Color Club!

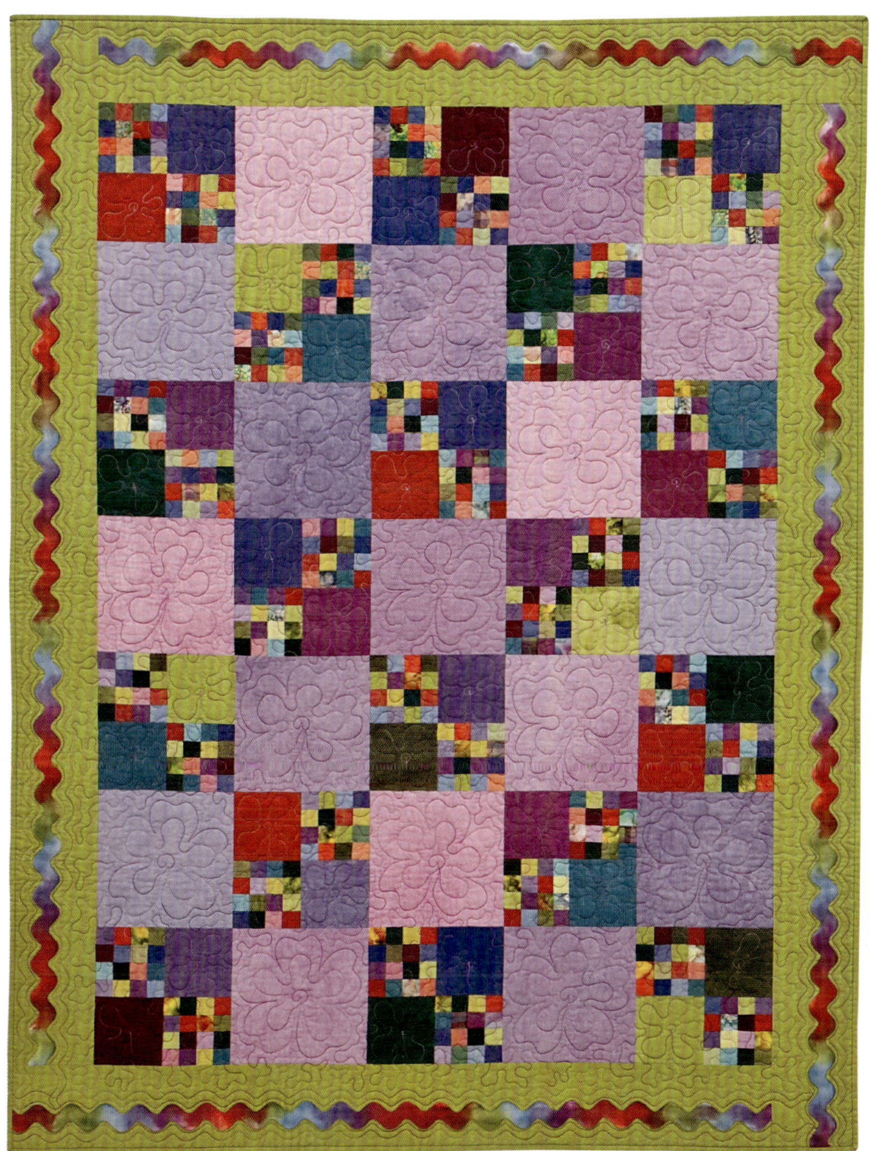

▶ *Tile Dance* pieced by Christine E. Barnes, machine quilted by Carol Walsh, 2023

BEYOND THE BASICS: LIGHT EFFECTS

By Christine Barnes

Have you ever looked at a quilt and said, "It just glows!" That's a special effect known as luminosity, an illusion based on light. Luster and transparency are two other light effects that captivate quilters. All three are surprisingly easy to achieve by manipulating value, visual temperature, and intensity (see page 28).

Luminosity

There's a simple "recipe" for luminosity in a block or quilt: When you surround a relatively small area of *medium-value, warm, intense color* with a larger area of *darker-value, cooler, less-intense color*, the design will appear luminous, as if light and warmth are coming from behind. You can see this phenomenon at work in *Luminaria* (right).

Like most recipes, you can modify this one. The contrast between the glow and the surrounding area can be subtle, as long as the difference is discernible. That is, the medium, warm, intense fabrics can be a bit *less* warm and *less* intense. (If the fabrics are too light in value, however, you'll lose the effect.) The surrounding darker, cooler, less-intense fabrics can be closer to medium in value, a little warmer, and a bit more intense. The result will be a softer glow.

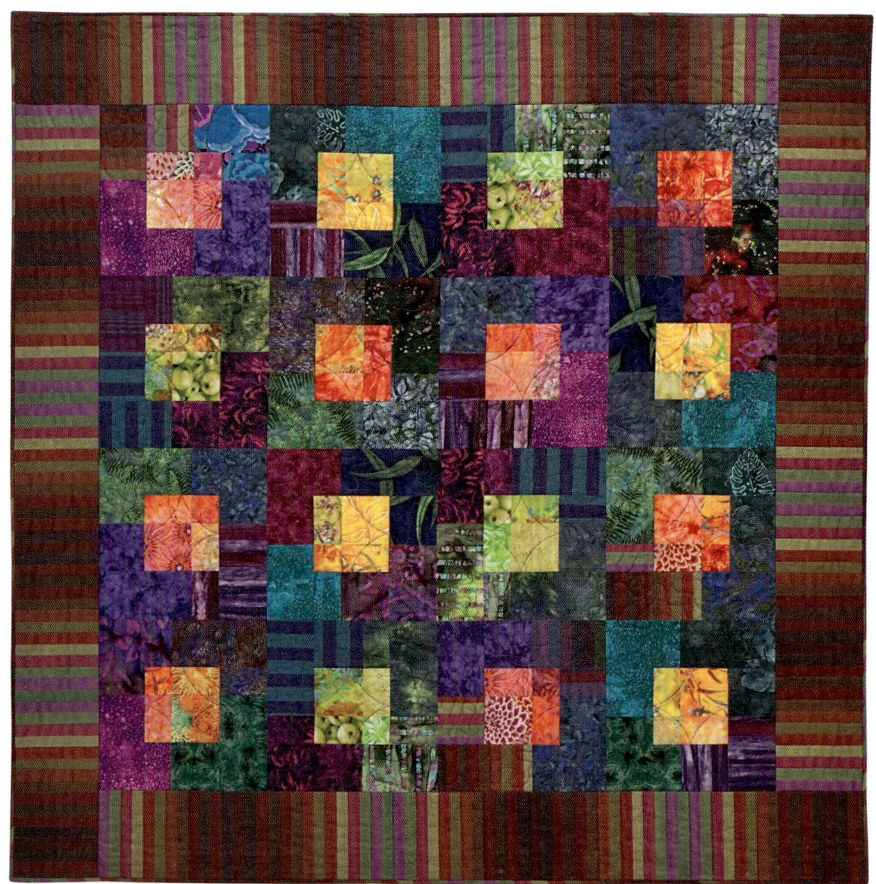

▶ *Luminaria* designed and pieced by Christine E. Barnes, machine quilted by Carol Walsh, 2008

◤ *Color Cue*

Luminosity is relative: That is, a slightly dull, warm color will still glow against a cooler, darker color that is even duller.

Exercise: Try Luminosity

Choose five fabrics that are medium, warm, and intense, and eight fabrics that are darker, cooler, and duller. Cut the fabrics into 1½-inch strips and make a Log Cabin sample block, placing the warmest, most intense fabric in the center square. Use the other four medium, warm, intense fabrics for the first round of logs, followed by two rounds of the darker, cooler, duller fabrics. Trim the paper and butt the blocks against each other when you critique them to see the full effect.

Luminosity is effective even when it's confined to small accent areas. Here, shafts of light and warmth run vertically through the quilt. The background pieces are both light and dark, but they are also dull, allowing the gold and orange slivers to appear illuminated.

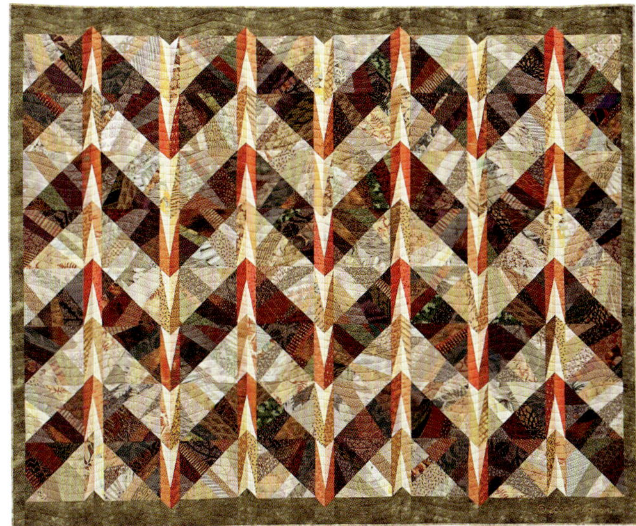

▶ *Sunlight in the Forest* designed, machine pieced, and machine quilted by Elaine Plogman, 63″ × 54″, 2000

Luster

This light-driven illusion imparts a sense of glow, but in this case the light source comes from above or one side, rather than from behind the quilt. Sometimes, it looks like a diffuse sweep of light; in other cases it's more of a reflective glow, sometimes referred to as sheen. For an example, see *Elegant Circles* (right).

For a focused lustrous effect— imagine light bouncing off curled ribbon—use light values where you want to imply the first strike of light. The fabrics surrounding the lightest areas should decrease gradually in value and intensity.

To create luster across an entire quilt, make the blocks on one side or in one corner the lightest, with adjoining blocks gradually darkening in value as your eye moves to the opposite side or corner. Keep the range of values fairly narrow, avoiding very light lights and very dark darks. Luster is a tricky illusion, but when it works, your quilt will pulsate with energy and reflected light.

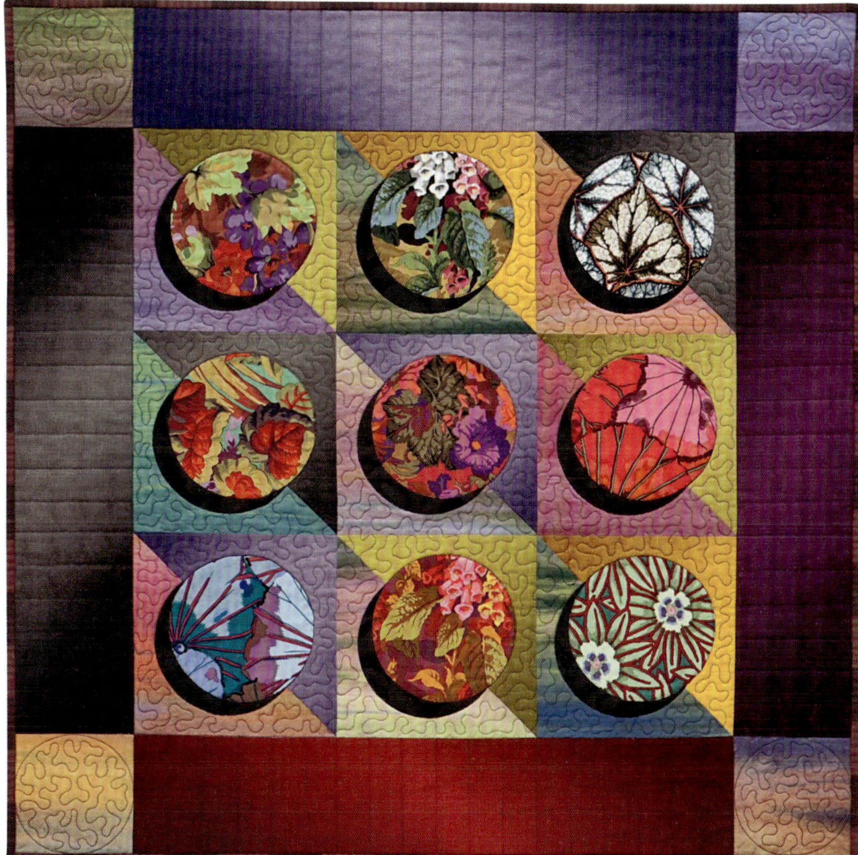

▶ *Elegant Circles* pieced by Christine E. Barnes, machine quilted by Carol Walsh, 32″ × 32″, 2010

Exercise: Try Luster

Gather at least 10 fabrics (more if you're working on your own), in light through medium-dark values. Avoid very light or very dark fabrics. Cut three 2-inch squares from each fabric, then swap squares among your Color Club members for greater variety. Arrange and glue 25 squares, 5 across and 5 down, on a 10″ square piece of paper so the squares flow diagonally from light to dark, starting in the upper left corner. Pin the completed blocks in the same orientation on your design wall and evaluate their effect.

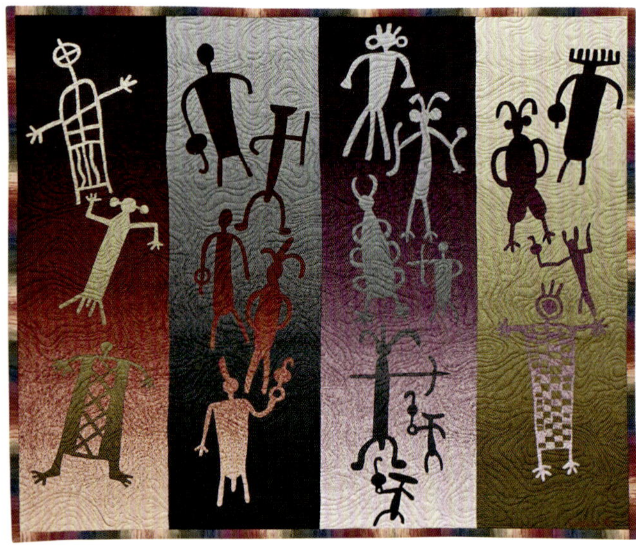

▶ *Coso Too* pieced, reverse appliquéd, and hand quilted by Charlotte Patera, 44″ × 42″, 1999

Gradated fabrics make lustrous backgrounds for Charlotte's graphic quilt. The reverse appliqué. figures were inspired by the rock drawings of Native Americans from the Coso Range in south central California. In the collection of the San Jose Museum of Quilts & Textiles.

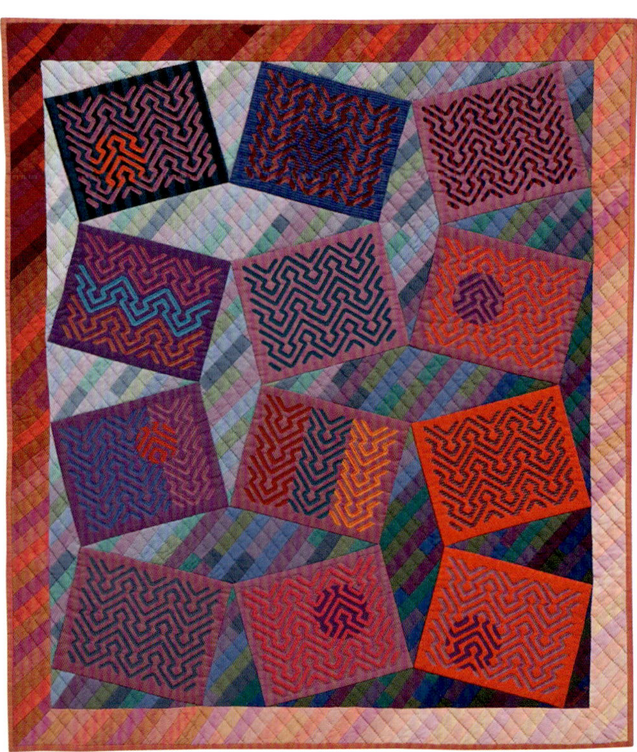

▶ *Hocus Pocus*, pieced, reverse appliquéd, and hand quilted by Charlotte Patera, 42″ × 52″, 1991

Light appears to sweep down the background from the upper left and up the border from the lower right in this dazzling quilt. Darker-value, more intense Molas dance on the surface. In the collection of the San Jose Museum of Quilts & Textiles.

Transparency

With transparency, we see something that makes sense, even though we know it can't be true. Think of it as trompe l'oeil—"fool the eye"—for the quilt world. Of all the light effects, this is the one that amazes, and occasionally confounds, quilters.

How does it work? Transparency assumes you can see *through* the colors. One color appears to lie on top of another, and where they overlap, a mixture of the two colors results. It's easiest to work with transparency if you consider the two source colors the *parents* and the mixed color the *child*. (Judi Warren Blaydon, an expert in creating transparencies, came up with these great terms.) The Nine-Patch blocks on page 86 illustrate simple transparencies.

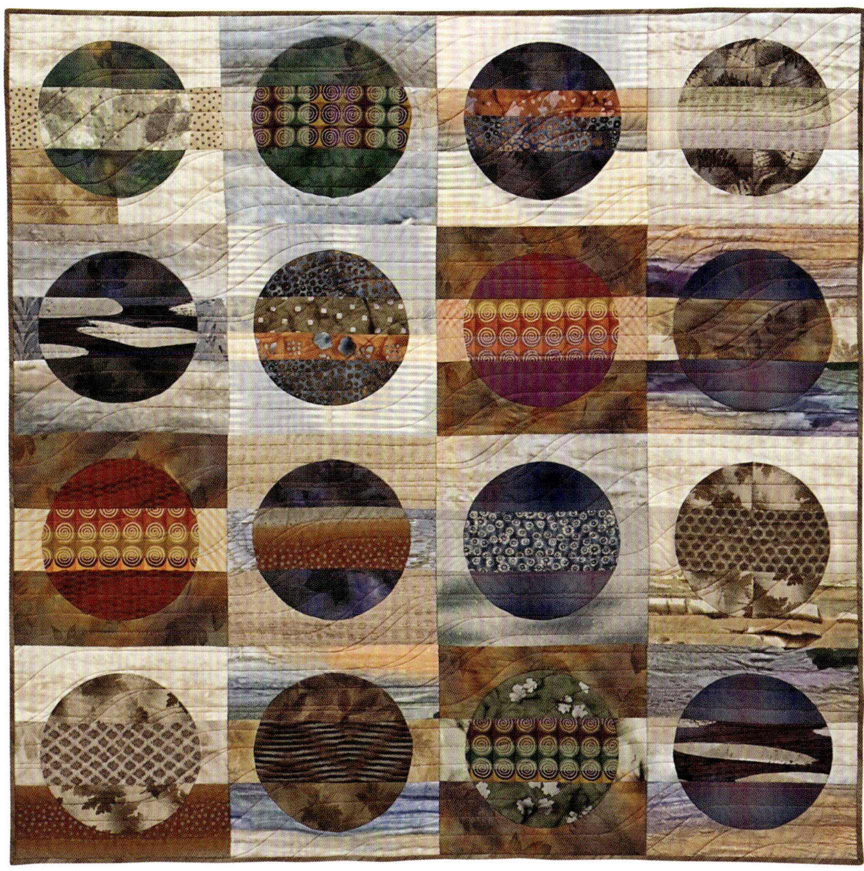

▶ *Untitled* pieced by Naoko Anne Ito, machine quilted by Rebecca Rohrkaste, 45″ × 45″, 2006.
Transparent bands of color flow through the circles in this ethereal quilt. Naoko made her quilt in a workshop taught by Judi Warren Blaydon, using cotton fabrics collected on her many visits to Japan.

TRANSPARENCY BASICS

A few guidelines will help you achieve convincing transparencies.

- The child fabric must be different enough from the parents to read as a separate shape.

- The child shape must be large enough to be noticed. A good rule of thumb is to make the child no less than one-fourth the size of the combined parents.

- The parent–child relationship must make sense in terms of value—a light-value parent, a dark-value parent, and a medium-value child, for example.

- The fabrics must have a similar intensity (page 32) for a convincing transparency. Marked differences in intensity will destroy the illusion.

- Batiks, hand-dyes, and mottled fabrics are excellent for transparency; their variations in value, color, and pattern establish a visual flow from parent through child. (See Magic Fabrics, page 86.) You can achieve the same sense of flow with many naturalistic and stylized patterns.

Create the following transparencies as 9″ Nine-Patch sample blocks. An easy way to audition fabrics is to lay a 3″ × 9″ rectangle of each parent crosswise, and then place the 3″ × 3″ child in the center, where the parents overlap. If you plan to sew these blocks, fussy cut the center squares for the strongest illusion.

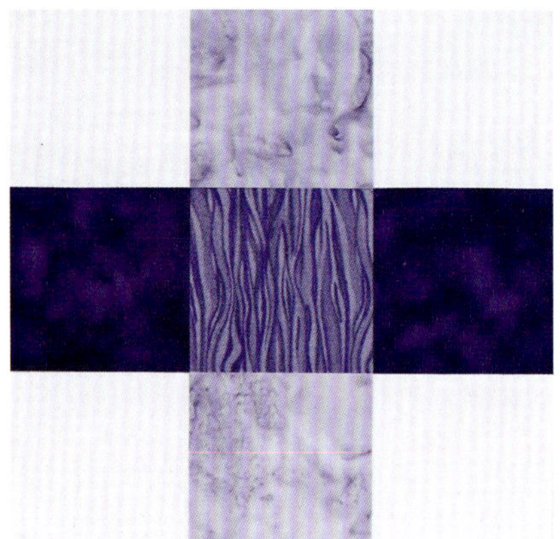

Transparency of value

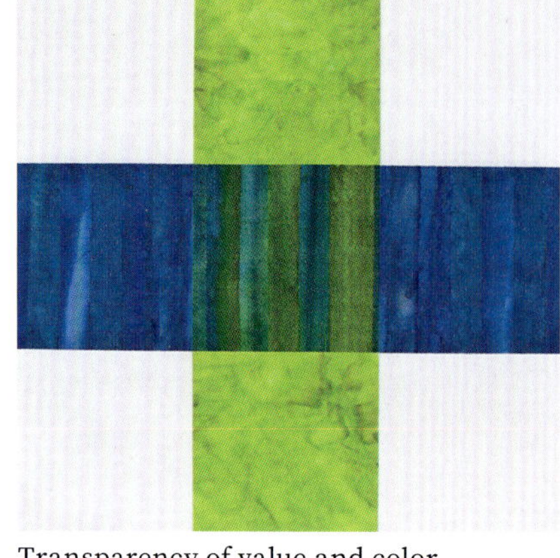

Transparency of value and color

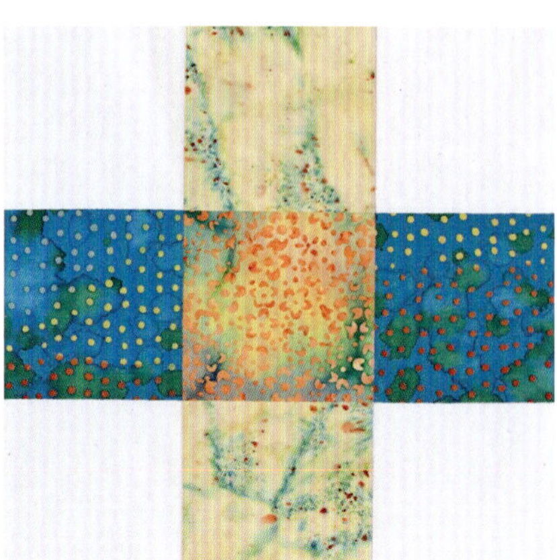

Transparency of value, color, and pattern

Value. For your first transparency, choose a light, dark, and medium value of the same color, such as the blue-violet fabrics in the block above. A medium-value fabric that lies midway between the light and dark fabrics will create the most successful transparency. Don't worry about pattern for this exercise; just focus on the values.

Color Cue

It's easy to let illogical colors creep into a transparency. If your child fabric contains violet, at least one parent must also contain violet. When evaluating fabrics for the parent and child roles, ask yourself, "Does this make sense?" It should. If you find yourself saying, "Now, where did that color come from?" keep trying. When you get it right, you'll know.

Value and color. Now bring color into the equation. The child should look like the logical combination of one lighter parent color and one darker parent color. In the block above, one parent is a medium yellow-green, the other is a dark blue-green, and the child contains each color, in medium-dark values.

Value, color, and pattern. In this complex transparency, the values, colors, and patterns of the parents appear in the child, as if you had poured two colors together and mixed them slightly. For the child, start with a patterned fabric that has at least two colors, and then search for the logical parent colors. Strive to find one parent with at least a hint of the child's pattern. Consider value, too—the child should lie midway between the light parent and the dark parent, as in the block above.

Magic Fabrics

I came up with the term *magic fabrics* when I was helping a student find the perfect fabric for a color exercise. I handed her a dappled golden-yellow piece. She cut it up, glued it to her mock-block sheet, and wow! Her block radiated light and warmth. From then on, I called it a magic fabric, and I soon began to see the potential for amazing effects in so many of my favorite fabrics.

Put simply, magic fabrics animate a quilt. Some suggest a light source coming from below the surface (luminosity) or bouncing across the surface (luster). Others imply that transparent colors overlap to create new color mixtures (transparency).

What constitutes a magic fabric? I describe many as "shot with light." They usually display variations in value—light areas among darker areas, or light-to-dark gradations—and they typically contain warm colors. (Cooler hues can convey light but rarely warmth.) Batiks, hand-dyes, and hand-painted fabrics have an organic quality, and they are among the most effective magic fabrics. Some commercial fabrics appear to be "smoldering," an illusion that lends depth and richness to even the simplest quilt.

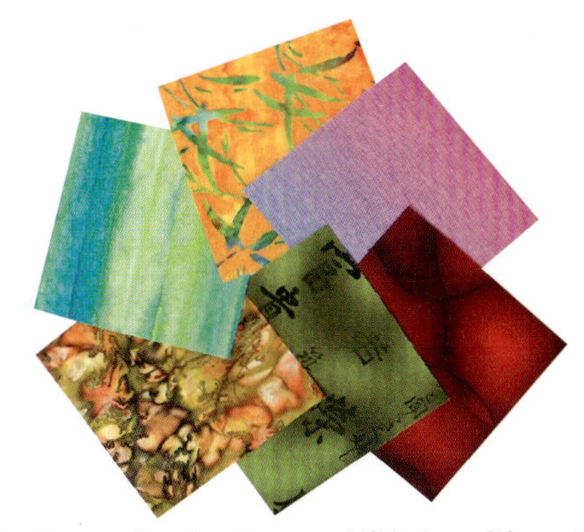

Batiks, gradated colors, and fabrics with gentle shifts in value add vitality to a quilt.

Irregular patterns—as opposed to patterns with crisp, evenly spaced motifs—suggest movement as well. And although they are technically geometric patterns, some woven plaids look nearly iridescent. See the center of *Concentric Squares* (below).

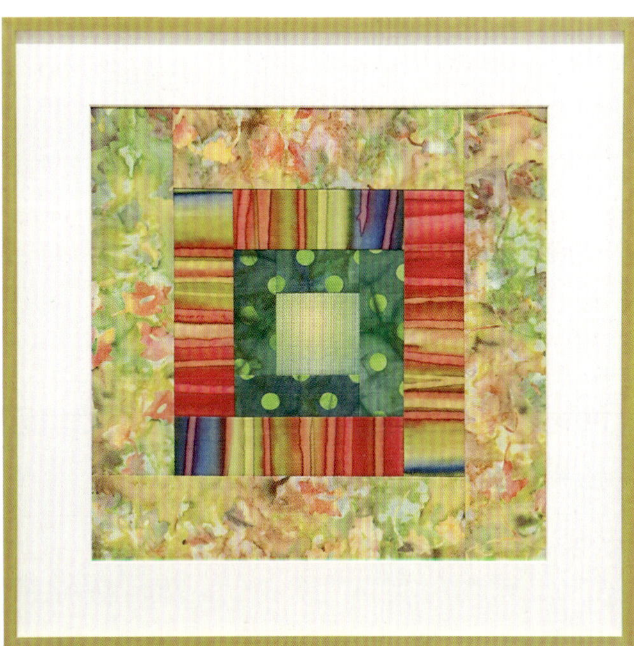

Concentric Squares designed and made by Christine E. Barnes, 16″ × 16″, 2012.

A Little Goes a Long Way

Use magic fabrics sparingly. Side by side or throughout a quilt, they tend to fight or—worse—result in visual chaos. Give your eye a place to rest and relax.

How you use a fabric can make it magical. When background stripes run outward in a block, their lines appear to "grow" the space. Juxtaposing a glowing fabric with one that is duller and darker accentuates the warmth; see *Squares and Stripes* (page 80). Placing a gradated fabric in the background implies a sweep of light.

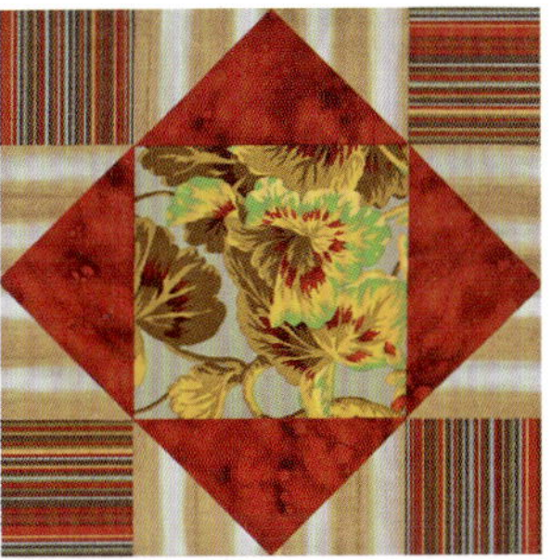

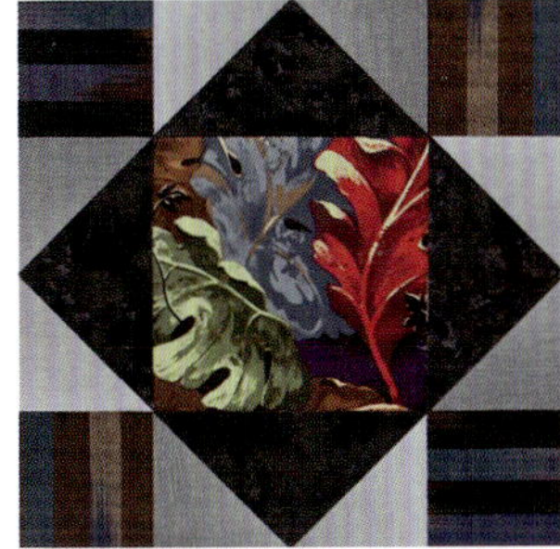

Background stripes running outward

Gradated background fabric.

Whatever their specific attributes, magic fabrics are invaluable, and it's well worth the time to seek them out and use them in your quilts. Once you see the possibilities, you'll buy fabric differently.

Exercise: Try Magic Fabrics

It's easiest to spot magic fabrics when they're on the bolt. On your own or with your Color Club, visit a quilt shop and pull bolts of fabric that have "magic" potential. Compare them and decide what qualities make them magical: Are they shot with light? Gradated? Do they have organic, flowing forms or motifs? Buy your favorites and try them out in a King's Crown block or in a simple shadowed circle quilt, like the one shown on the following page.

THE MAGIC OF COLOR

By Jean Wells

Color is powerful! It can emphasize feelings, portray ideas, and influence style. It is the most emotional element that the quilter has to work with. What a gift to truly be able to use color in a way that expresses the Big Idea in a quilt. Look for ways to be unpredictable to create a sense of mystery and intrigue.

How can you capture the eyes of viewers and keep them interested in viewing the quilt?

Going beyond structured color theories is the way to begin to develop your own voice of personalized color themes. You will be a student your whole life—capitalize on the joy of discovery!

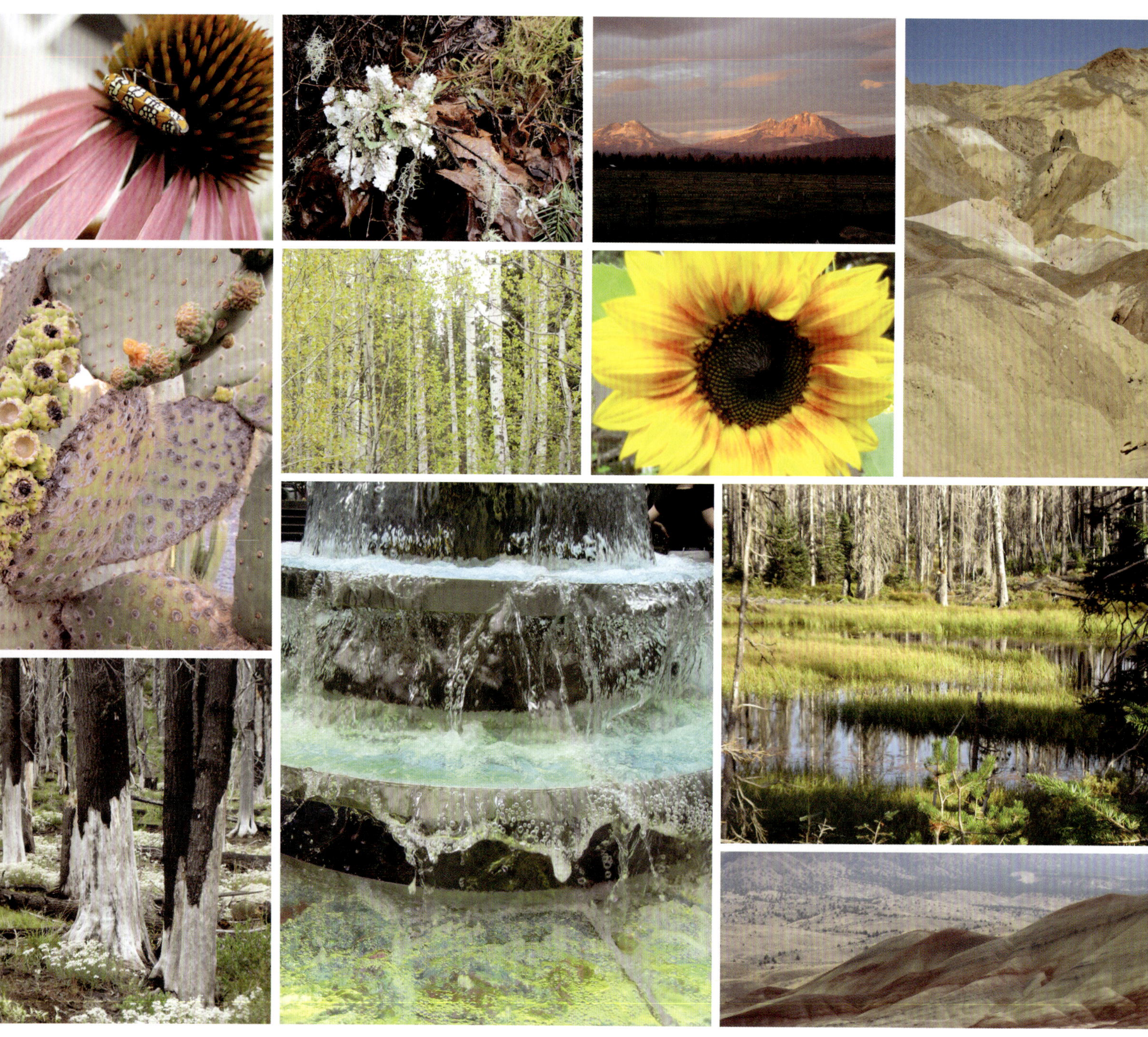

Color is one of the elements of design available to you in your journey. It can be literal. It can create a mood. It is what makes quiltmaking exciting to me regardless of whether I am working with subtle desert tones in an understated way, interpreting the vibrant colors of a summer garden, or using the rich tones of the earth seen on a hike. Color is an individual choice, and we all see it differently.

Repeating Colors

Repeated color combinations can lead the viewer's eye through a composition. It also can help to unify a composition. I have discovered through the years that I am happier working intuitively, developing a spontaneous approach to color in my quilts—more of a "what does the quilt need?" line of thinking after the Big Idea has been determined.

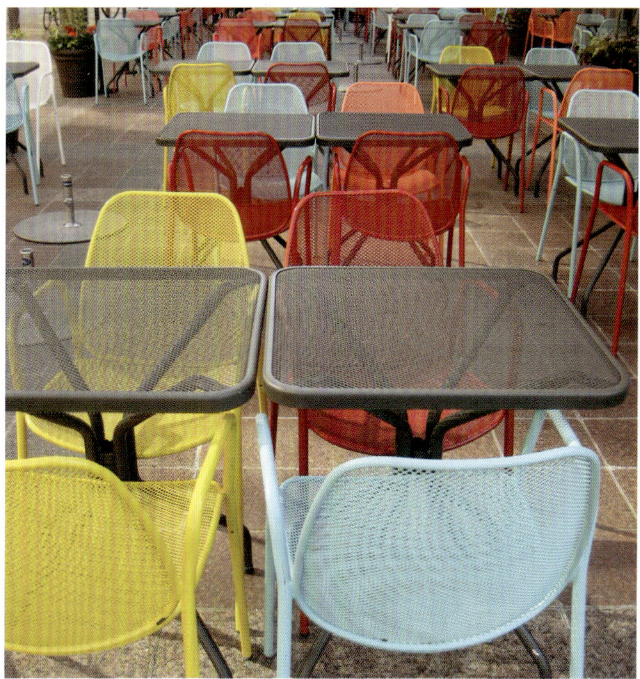

The yellow pulls your eye through the photo.

Pushing Colors

I often find myself pushing a color. What I mean by this is that I get as much mileage out of the color as I can. This extends the life of the color in the quilt and makes it more interesting. I might look to the neighboring colors on the color wheel and choose a red with a bit of blue in it to make it cooler, or find a red that has some yellow and white so it is more of a melon-like red, or look for a rusty red that has some black and a touch of yellow to it. It is all still red in the end. *Hidden Stone* is a good example of pushing red.

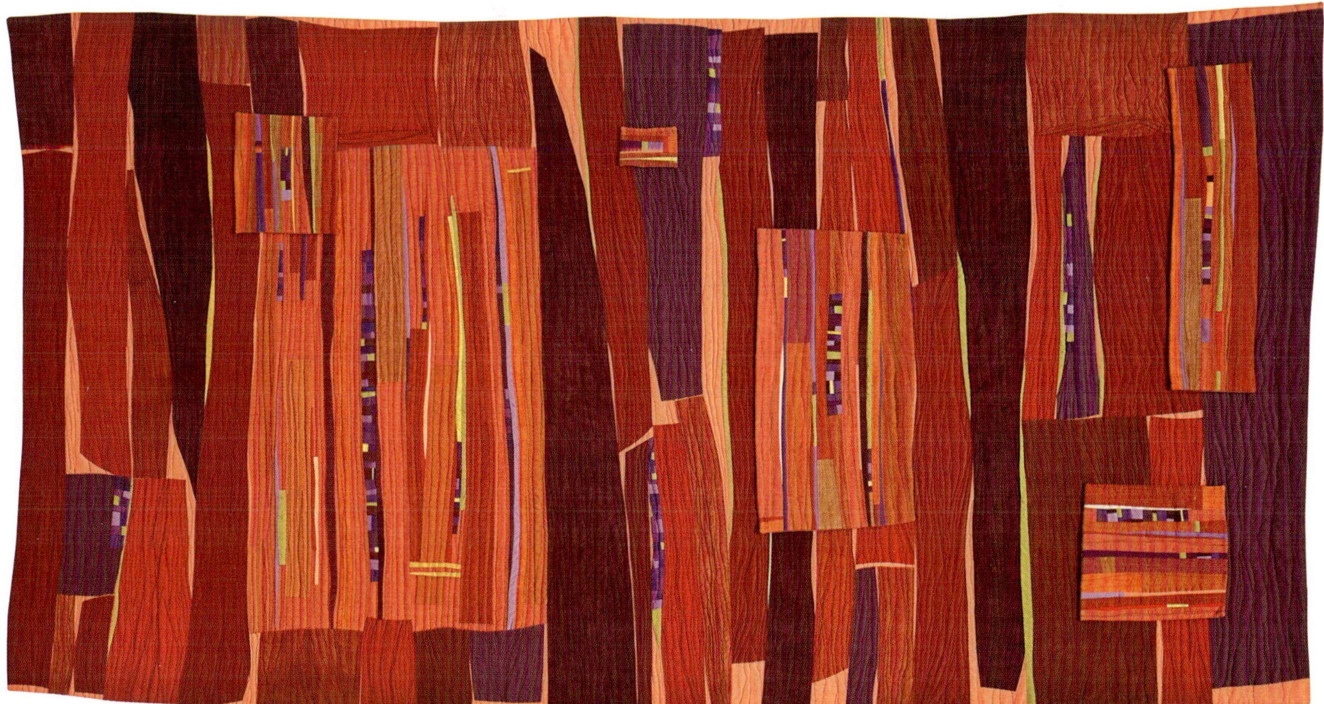

▶ *Hidden Stone* by Jean Wells, 83″ × 45″

Using Color as a Big Idea

The Big Ideas for *Hidden Stone* are stacked stone and the color red. I like to give myself challenges when I take on a new piece. I had taken a photograph of an ancient stone wall at an Indian ruins in Arizona. I was fascinated with how the stones were balanced on each other, so I thought about balance repeatedly while I cut and sewed the pieces together. As I worked with the red colors, I realized that the quilt needed a spark of some kind. I tried violet, but it had too much red in it and not enough spark. The bits of green worked for me. After the quilt was pieced, it felt more complete to orient it as a horizontal composition. It was a stronger piece as a result. Look at how the red appears in the images at right.

Colors have a major role in the composition, but that role will vary depending on the other players. Don't get so attached to using a particular color that the mixture gets out of balance. In a recipe you are not going to add so much salt that it becomes distasteful. Use the same discretion with color. Follow your instincts, knowing that your first impression is probably the best.

WORKING WITH COLOR IS LIKE DIRECTING A PLAY

Most successful quilts will have main colors, supporting colors, and accent colors. These colors all have roles that develop during the design process. And, if needed, the roles can change during the creation of the quilt. You are the director, but a time will come in the design process when the quilt takes on a life of its own and directs its own destiny. Embrace that time when it arrives.

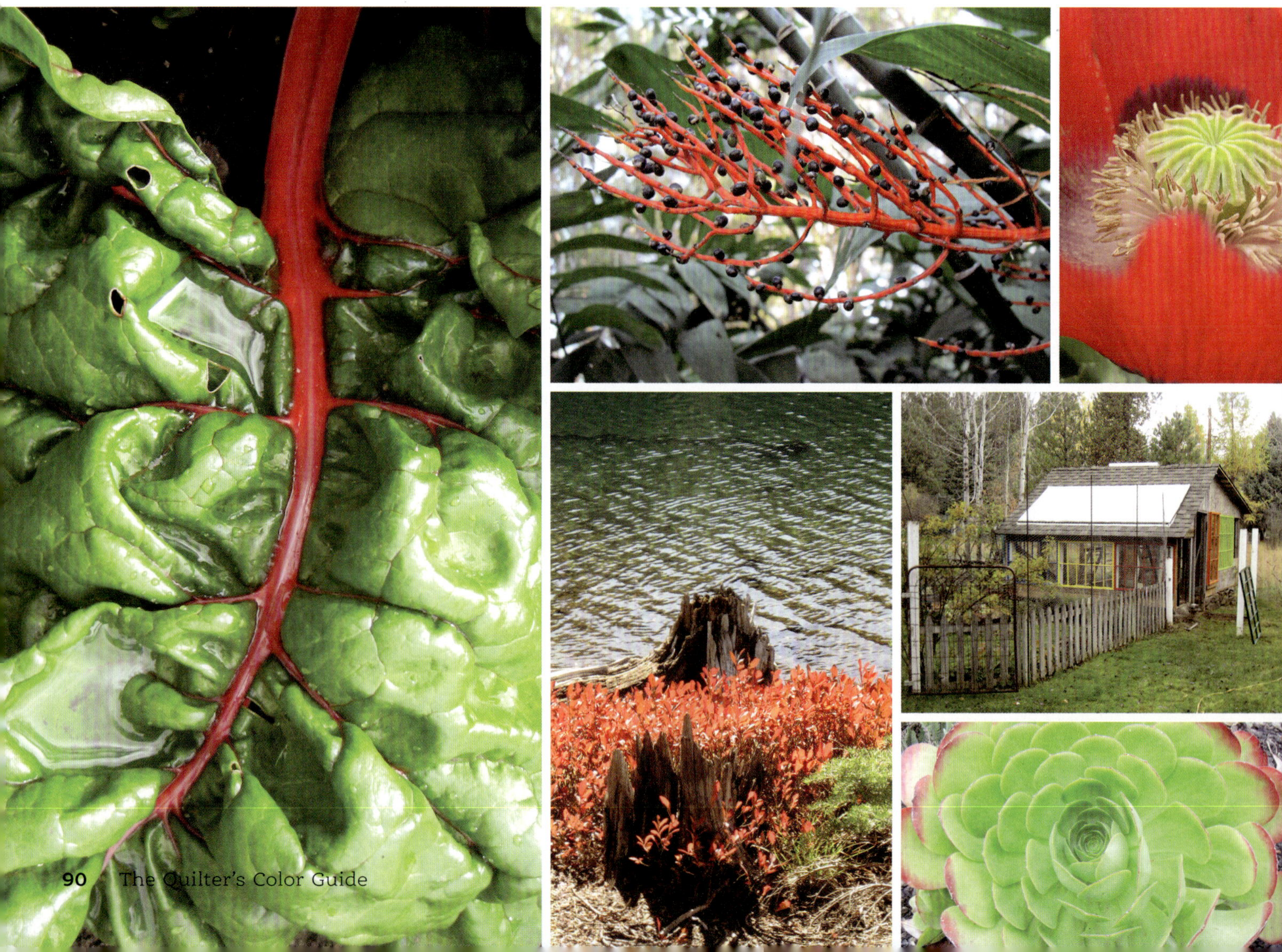

Exercise: Go On a Color Adventure

In the process of becoming a colorist, you will create your own rules to reflect your style and desires for the quilts that you make. Inspiration and ideas are everywhere.

1. Become a detective, sorting out what you see and actively learning from the inspiration.

2. Study paintings, collect pictures from magazines, and take photos. In the process of being a student, you will begin to develop a color sense that is unique to you.

3. Challenge yourself to find unexpected combinations of color.

4. Give yourself the assignment of completing two journal pages a week that focus on color.

5. Set aside a designated time when you can devote at least half an hour to concentrating on color. Look forward to your creative journaling and enjoy learning to develop ideas from inspiration.

Knowledge and observation are the keys.

Color Contrasts

Practice creating contrast that adds excitement, remembering that opposites attract. A significantly larger amount of one color will play well with a smaller amount of its opposite.

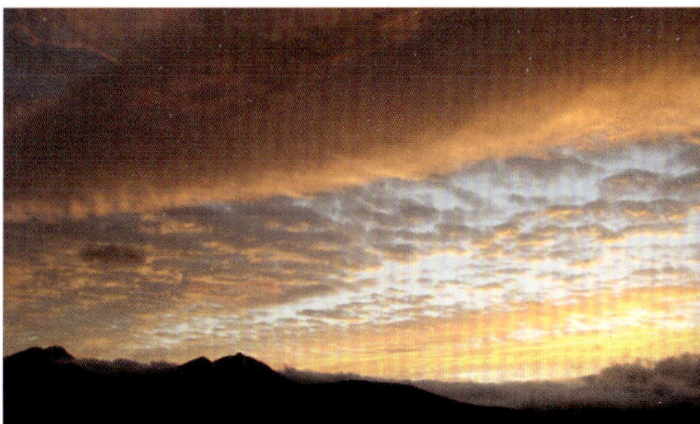

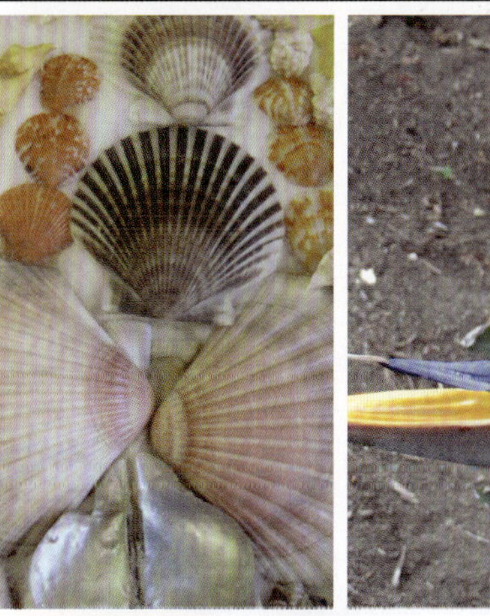

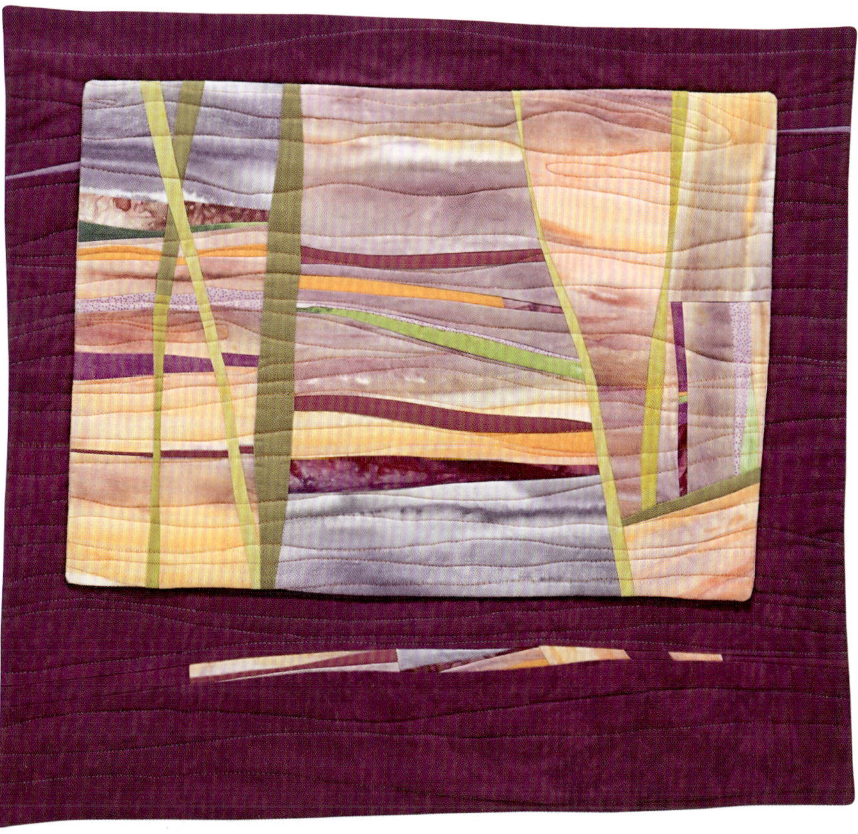

▶ *Summer Breeze* by Jean Wells, 21″ × 19″

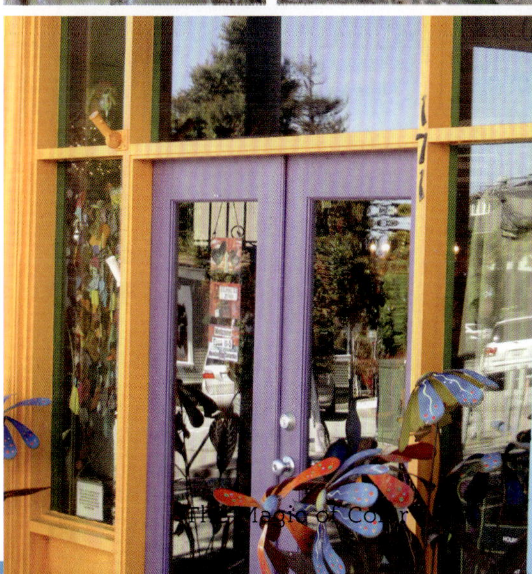

CONTRAST: COMPLEMENTARY COLORS

Using complementary colors is a good way to add contrast. For example, use mostly reds with acid green or mostly violets with a sliver of yellow, as seen in *Stone I*. My color reference was a picture from a calendar photo of cactus and yucca in the desert. A tiny yellow flower appeared in one of the corners of the photo, so I slipped a few slivers of yellow into the piecing. It wasn't until I was finished that I realized I had used two sets of complementary colors in the composition: red/green and violet/yellow. The quilt is so much better because of the yellow.

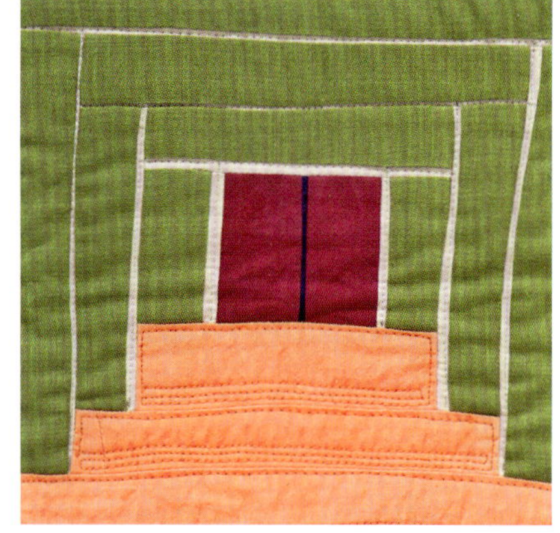

Detail of *Mom's Houses* by Jody H. Rusconi, 48″ × 79″

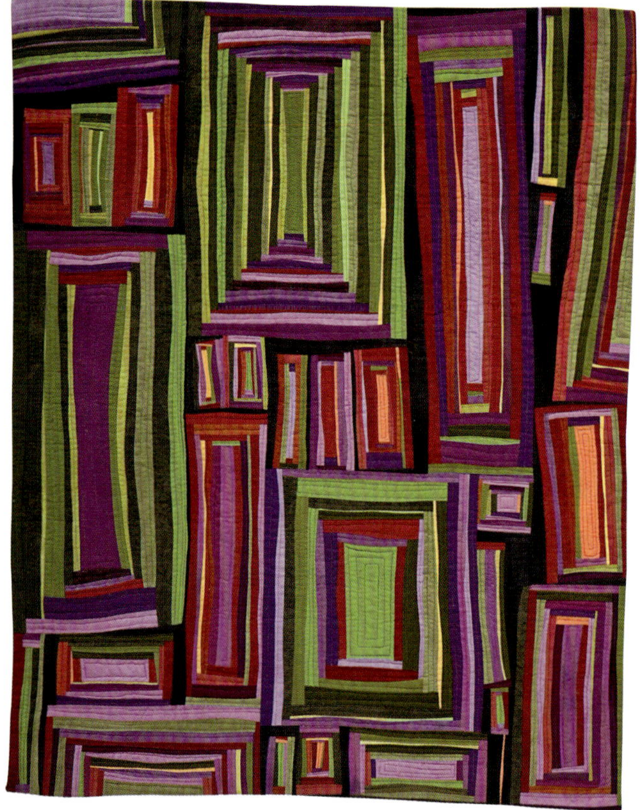

▶ *Stone I* by Jean Wells, 35″ × 45″

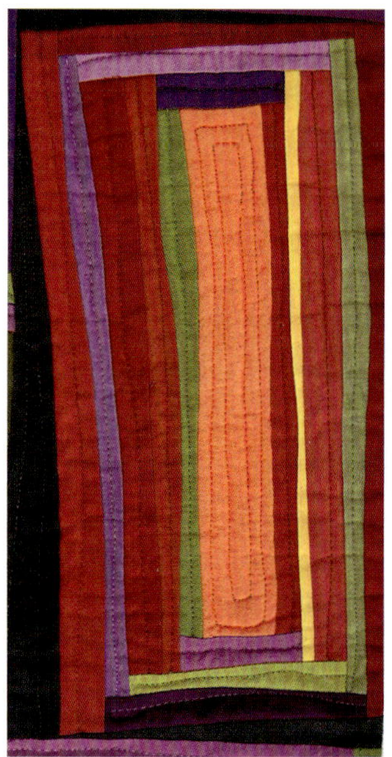

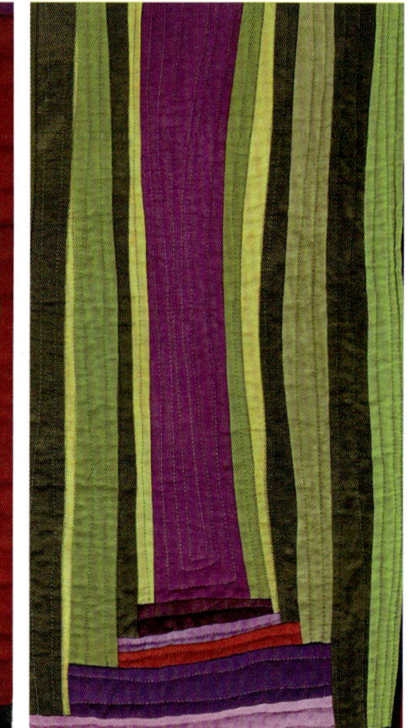

Double complementary colors

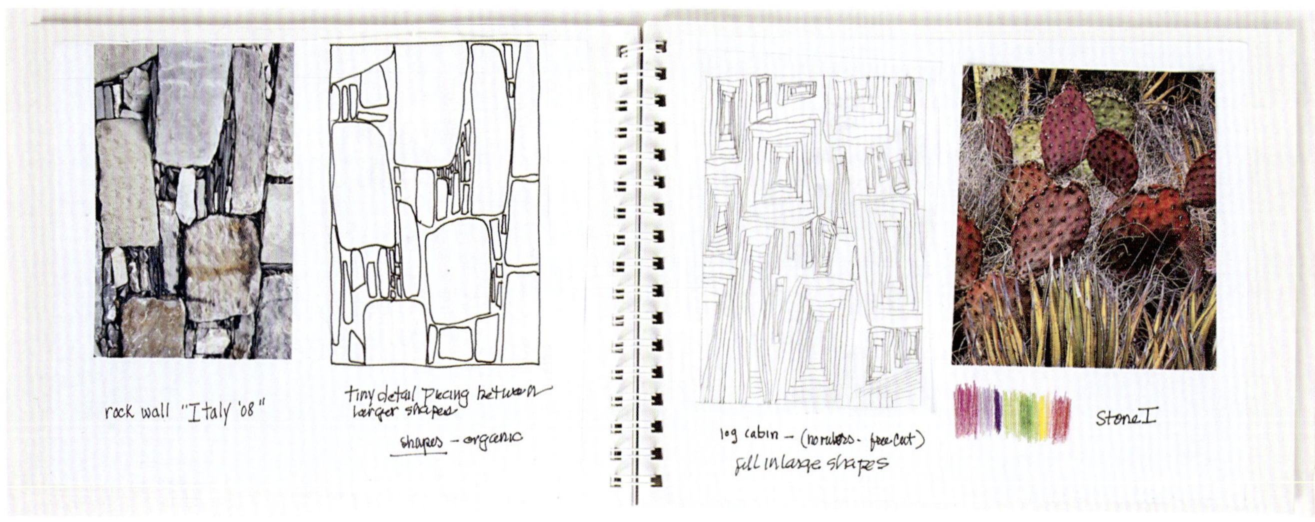

CONTRAST: WARM AND COOL COLORS

Color temperature is another type of contrast. In the past, I didn't think about warm and cool as a form of contrast, but now that I do, this contrast has become a good tool to use when I am stuck. I have a tendency to use mostly warm colors in my quilts, but lately I have been consciously throwing in a cool color, which helps to make all the colors sing in tune. In After the Rain, the sky is a stormy, cool blue-gray, but much of the stonework is warm in tone. This contrast creates a touch of moodiness. The blue-green edging enhances the warmth of the brown and orange stone, and at the same time it makes the cool whites and the blue-grays even cooler.

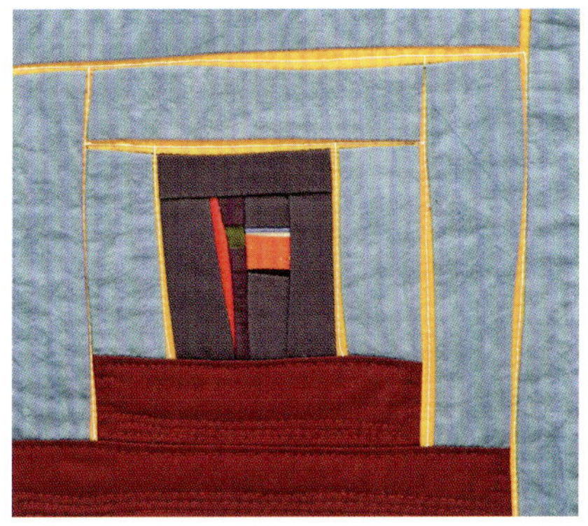

Detail of *Mom's Houses* by Jody H. Rusconi, 48″ × 79″

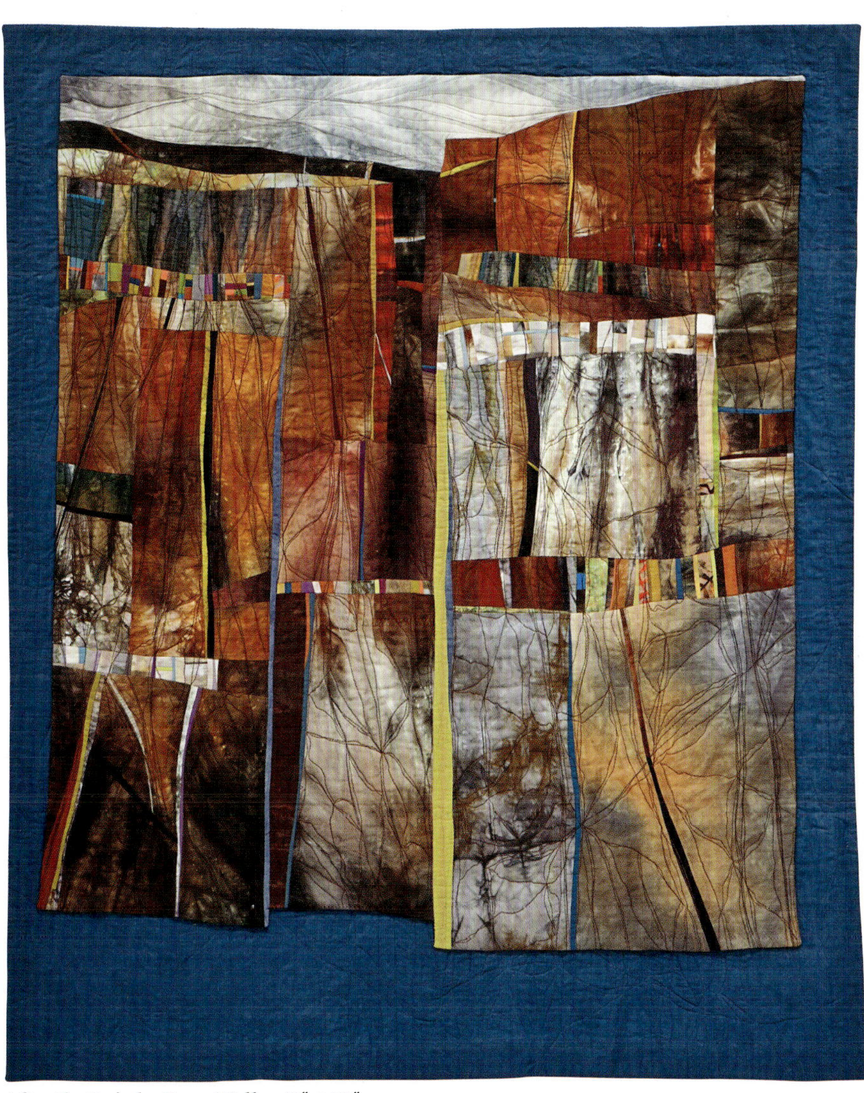

After the Rain by Jean Wells, 41″ × 51″

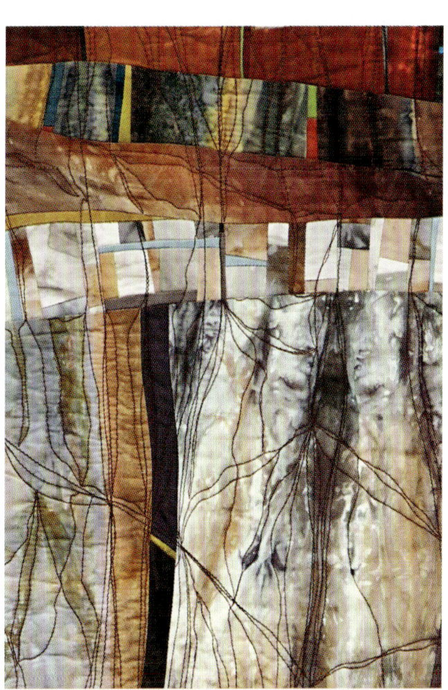

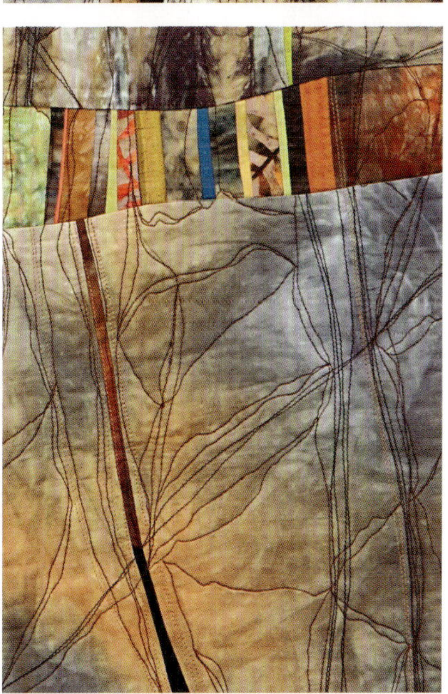

Most of the colored fabrics in August Sage are bright in mood. The various grays and whites appear dull, and the texture of the nubby cottons and linens contributes to the dullness. They make the shiny taffeta, yellow, aqua, and green appear even brighter against those duller, quieter colors. The rabbit brush that blooms in August next to my house was the inspiration for this quilt, and I just can't get enough of these colors. When I look closely at the plant, the stems seem to be a tinted grayish aqua. Who would have thought there was such a color? This is what I love about being a detective. Nature has many valuable lessons to teach us.

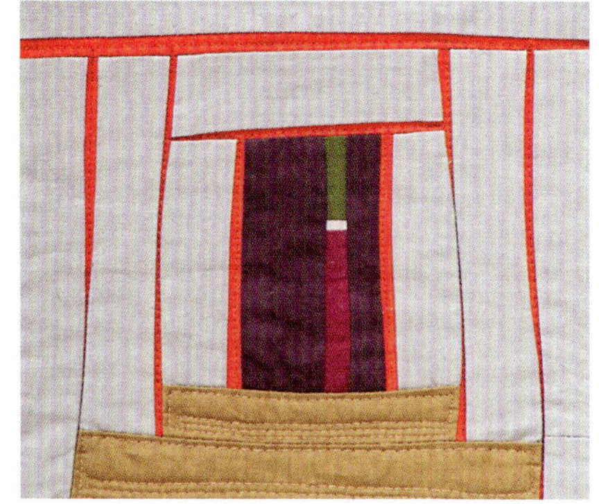

Detail of *Mom's Houses* by Jody H. Rusconi, 48″ × 79″

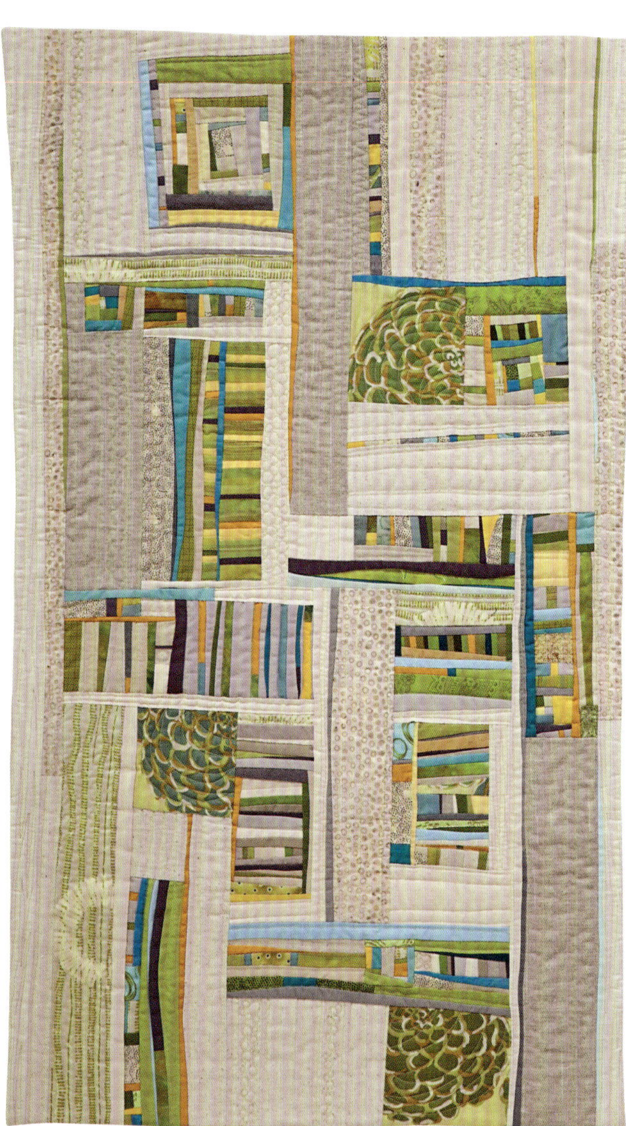

August Sage by Jean Wells, 42″ × 41″

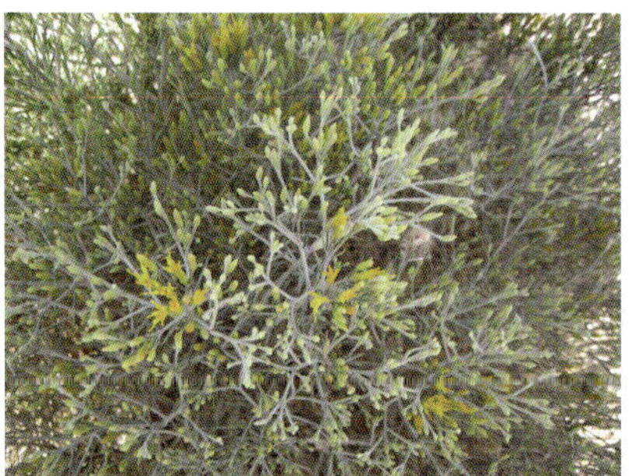

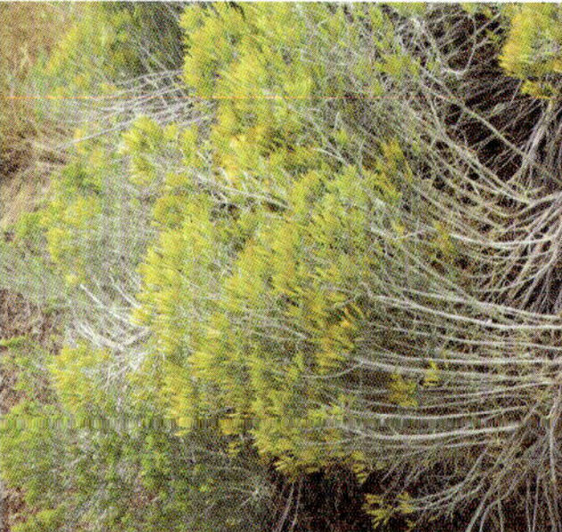

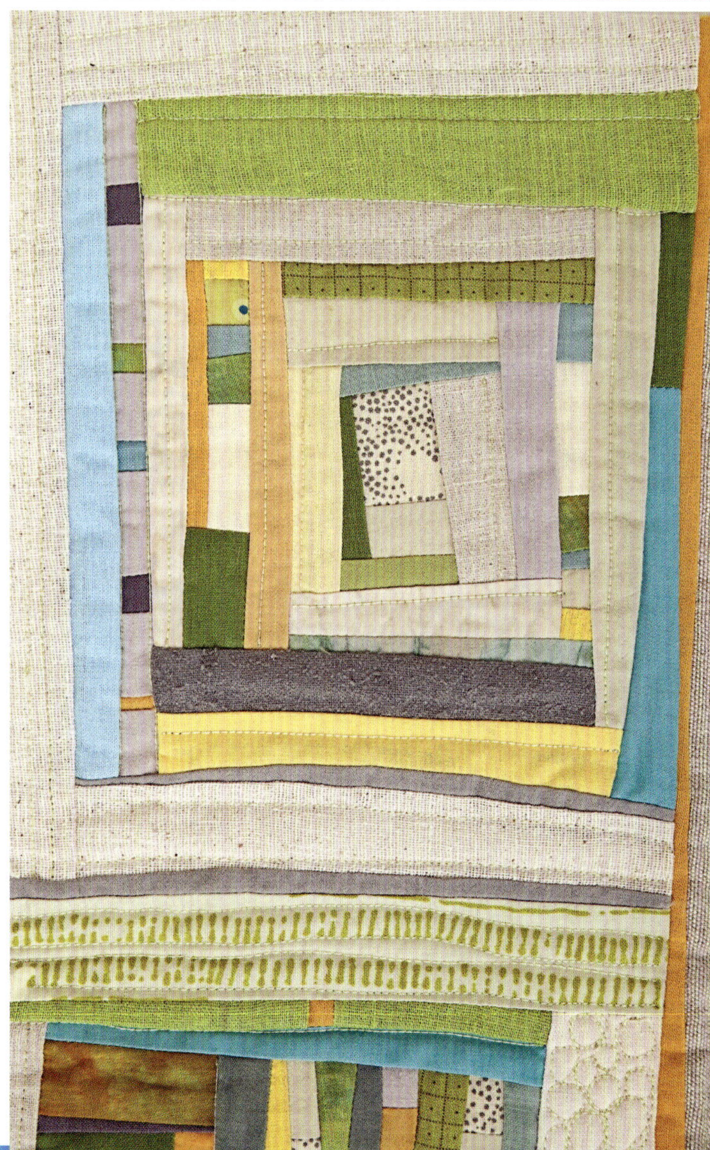

CONTRAST: LIGHT AND DARK COLORS

During a trip to Death Valley, California, I couldn't get the mood of the light colors out of my mind. It was interesting to see everything so very light in value with tiny touches of darker colors scattered throughout. Every once in a while there was evidence of water, but it took on the desert tones—the darks in the photos are deep purple, coppery red, and brighter green, but all you see are just little bits of earth. You don't have to go to the desert to see this kind of contrast. Notice how the weathered structure contrasts with the tall grasses on the beach. Working in low contrast takes patience and the ability to capture enough contrast of light and dark to make the composition work.

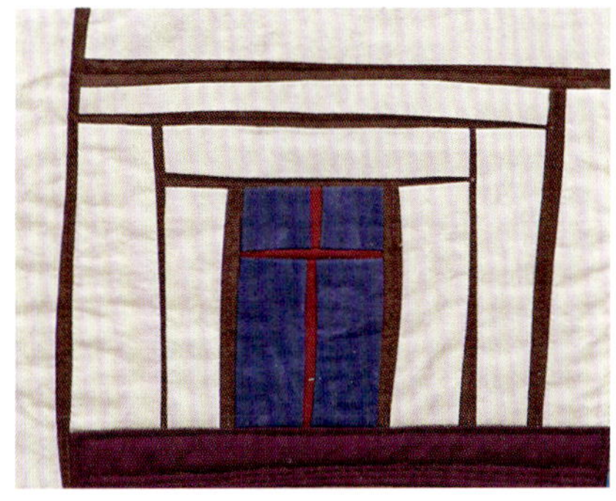

Detail of *Mom's Houses* by Jody H. Rusconi, 48″ × 79″

VIEW FABRIC FROM A DISTANCE

Be sure to lay fabric out that you are considering for a quilt and look at it from a distance to see the value changes. If you are unsure, you can cut swatches from each fabric, glue them to paper, and photocopy them in black and white. Then you will see the value of each fabric and know which is light and dark in relationship to the others. It is useful to cut the swatch strip and glue it next to the colored fabric.

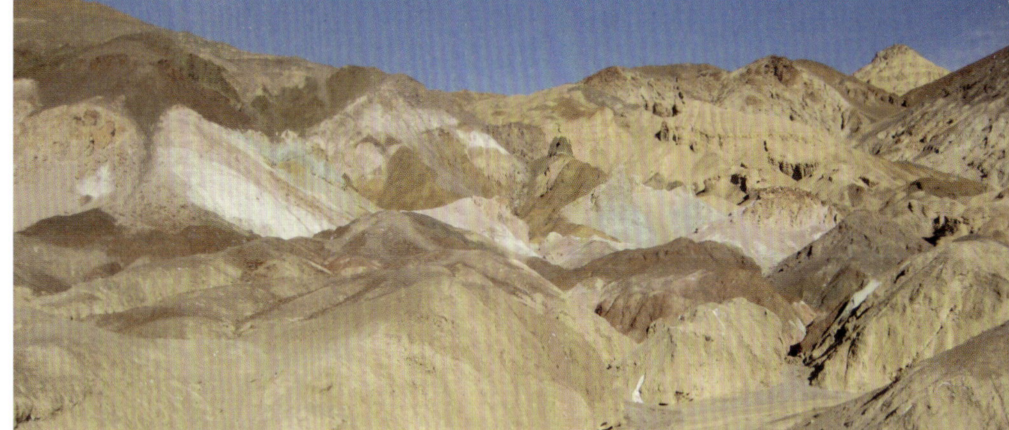

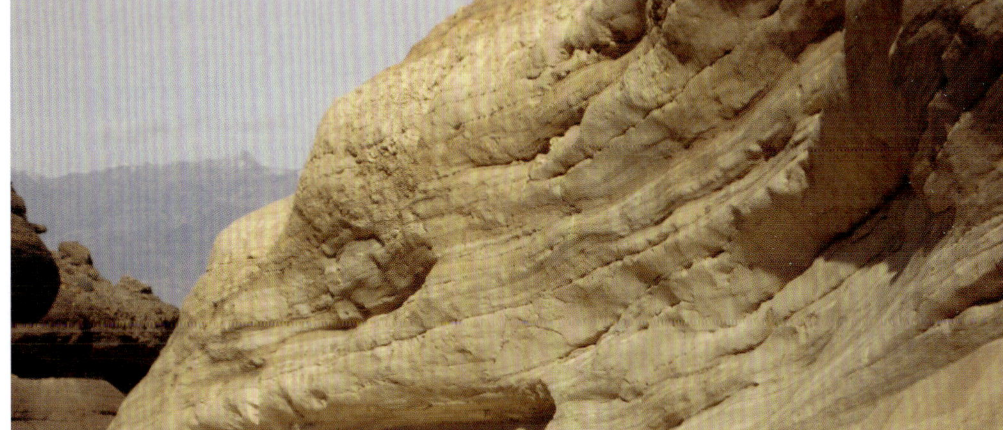

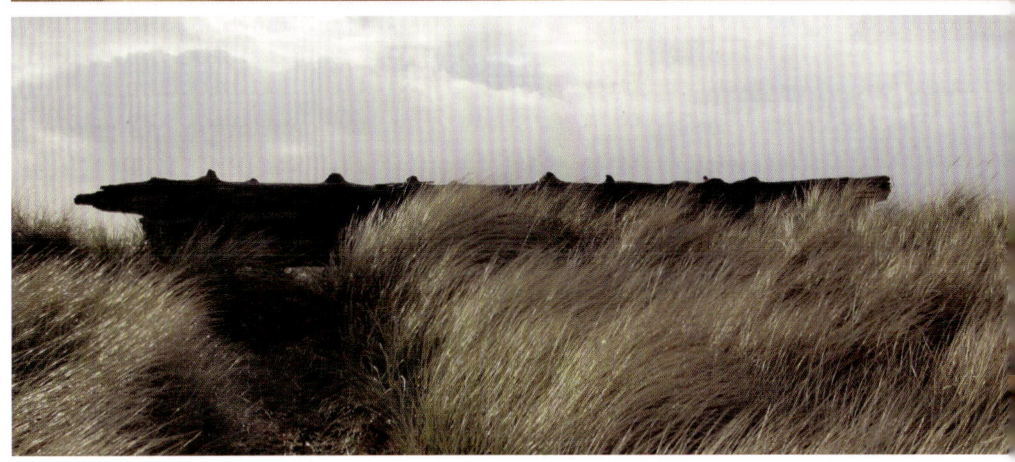

CONTRAST: DOMINANT AND SUBORDINATE COLORS

Equal amounts of two colors in a quilt will confuse the eye because they both compete for attention. Because of this, one of the colors needs to dominate. The subordinate color ends up with a supporting role, but that does not mean it is not important. Without it, the composition would be lacking.

Exercise: Understanding Color and Contrast

The purpose of this assignment is to help you understand the use of contrast in a composition by isolating these elements in a small study. The right amount of contrast can make a quilt a work of art. Be conscious of the decisions you are making in the design process. Fresh eyes in the morning are the best for looking objectively at your work from the previous day.

1. Pull fabrics from your stash that represent one of the types of contrast discussed in this section.

2. Make a composition that is approximately 6″ × 8″. Think about proportion when you choose the colors. Equal amounts of the two elements will fight. Choose a greater amount of one color.

3. Use simple piecing techniques, such as free cutting strips of different widths, keeping the line work simple, such as in *Stone I*, page 92, and *Hidden Stone* page 89.

4. When your piece is finished, audition border colors. You may choose to do one or two borders—with a single fabric or multiple fabrics. One of the border fabrics should represent a fabric from the opposite element. (For example, if most of your fabrics are bright, use some dull fabrics in the border.) Be conscious of the width you make the borders so that they do not overwhelm the piecing. Finish your piece as you wish.

5. Try this assignment several times, using different pairs of contrast. This is how you develop and learn to sense contrast possibilities. Both of the small quilts at right were contrast assignments.

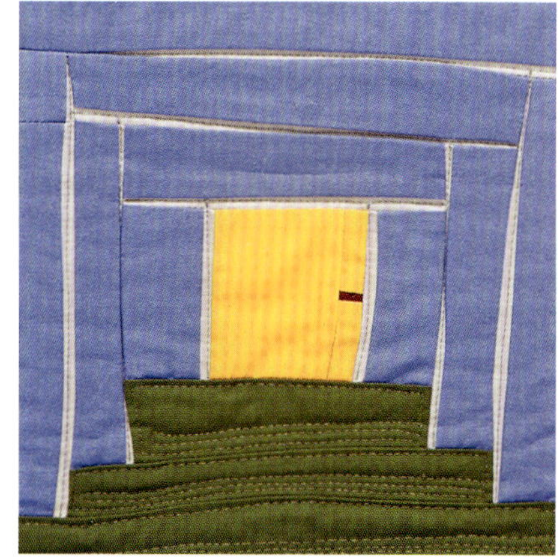

Detail of *Mom's Houses* by Jody H. Rusconi, 48″ × 79″.

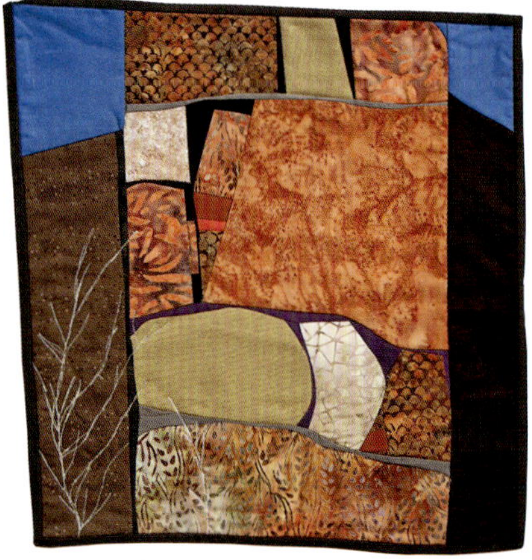

Sedona Rock Pillar by Nora Briggs, 14½″ × 15¼″

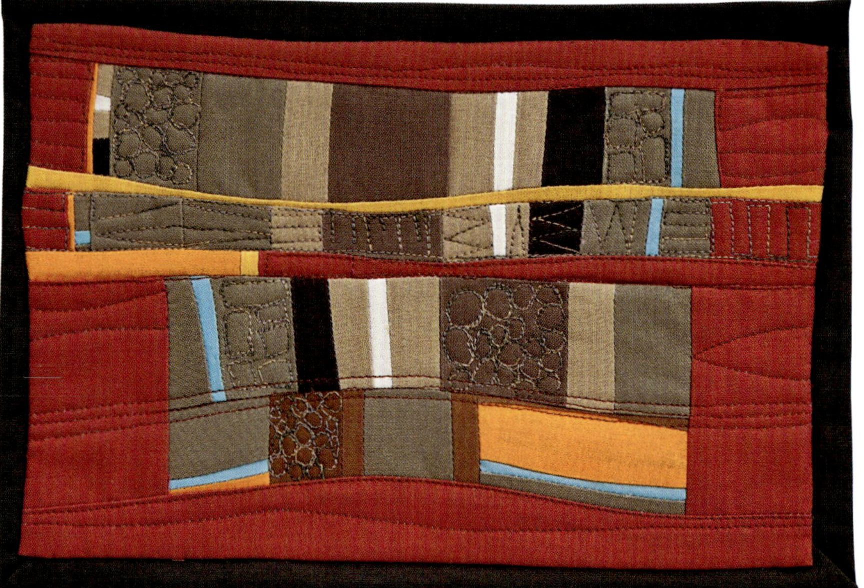

Red Color Study by Linda Weick, 9¼″ × 6½″

Color Proportion

PROPORTION: A LITTLE COLOR CAN GO A LONG WAY

The acid green lichen on a juniper tree is startling to look at, but a whole tree of it would not be nearly as interesting. Nature is one of your best sources of information when it comes to color.

I also look to the professionals. Look at what I call beauty shots in magazines. A stylist or art director had a definite idea in mind when planning those shots. You most likely will find a small amount of a color that is a lot darker, brighter, or lighter and that makes the other colors work together. Look at paintings that you admire and see how the artist uses color in a proportionate way.

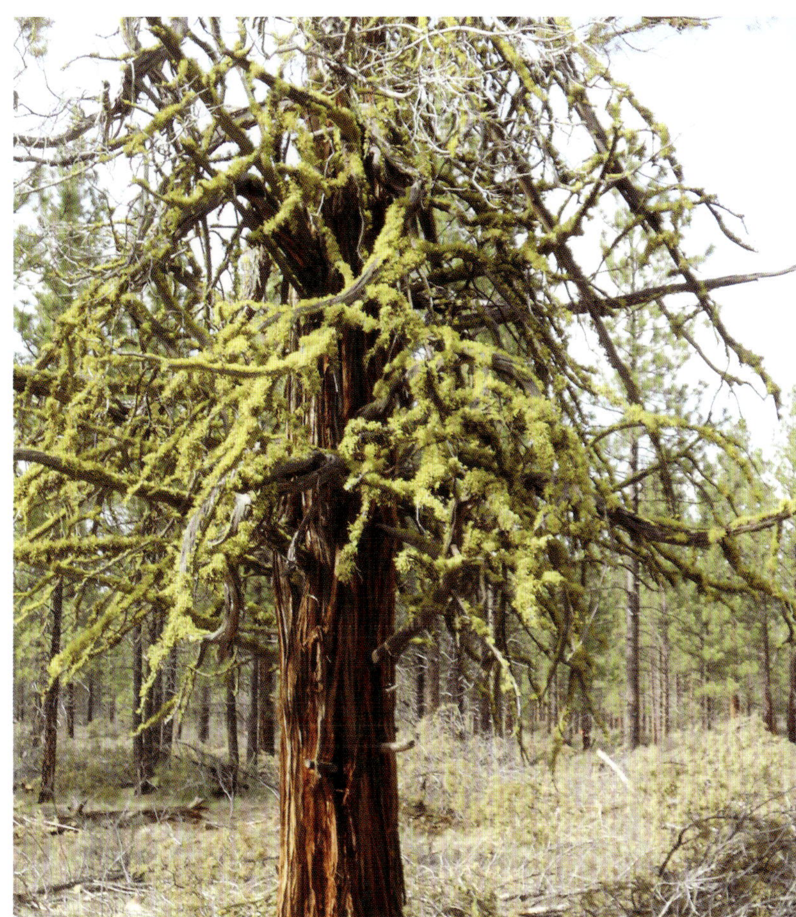

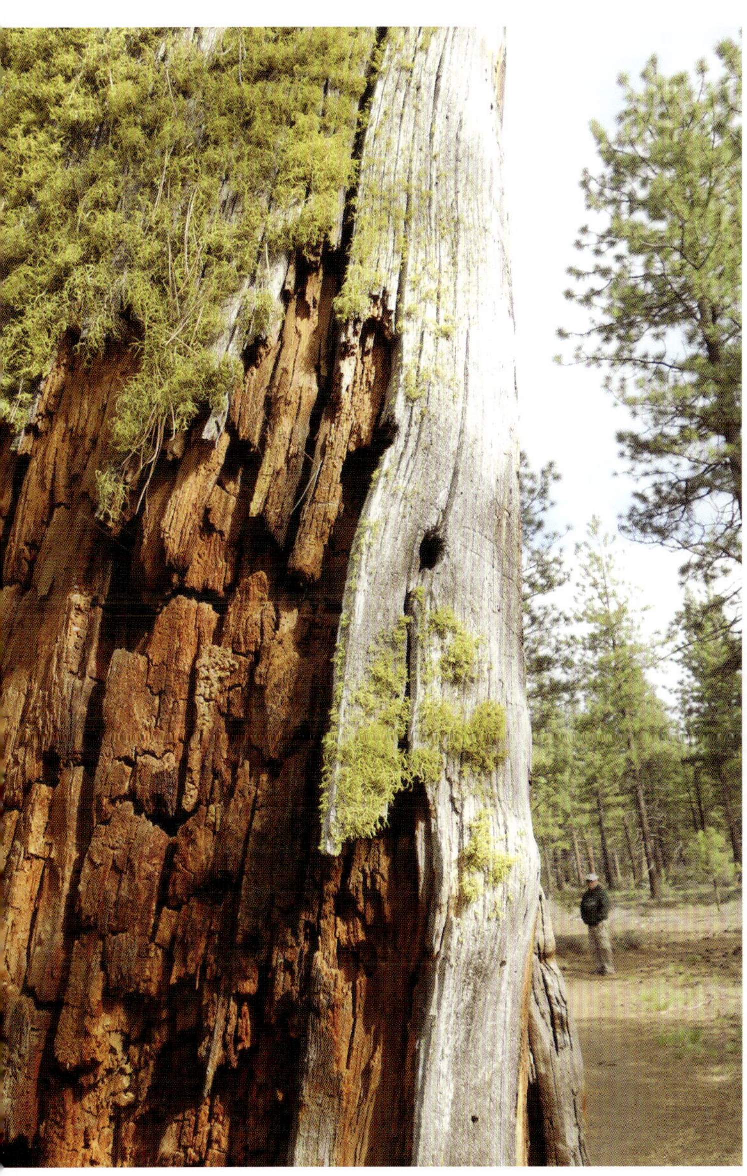

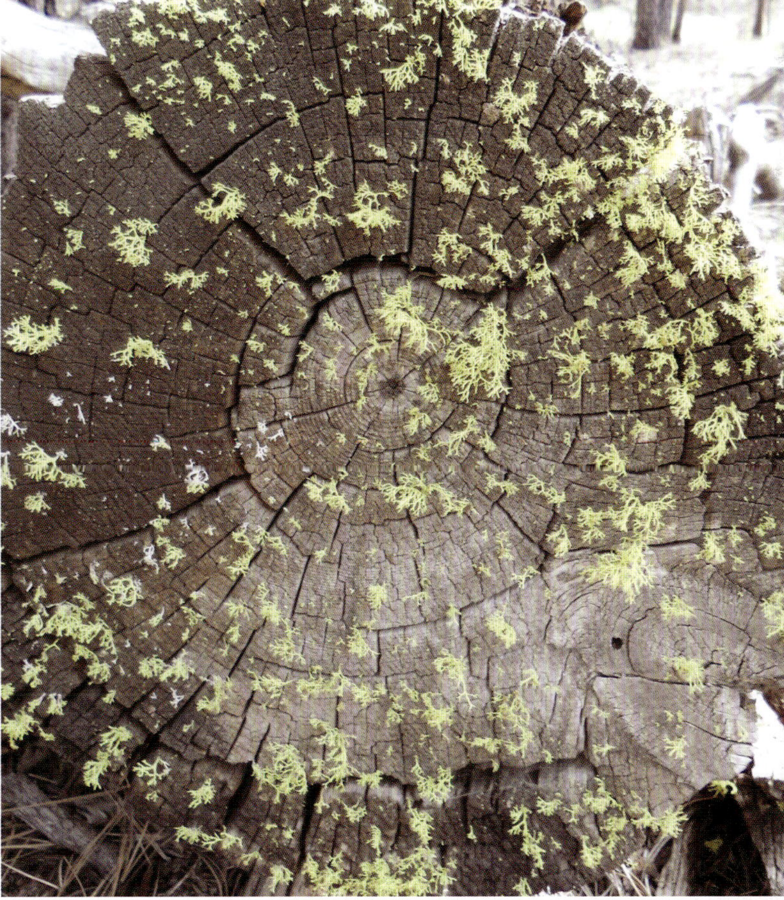

PROPORTION: GIVE IT A PUNCH

In working on *Small Wonder*, I found that my original choice of fabrics did not give the quilt the punch that was needed. As I auditioned other fabrics, it turned out that very bright Pepto-Bismol pink and bright orange in small amounts made the difference in the quilt. It is easy to overlook this kind of contrast because even an eighth of a yard of these mixed in with the remaining colors on the worktable can look overpowering. But a 2″ strip tossed in the pile of fabrics is just fine.

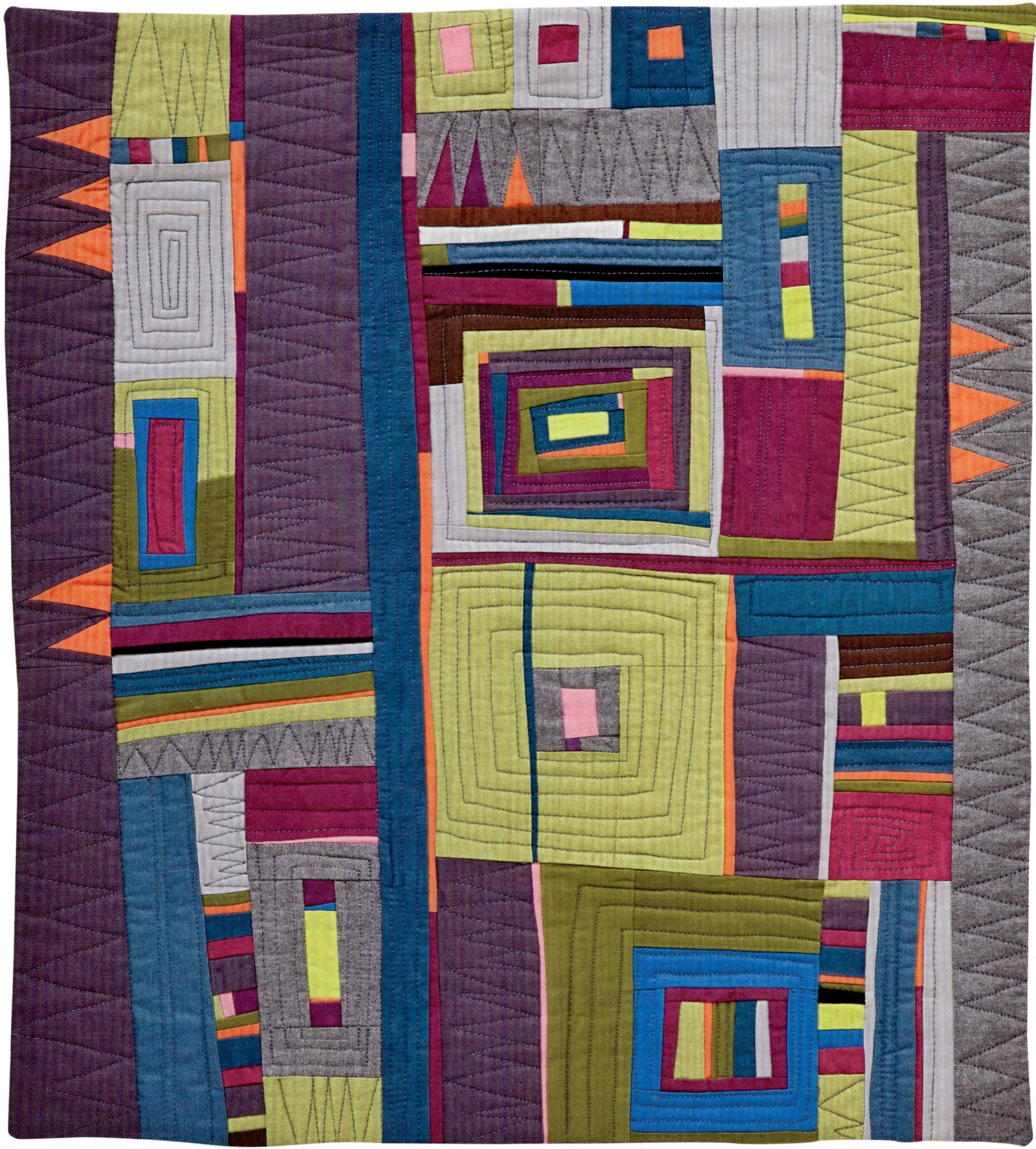

Small Wonder by Jean Wells, 24″ × 24″

PROPORTION IS THE KEY

Keep working with the amount of color until it feels right and does the work it needs to do with the rest of the colors. Think of a painter using a thin brush stroke. In a quilt it might be in the form of squares and rectangles. As you observe the quilts in this book, you will see examples of this concept. Mother Nature does this beautifully as the sun sets in the western sky.

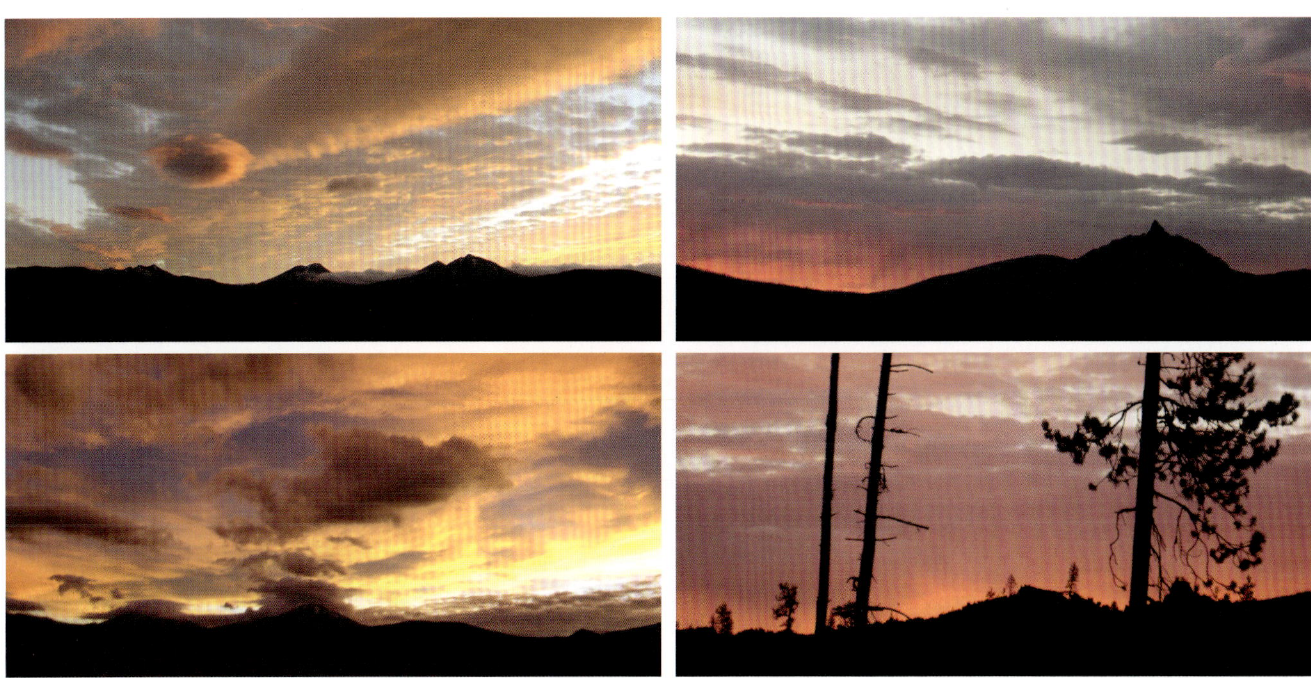

MORE ON THE PROPORTION RULE

In *Intuitive Color & Design*, I wrote about looking at a picture, identifying the color families, and then determining what percentage they are of the whole. If these same percentages are followed in your quilt, you will capture the essence of the color inspiration. Take a second look at your inspiration. This can give you more insight into color. Proportional use of colors can make or break a color scheme.

Exercise: Sketching Contrast

Tracing the main lines of a photograph gives you line work and structural lines to use as a launching pad when you begin a quilt. But if you think about it, you were also subtly attracted to the photograph because of the contrast.

1. Select some of your sketches.

2. Use a pencil to shade in the dark and medium areas, leaving the light areas without shading. This is a helpful tool to use when you are choosing colors. After you have the values nailed down, you can focus on the palette. It would be interesting to work

with a monochromatic scheme and throw in a small amount of a very deep shade of something from another color family to pull it off.

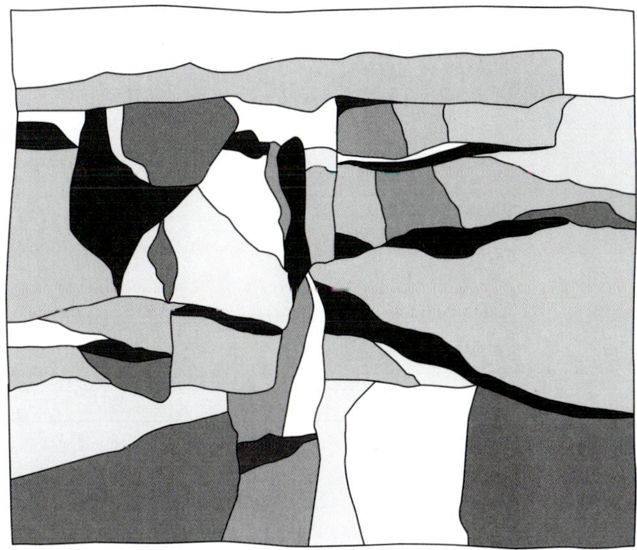

Shade in the sketch more than once and you will begin to see contrast differently. Become a detective! If a sketch feels unbalanced, then do it again and change things up.

EXPANDING YOUR KNOWLEDGE

By Katie Pasquini Masopust and Brett Barker

In this chapter, we'll show you ways to expand on your newly found color knowledge by considering transparency, colors from nature, and geometric focal points.

Exercise: Create Transparency

Transparency is the effect of being able to see through to another layer, as if two pieces of colored cellophane are overlapped, creating a third color as they cross. Instead of using sheer fabric to create transparencies, you will create the effect with opaque fabrics. When mixing paints, equal amounts of red and yellow create orange. As a textile artist, you can visually mix these colors by using the techniques in this exercise.

Materials

- Fused fabric in all the colors from the color wheel, including the tints and shades
- Gray fabric: 1 piece 8½″ × 11″ for background
- Pencil
- Rotary cutting ruler
- Rotary cutter
- Cutting mat
- Scissors
- Iron

DIRECTIONS

1. Cut several 2″ × 2″ squares of each color. Remove the paper backing from the fabrics as you cut them.

2. Lay a square of red and a square of yellow so that they overlap in the middle of the gray fabric. Touch the tip of the iron to each of the squares to hold them in place.

3. Use a pencil to draw the edge of the piece hidden underneath the top square. Cut out this overlap shape, and use it as a template to cut the transparency color—orange. Flip the little template over onto the back of an orange square, mark, and cut out. Remove the paper backing from the fabric.

4. Place the orange piece in the proper position so its edges complete the edges of both the original squares, creating the look of 2 squares overlapping. Fuse the orange piece in place.

5. Lay a blue square over a portion of the yellow square. The place where they overlap will create a transparency of green. Use the same process as above and draw the overlap, cut it away, and use it for a template to cut the green. Place the green in the proper spot, making sure that it completes each square.

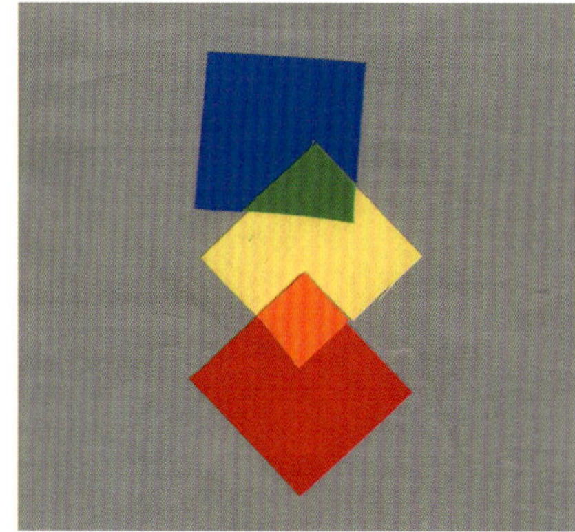

Blue added to yellow for green transparency.

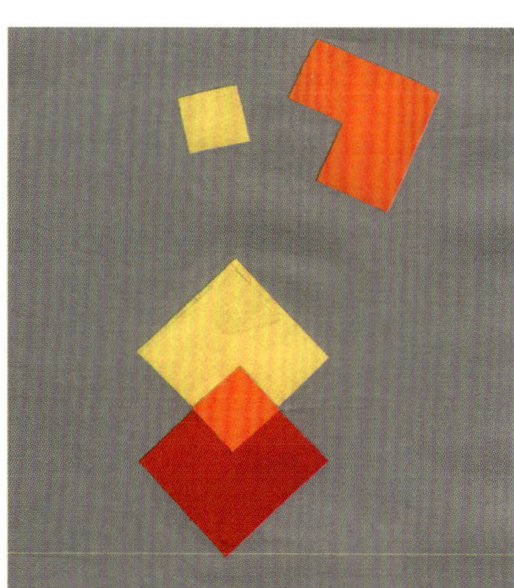

Red and yellow create orange.

6. Lay a blue square over a portion of the red square to create a transparency of violet. You have now used all the primary colors—red, yellow, and blue—to create the secondary colors of orange, green, and violet.

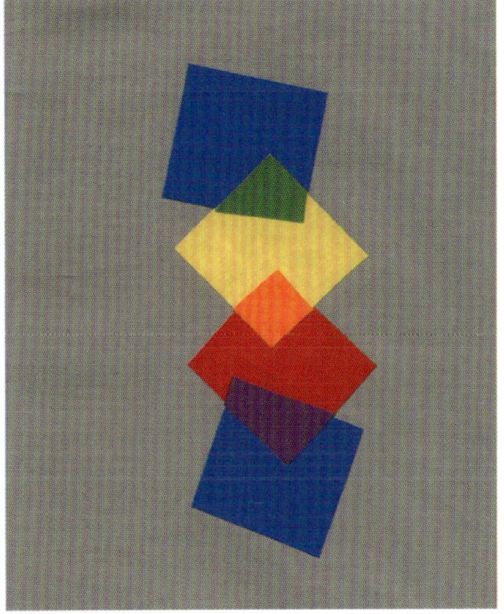

Blue added to red for violet transparency.

7. Use this same process to create the tertiary colors.

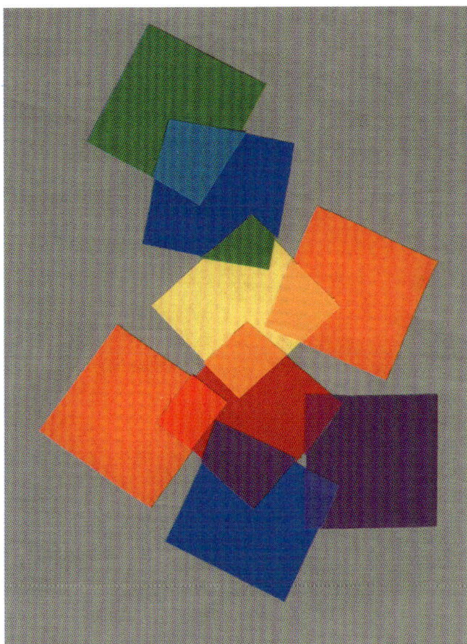

Combining to create the tertiary colors: orange and yellow to create yellow-orange, red and orange to create red-orange, violet and red to create red-violet, blue and violet to create blue-violet, green and blue to create blue-green

8. Add white to create the tints. The difference in value also creates the effect of a transparency.

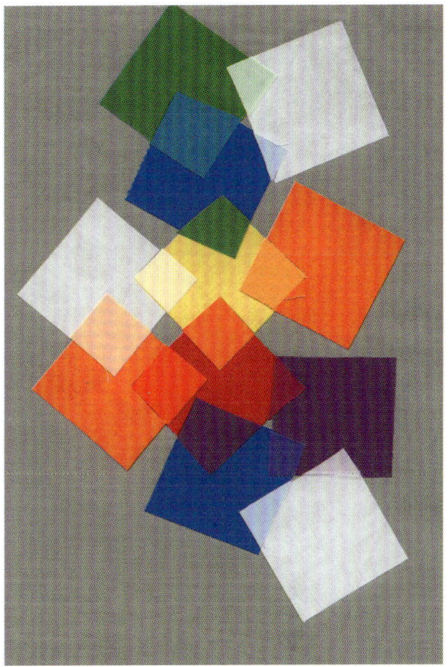

White added to several colors

9. Add black to these colors to create the shades. Differences in value create the transparency.

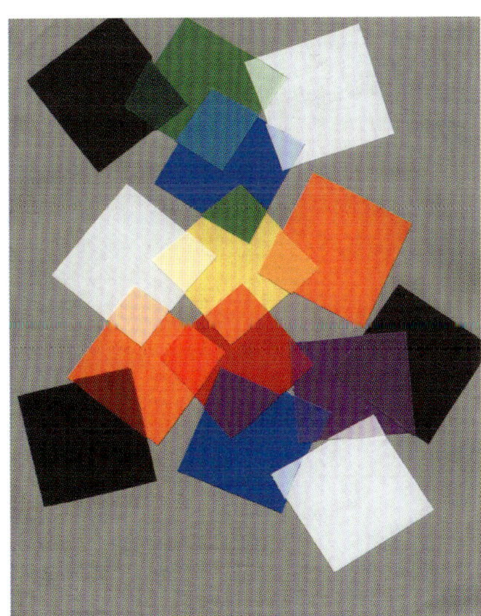

Black added to several colors

Be sure that the overlays create a continuous line to represent the perfect square.

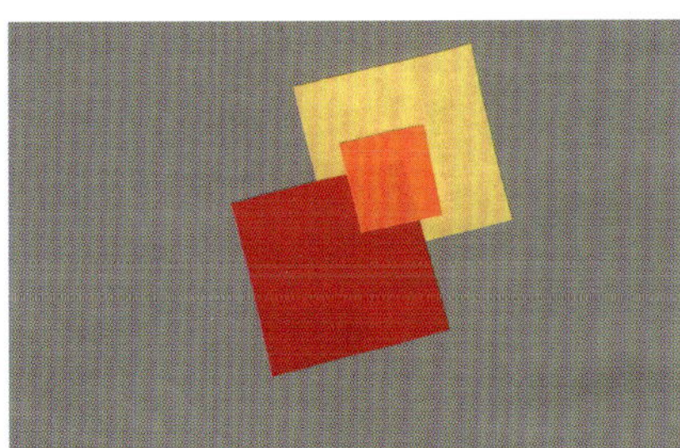

Incorrect placement of transparency square

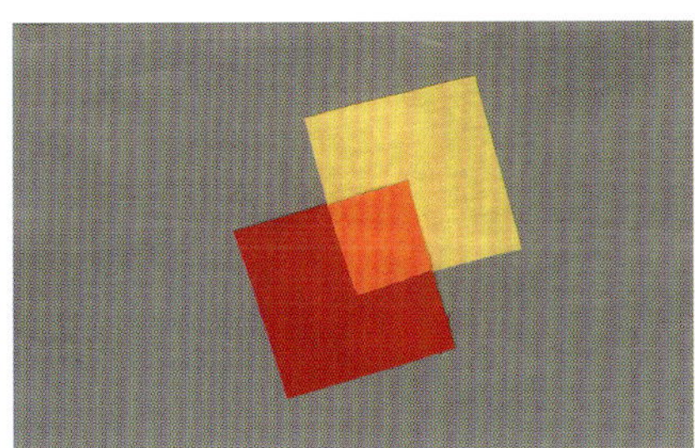

Correct placement of transparency square

Why Transparency

This exercise demonstrates the use of the color wheel for visually mixing fabrics to create transparency. By adding transparencies to your quilts, you give them a light, multilayered, airy feeling.

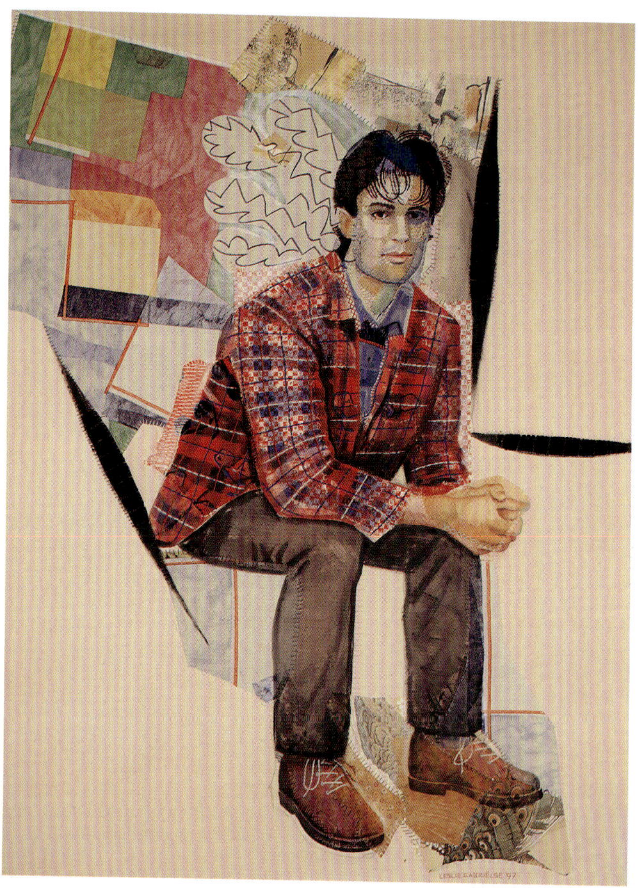

▶ *Joris Lutz* by Leslie Gabrielse, 52″ × 72″
Photo By Eric Kievit

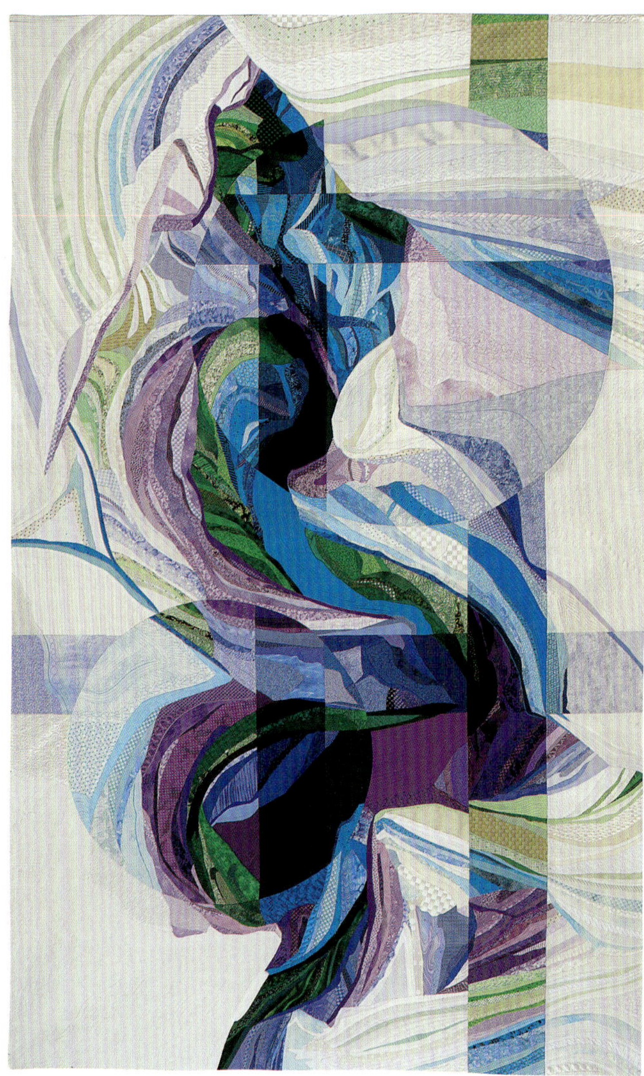

▶ *Ice Cave* by Katie Pasquini Masopust, 54″ × 90″
Photo By Hawthorne Studio

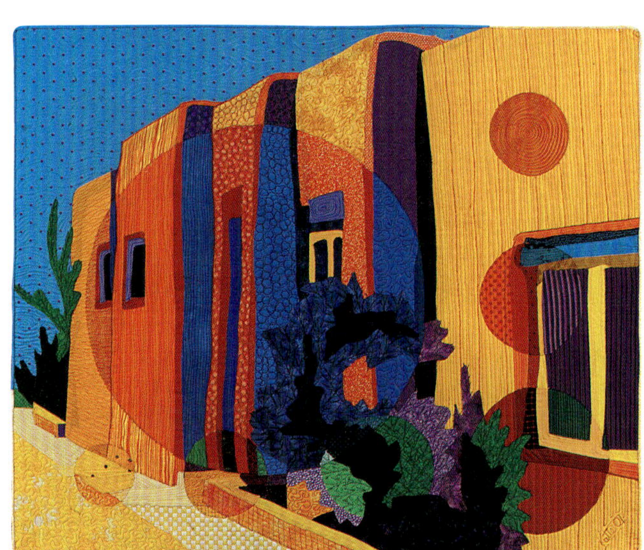

▶ *Sunny Side Up* by Katie Pasquini Masopust, 44″ × 44″
Photo By Hawthorne Studio

Exercise: Colors From Nature

There are many color schemes beyond the classic color schemes (page 12). Mother Nature is a true colorist, providing inspiration through the color combinations of the flora and fauna around us. In this exercise, you will create a series of 3″ × 5″ cards that capture these color schemes.

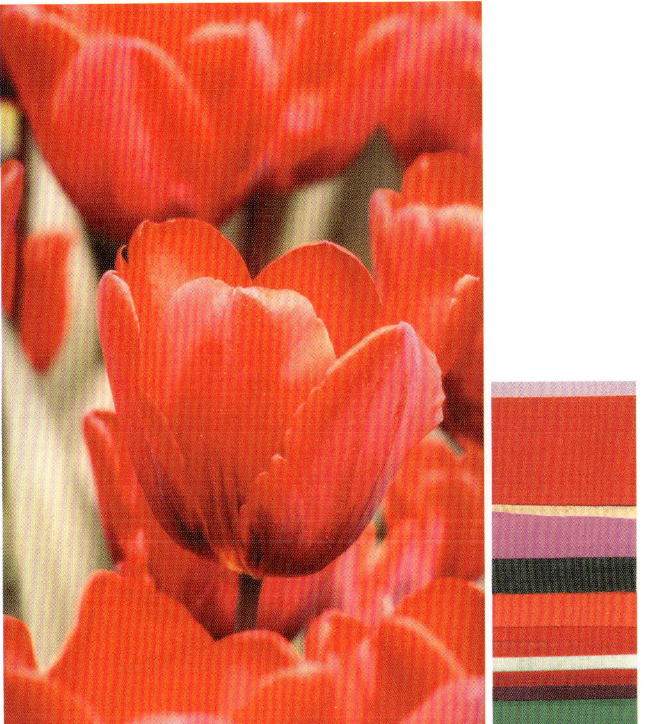

Flower and its proportional colors

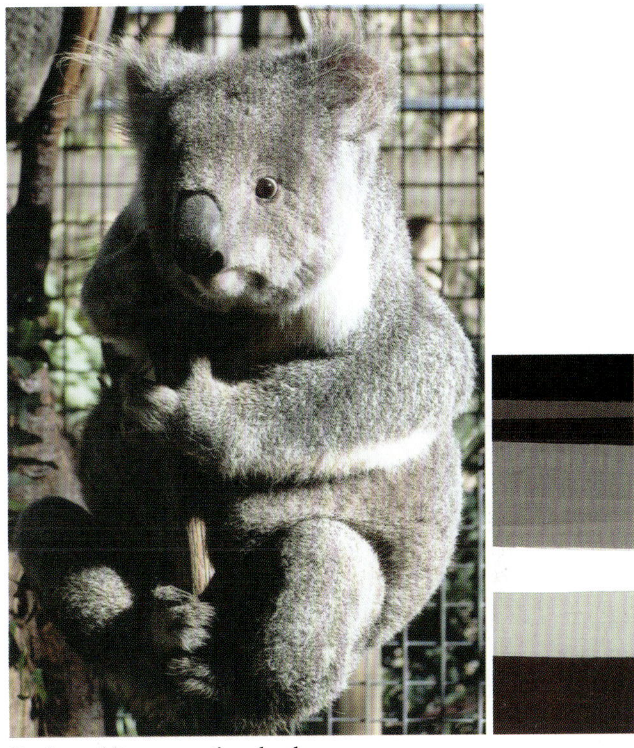

Koala and its proportional colors

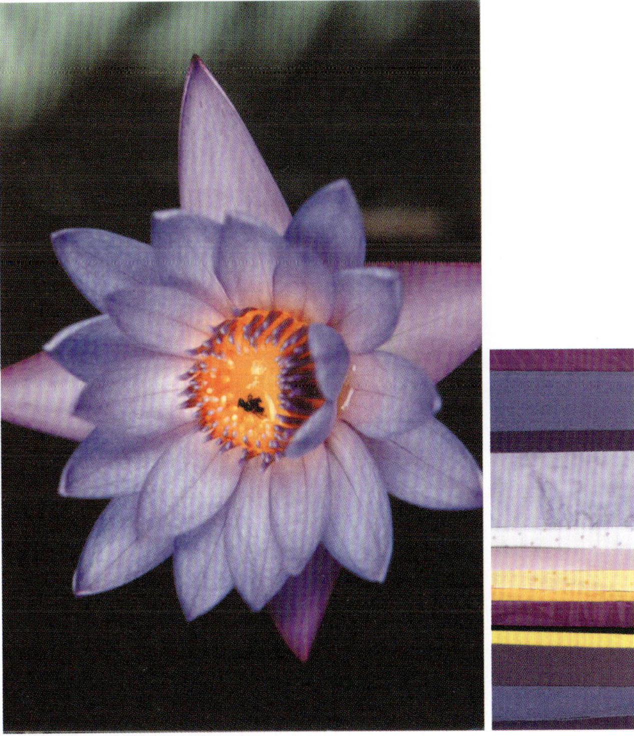

Flower and its proportional colors

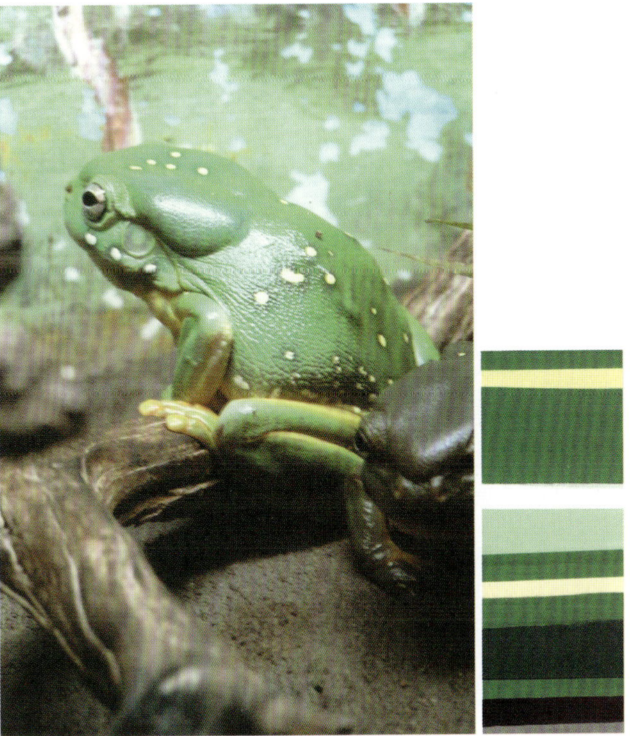

Frog and its proportional colors

All photos on this page by Katie Pasquini Masopust

Materials

- Pictures of a flower and an animal
- Magazine ad (optional)
- Fused fabrics in the colors of the flower and animal
- 3″ × 5″ index card
- Rotary cutting ruler
- Rotary cutter
- Cutting mat
- Iron

DIRECTIONS

1. Look closely at the picture of the flower. Be sure to notice all the subtle differences in the colors. Work with proportion by filling the 3″ × 5″ card with the same proportion of color as is found in the flower. Pick the most prominent color, and cut a strip of that color in the amount that you see in the picture. If it is a red flower and about 40% of the picture is red, cut a strip that covers 40% of the 3″ × 5″ card (use your eye to discern the proportions rather than measuring). If the yellow center is about 5% of the picture, cut a yellow strip that covers 5% of the card, and so on.

2. Use all the colors and their subtle value changes. Continue until the entire card is covered proportionally and you have used all the colors in the flower.

3. Fuse the strips to the 3″ × 5″ card.

4. Repeat the process, using a picture of an animal. Look closely for all the different colors. Approximate the percentage of each color, and cover that percentage of the 3″ × 5″ card for each.

OPTIONAL EXERCISE

Repeat the process of the exercise above, this time using a magazine ad that caught your eye because of the color. It is always fun to see how advertising designers use color.

◣ *Saving Your Results*

Subtle color changes and varying proportions make a more interesting color scheme. The 3″ × 5″ cards make a great reference tool. Save these cards in a card file box and pull them out when you start a quilt to find ideas for your color schemes. Whenever you feel stuck for ideas, reach for a picture and do this fun exercise.

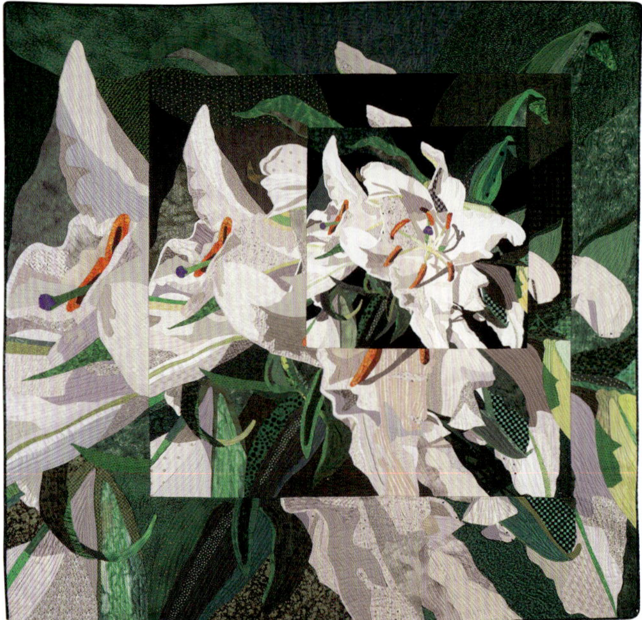

▶ *Casa Blanca Lilies*, 54″ × 54″, by Katie Pasquini Masopust
Photo By Hawthorne Studio

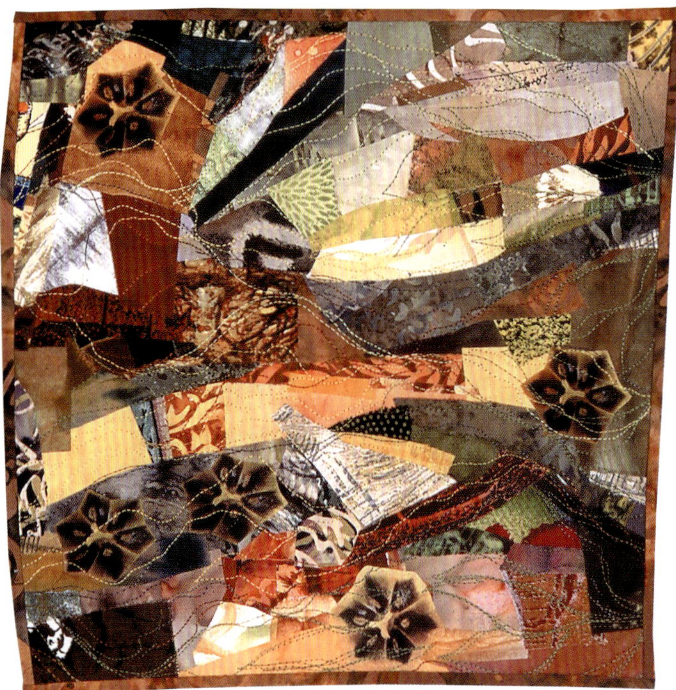

▶ *River* by Darcy Falk, 10″ × 10″
Photo By Gene Balzer

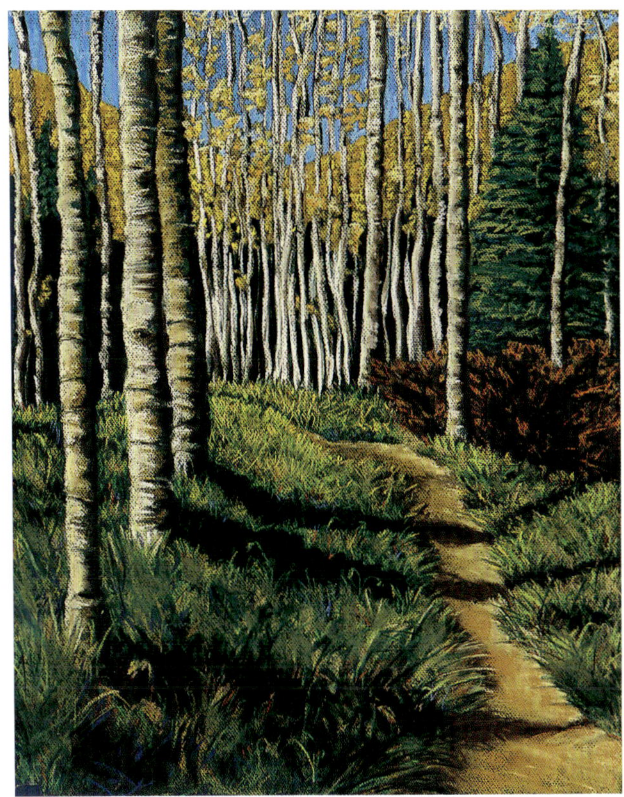

▶ *Tesuque Aspen* pastel painting by Brett Barker, 19″ × 25″
Photo By Hawthorne Studio

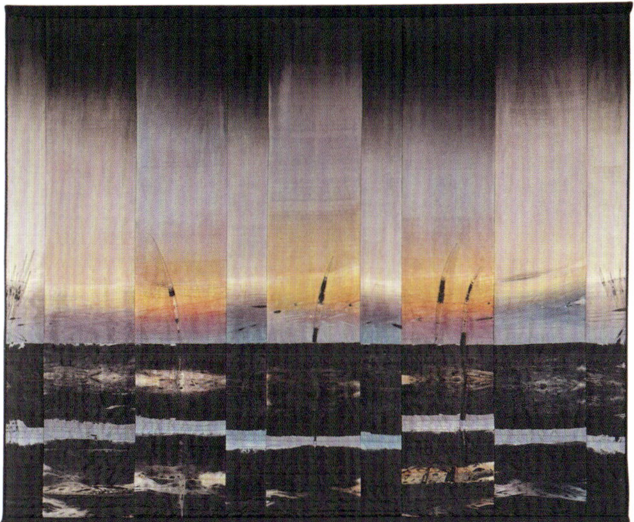

▶ *North Light* by Judith Content, 68″ × 56″
Photo By James Dewrance

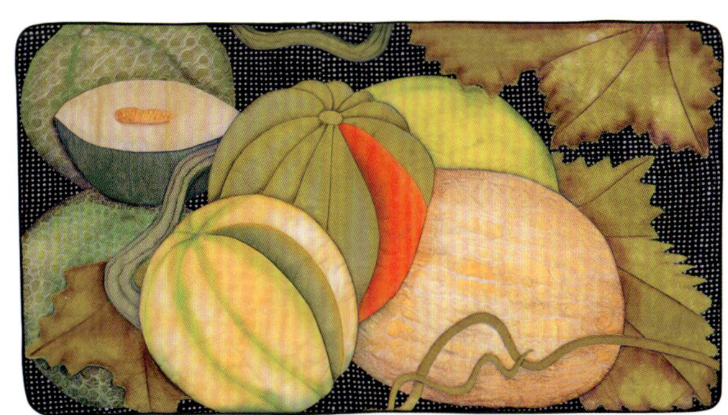

▶ *Melon Study* by Velda Newman, 36″ × 20″
Photo By Steven Buckley, Photographic Refelections

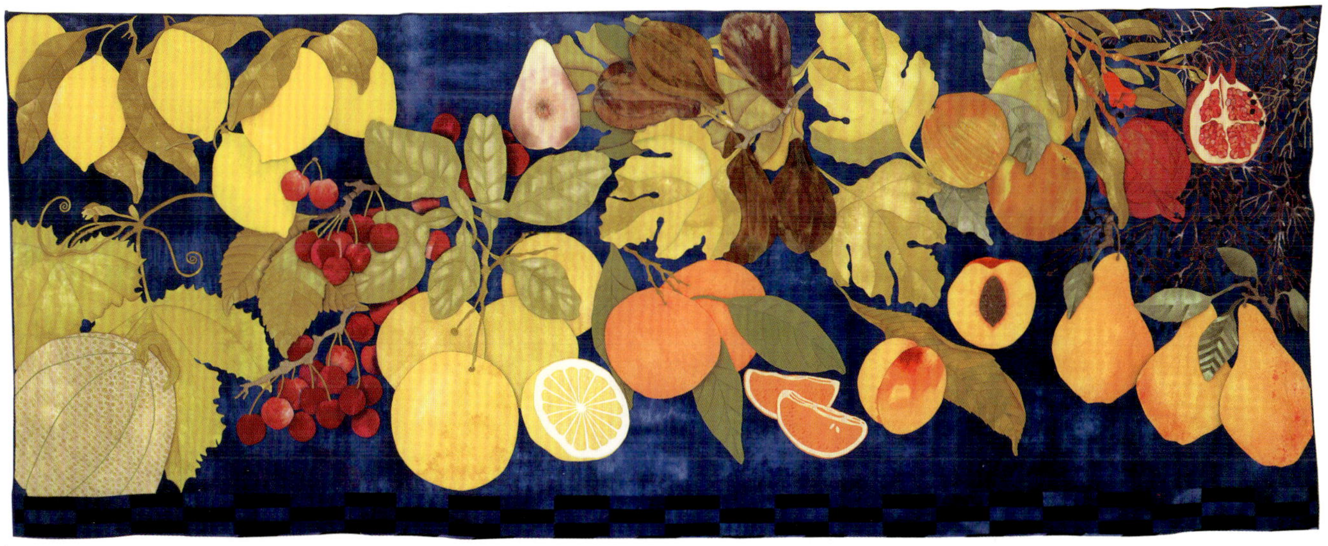

▶ *Sun Kissed* by Velda Newman, 168″ × 65″
Photo By Steven Buckley, Photographic Refelections

COLOR TOOLS

By Amy Barrett-Daffin

In 2002, Joen Wolfrom's *Color Play* was turned into a color tool, a fan deck of hues, tints, tones, and shades. There have been three editions, each one adding and improving on the previous version. It is packed with color theory and each color has five color plans so you can see what colors play well together and learn while playing. It has also morphed into a variety of other formats based on customer requests. Twenty years later, we now have six unique products that have helped crafters find pleasing color every time. From the Take-Along Mini Color Wheel to the Studio Color Wheel, these tools are here to help you come up with a color plan that is visually appealing. We have sold hundreds of thousands of these tools and they continue to delight and inspire makers.

Every time I demo these tools I see the lightbulb go on over someone's head and I know that they are on the road to gaining color confidence. Each of these products is based on the Ives Color Wheel by Herbert Ives. Here is a brief overview of all six of Joen's tools and a few additional products I think you will find helpful on your color confidence journey.

TAKE-ALONG MINI COLOR WHEEL

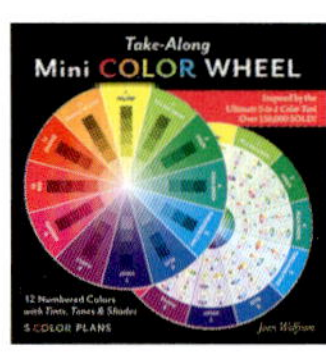

by Joen Wolfrom: Running to the quilt shop to find the perfect colors? This mini color wheel has 12 colors, fits nicely in your purse and is easy to use.

STUDIO COLOR WHEEL

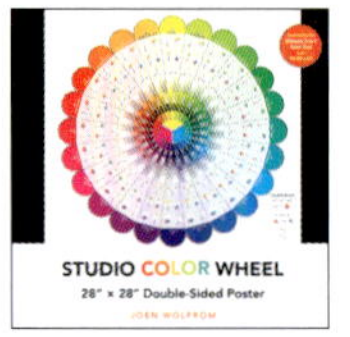

by Joen Wolfrom: This two-sided poster will brighten up any creative space, on one side you have the 24 hues, each with 4 color families and on the other fun artwork in those same colors.

ESSENTIAL COLOR WHEEL COMPANION

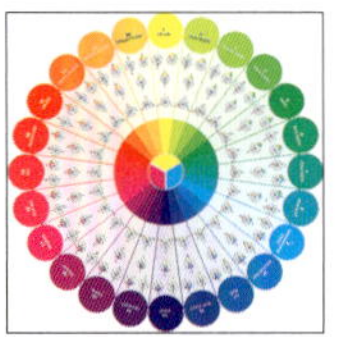

by Joen Wolfrom: With the rounded petals, this color tool is great for the design and cutting table. grab your fabrics, select a color story and start planning your quilt.

ULTIMATE 3-IN-1 COLOR TOOL

by Joen Wolfrom: Our flagship color tool has everything you need to design with pleasing color. With 24 hues, tints, tones and shades it has over 800 color samples. It also includes CMYK, HEX and RGB color formulas.

PALETTE-BUILDER COLOR TOOL

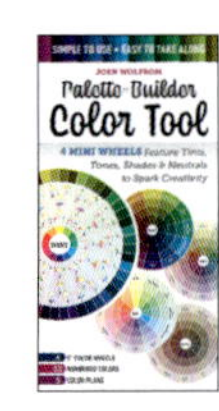

by Joen Wolfrom: Pick your own color story with these four mini color palettes! From rich tones to pastels and neutrals this palette builder will aid in your design process. It also has a bonus greyscale on the back cover.

ESSENTIAL COLOR CARD DECK

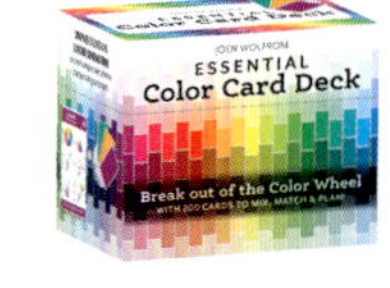

by Joen Wolfrom: My favorite tool of all time! With over 200 cards, this deck of huge color swatches makes selecting and telling your color story a breeze. Included are neutral cards that add red, blue and yellow and grayscale cards from black to white. This versatile tool has quickly become my go to for all my quilt projects.

FOOLPROOF COLOR WHEEL SET

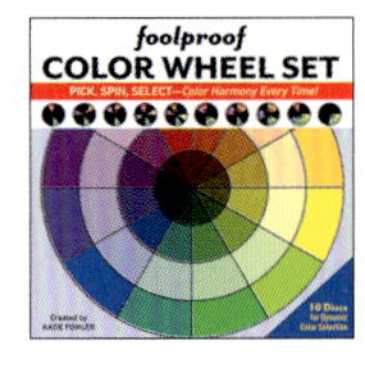

by Katie Fowler: A great color wheel for beginners, this tool masks all the other colors so that you can focus in on the colors of your choosing. With 10 die-cut discs finding matching colors is a cinch.

FOOLPROOF COLOR WORKBOOK

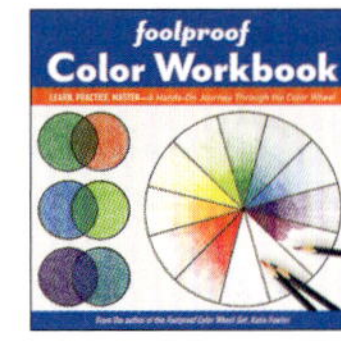

by Katie Fowler: This book is a fun way to get creative, you select a color plan and color in the images with pencils or crayons. A great way to unwind and get to draw.

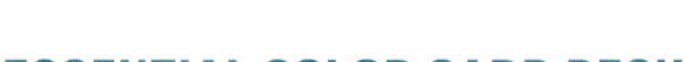

SWATCH THIS, 3000+ COLOR PALETTES FOR SUCCESS by Haruyoshi Nagumo: This book is packed with lucious and inspiring color combinations by a world class graphic designer. Learn how to use colors, evoke emotions and create stunning designs. A great addition to your color library.

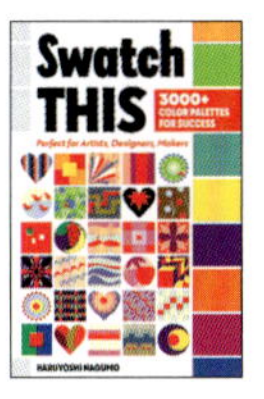

ULTIMATE VALUE TOOL by Marci Baker: Color gets the credit, but value does the work. This no-nonsense value tool will help you to create transparency and illusions in your quilts.

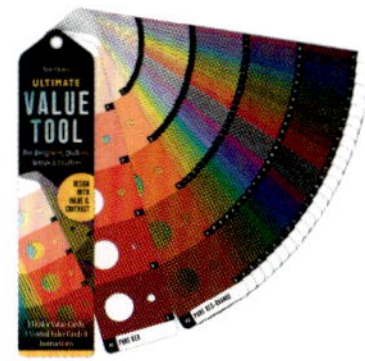

TITLE	FOOLPROOF COLOR WORKBOOK	TAKE-ALONG MINI COLOR WHEEL	STUDIO COLOR WHEEL	SWATCH THIS	ESSENTIAL COLOR WHEEL COMPANION	FOOLPROOF COLOR WHEEL SET	ULTIMATE 3-IN-I COLOR TOOL	PALETTE-BUILDER COLOR TOOL	ESSENTIAL COLOR CARD DECK	ULTIMATE VALUE TOOL
Instructions	yes	yes		yes	yes	yes	yes	yes	yes	yes
Beginner Friendly	yes	yes	yes		yes	yes	yes	yes	yes	yes
Theory	yes	yes		yes	yes	yes	yes	yes	yes	
Portable	yes	yes		yes	yes		yes	yes	yes	yes
Number of colors	12	12	24	3000	24	12	816	48	200	120
CMYK, HEX, RGB Codes							yes		yes	
Ives		yes	yes		yes		yes	yes	yes	
Neutrals								yes	yes	
Grayscale								yes	yes	yes

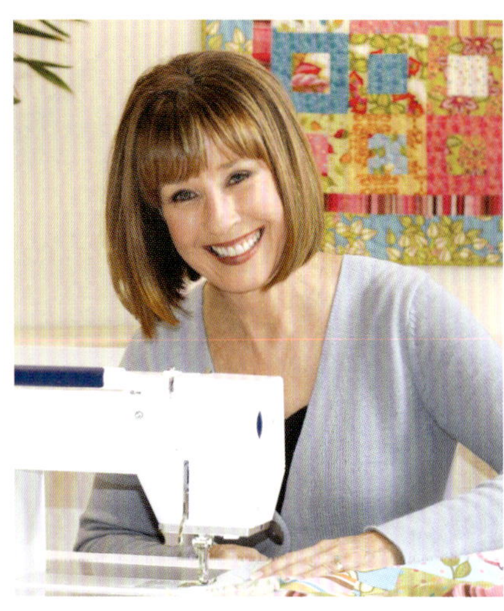

ALEX ANDERSON

Alex Anderson's love of quilting began in 1978 when she completed a Grandmother's Flower Garden quilt as part of her work toward a degree in art from San Francisco State University. She has an intense appreciation of traditional quilts and beautiful quilting surface design. She is the author of 30 books in four languages selling more than 1 million copies worldwide. Alex is a founding partner of *The Quilt Show* with Ricky Tims.

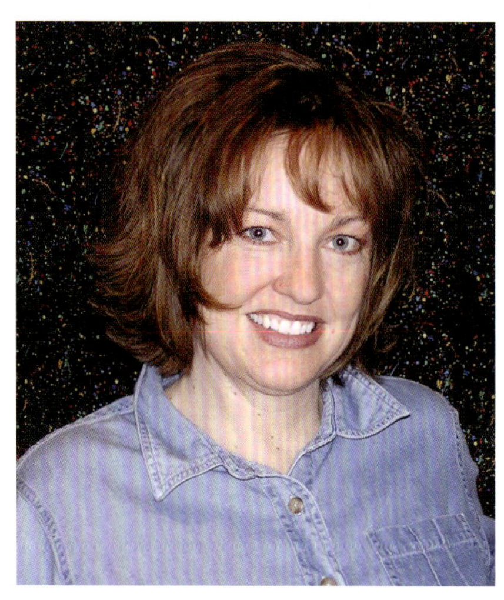

BRETT BARKER

Brett Barker, MAEd., BFA, BA, is a creative director, painter, graphic and surface designer, college faculty member, and writer. Brett creates fine art as well as graphic, fashion, and home decor designs for clients in the US, Europe, and Japan. Brett is currently an adjunct faculty member at Otis College of Design and has previously been an adjunct faculty member at ArtCenter College of Design.

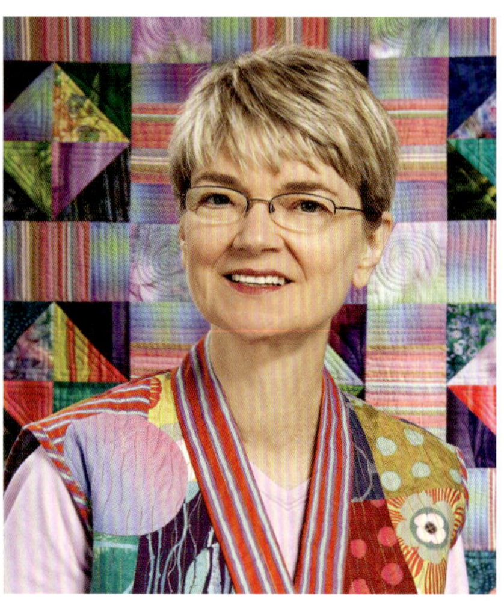

CHRISTINE BARNES

Christine Barnes is a contemporary quilt designer/teacher specializing in color theory for quilters and modern sewists. "Many quilters think there are no rules when it comes to color, but there are concepts and strategies, and they *work*—it's really more about practice than talent." Degrees in Design and Journalism led to a career writing books for Sunset Publishing, as well as two books on color for quilters. She lives in California's Gold Country and works in a "light-filled studio where I am always happy."

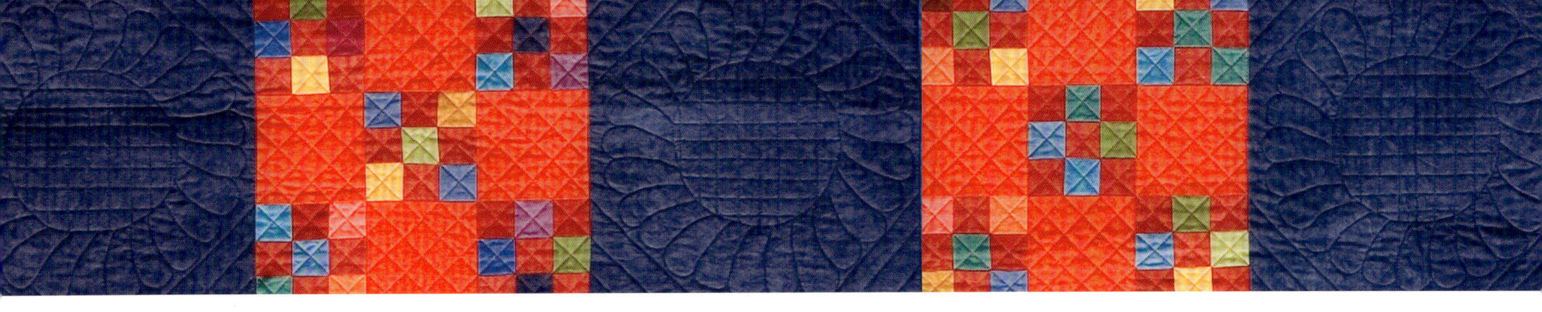

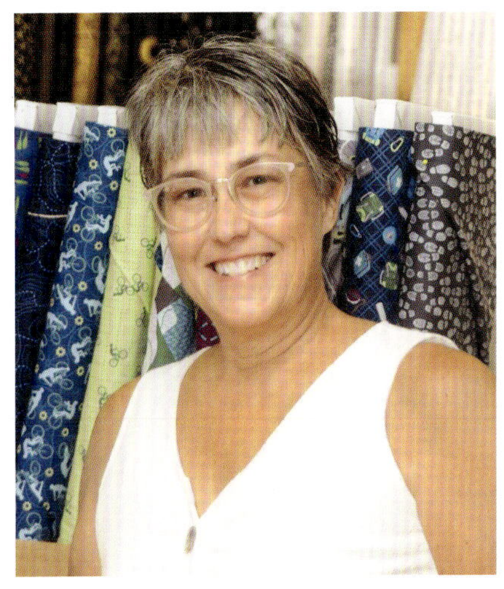

JUDY GAUTHIER

Judy Gauthier is an author of 6 books for C&T Publishing. She is a shop owner, and a designer for Studio e Fabrics. She has been dubbed "The Scrap Whisperer" by her friends at C&T. With a husband of 37 years, 4 adult children, several grandchildren and a Golden Retriever, she barely gets time to sit down. But, when she does, it's usually at her sewing machine or computer dreaming up new designs.

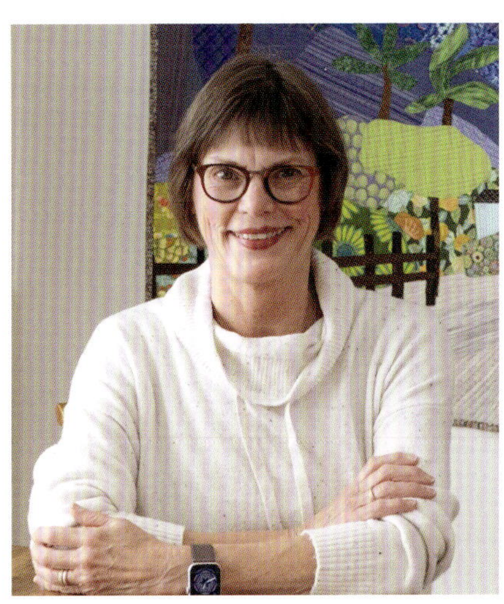

BECKY GOLDSMITH

Designing and making quilts and teaching others how to make quilts is a better career than Becky Goldsmith could ever have imagined. She has written patterns and books on her own and as part of Piece o' cake Designs. Becky has gained even more followers as a course instructor on the innovative and interactive platform Creative Spark Online Learning (by C&T Publishing). Quilters are wonderful people, and Becky loves being a part of the global quilt world.

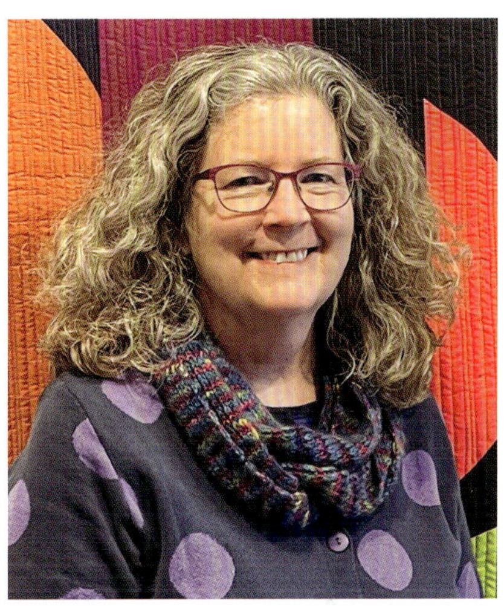

CINDY GRISDELA

Cindy Grisdela is an artist, teacher, and author of *Artful Improv* and *Adventures in Improv Quilts*, both books about creating original quilts without patterns. She specializes in improv design and using color fearlessly in textile art, and she travels all over the country giving lectures and teaching workshops. Her work has won awards in both quilt venues and art venues and can be found in private collections all over the country.

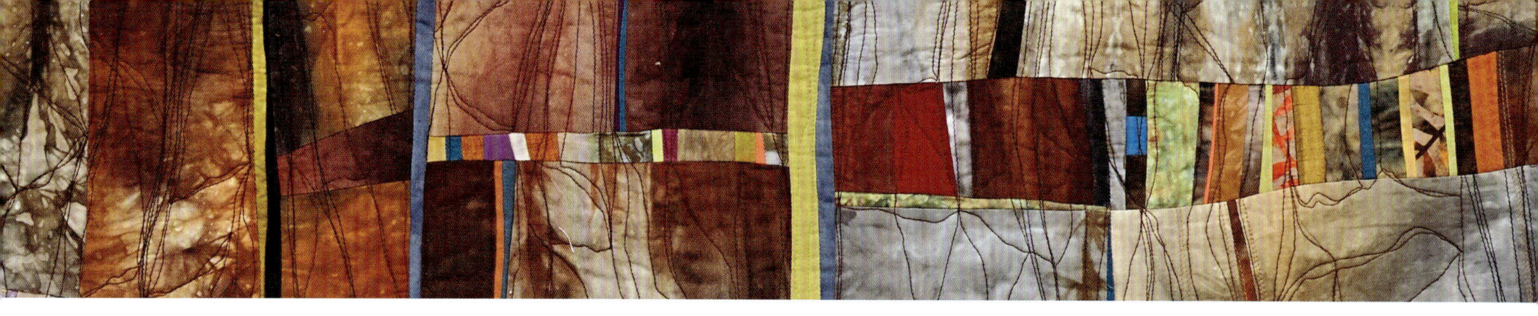

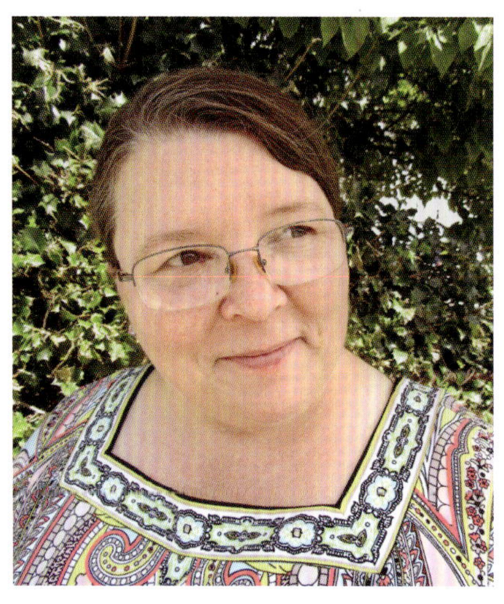

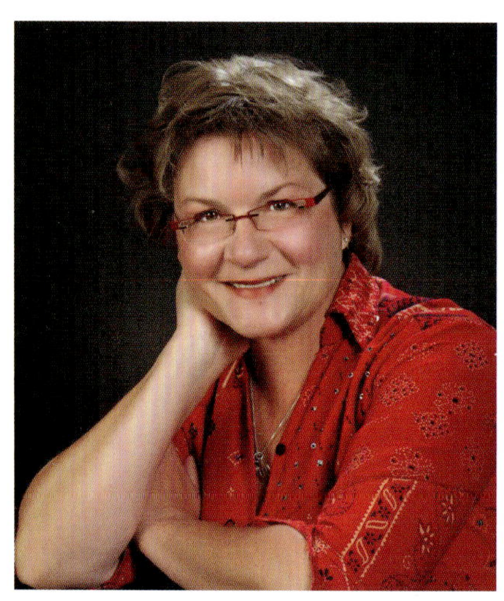

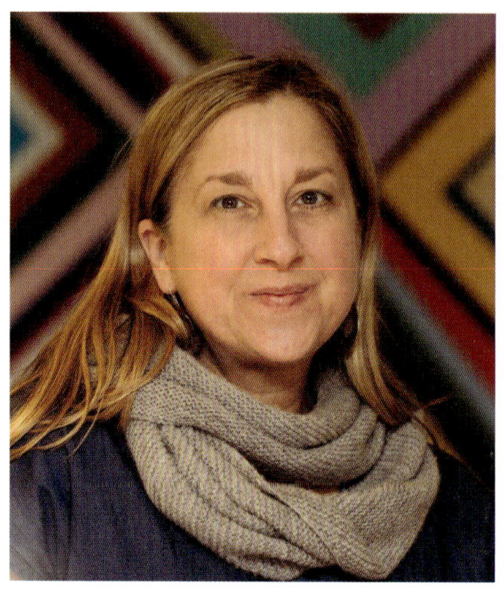

TERI LUCAS

Teri Lucas is a long time quilter, author, machine quilting teacher and former Community Editor, who is so in love with thread and color, and the playful interaction of the two. She loves listening to the machine get to just the right speed as it forms stitches over the surface of a quilt. Teri is inspired by beautiful skies, the riot of flowers, and most importantly, each quilter she encounters.

KATIE PASQUINI MASOPUST

For nearly 40 years, Katie Pasquini Masopust has created high-quality contemporary art quilts that have been coveted and collected by a broad range of admirers. Katie's easy, energetic manner has made her a very popular teacher and lecturer. When not in residence at her studio in Northern California, she travels, presenting her contemporary quilting theories and techniques to classes in North America, Europe, Asia, Australia, and New Zealand.

MARIA SHELL

Maria Shell's work is grounded in the tradition and craft of American quiltmaking. She strives to take the classical components of traditional bed quilts and manipulate them to create surprising combinations of pattern, repetition, and color for the viewer. Maria is the recipient of a Sustainable Arts Foundation 2011 Winter Award, a Rasmuson Foundation Project Award, and a Rasmuson Foundation Fellowship. She is the author of *Improv Patchwork*.

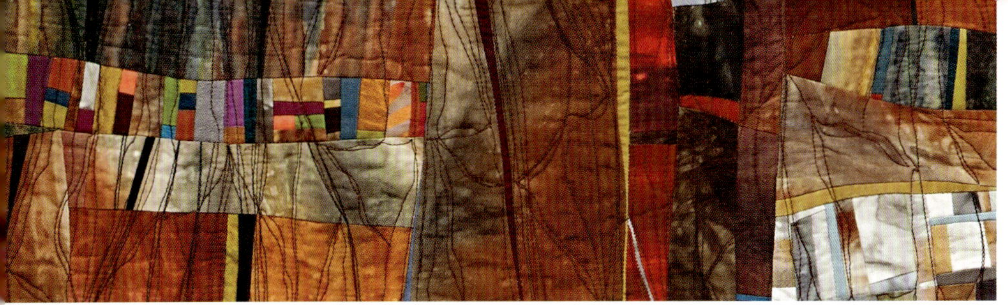

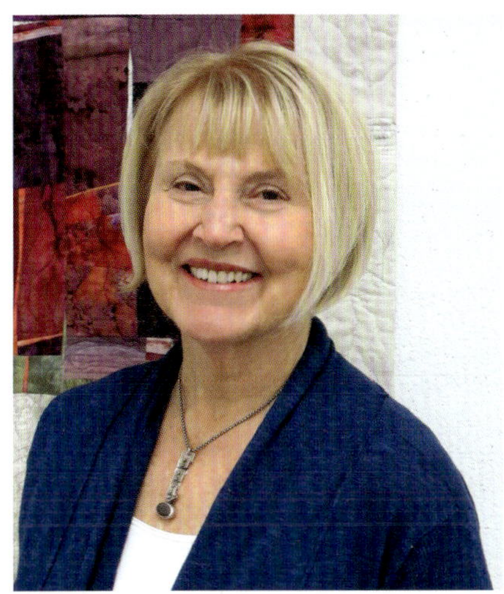

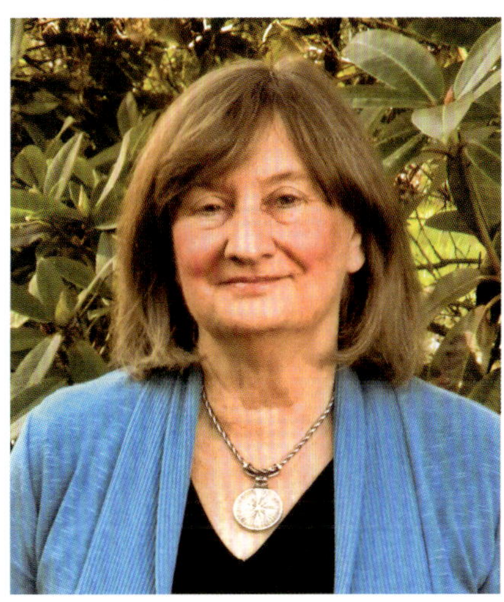

JEAN WELLS

Recurring themes in Jean Wells's textile art have to do with natural configurations: rocks, trees, grasses, flowers, and the land. She is fascinated with line, pattern, shape, color, and texture, and how to design with these elements. While co-owner of The Stitchin' Post with her daughter Valori in Sisters, Oregon for 49 years, Jean has been involved in quilting industry as an author, workshop/lecture presenter, and founder of the Sisters Outdoor Quilt Show.

JOEN WOLFROM

Joen Wolfrom is an author and teacher. She began quilt making in 1974 after leaving her career in education to become a homemaker and a stay-at-home mom. As a guest lecturer/instructor on color and design, Joen has taught throughout the globe. Joen is the creator of various color tools, including *Essential Color Card Deck*, *Take-Along Mini Color Wheel*, *Ultimate 3-in-1 Color Tool*, and many more!

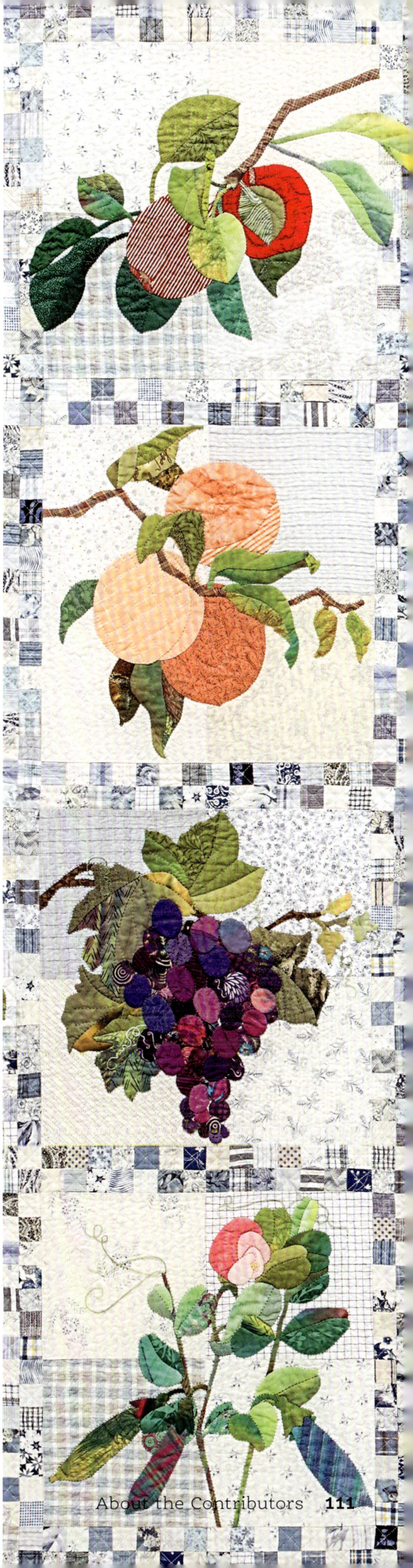

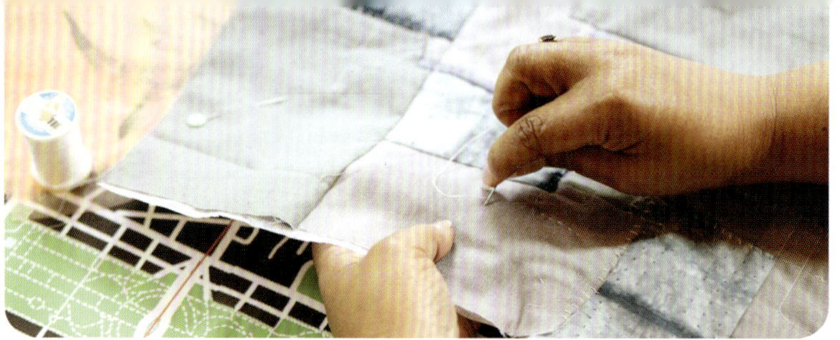
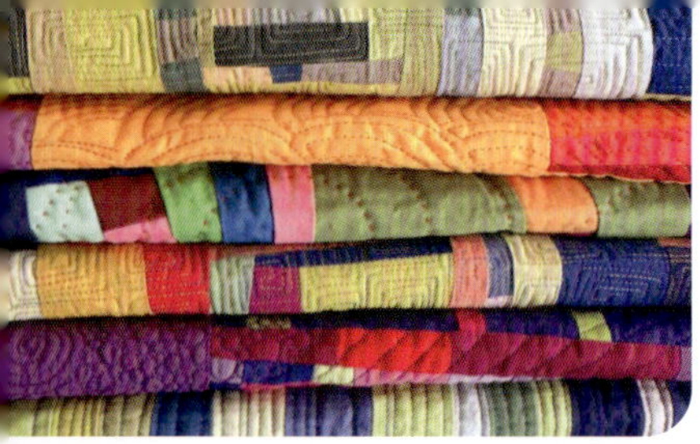
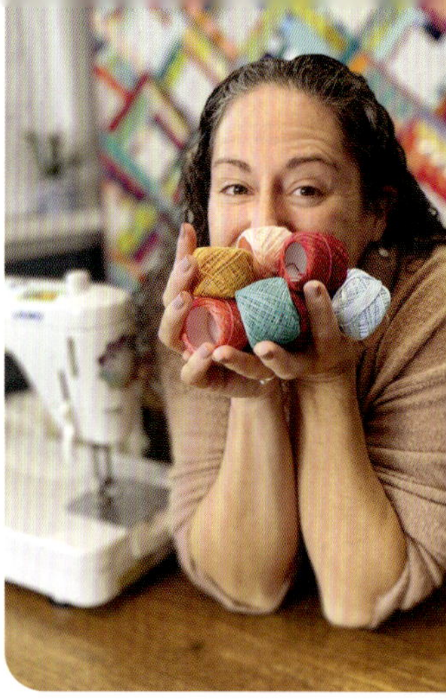

CREATIVE SPARK
ONLINE LEARNING

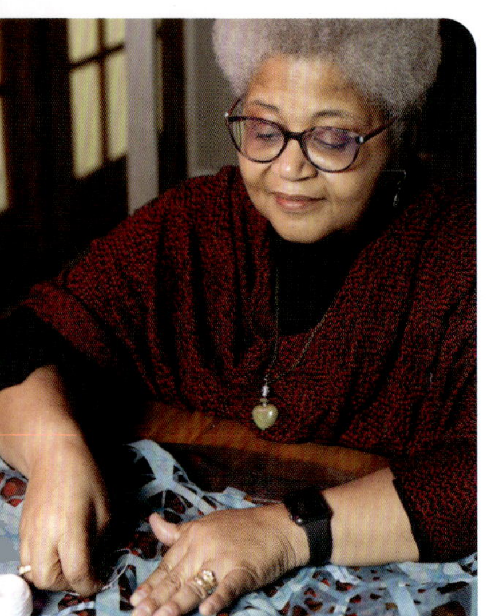
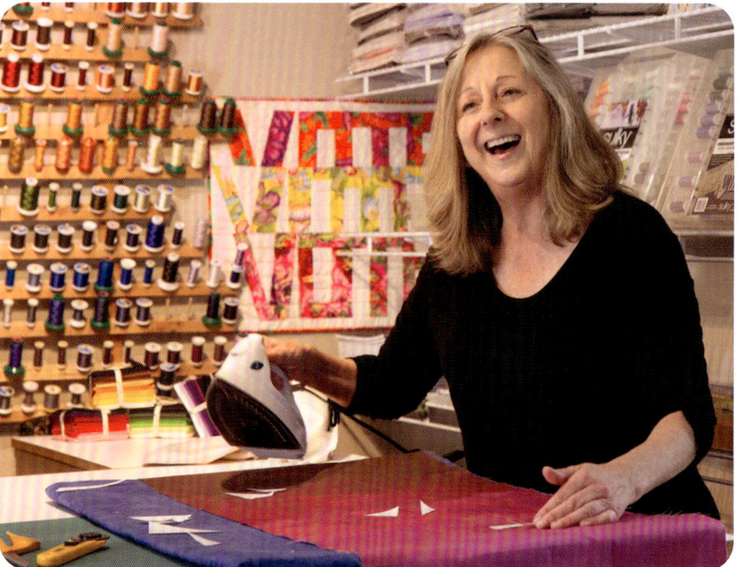
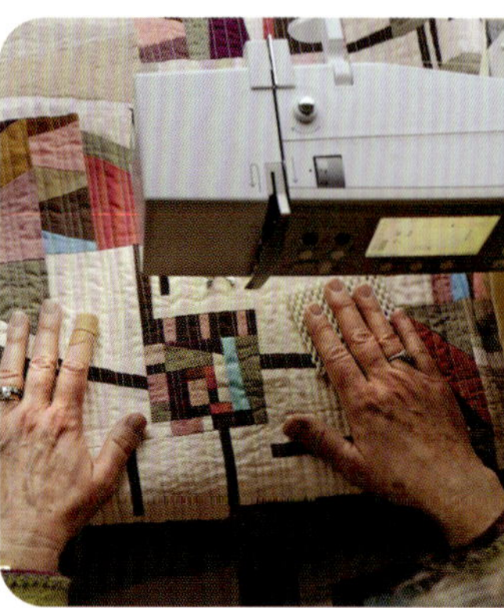
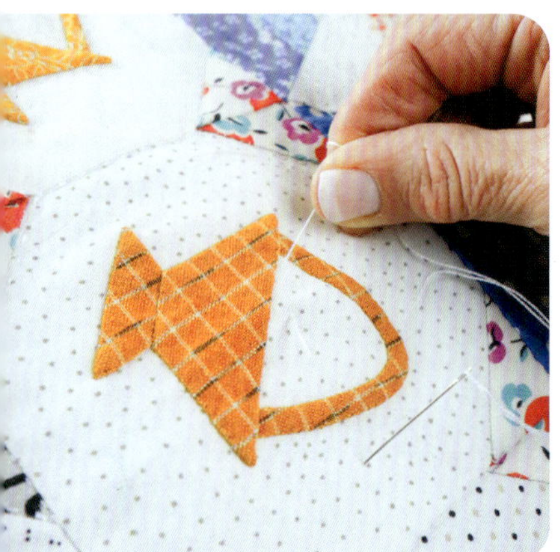
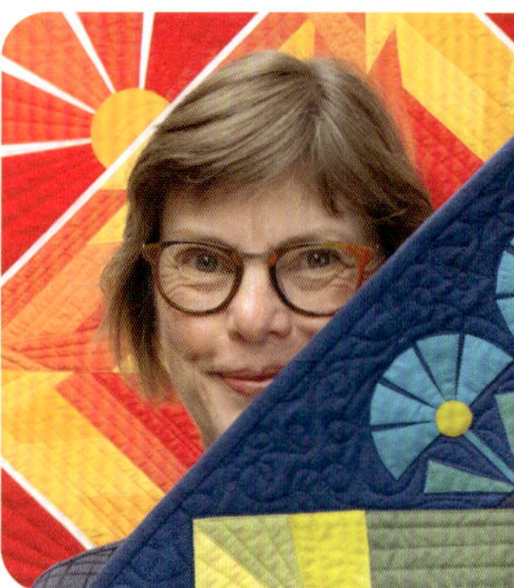

Quilting courses to become an expert quilter...

From their studio to yours, Creative Spark instructors are teaching you how to create and become a master of your craft. So not only do you get a look inside their creative space, you also get to be a part of engaging courses that would typically be a one or multi-day workshop from the comfort of your home.

Creative Spark is not your one-size-fits-all online learning experience. We welcome you to be who you are, share, create, and belong.

creativespark.ctpub.com